Table of Contents

CU01507169

London and Oxford

I was born at 103 Genesta Road in Plumstead, a south-east suburb of London, England, on 16th December 1912. My sister Barbara had been born fourteen months earlier, lower down the street at 49. I am not sure why we moved, but it was probably for financial reasons. My father, Ernest, and my mother, Annie Maud Johnson, married in Broughton Congregational Church in Manchester, and my father's first job had been as a library assistant in the Reference Library, King Street, Manchester, in the Manchester Public Free Libraries system. His letter of appointment, dated June 16th 1894, reads as follows:

> Mr Sutton has to inform Ernest Luke that he has been appointed as an assistant in the Reference Library at 7 shillings a week, and he will be obliged if he will commence his duties on Monday morning June 18th at 9 o'clock.

My father stayed with libraries, and after some years moved south to London to work in the Woolwich Public Library, while living in Genesta Road, upper Plumstead. I remember various events at No. 103. We rented the upper floor from a Mr and Mrs Martin, and my sister attended Plum Lane London County Council School, which was just across the road from our house. I remember as a very small boy – three or four perhaps – swinging on the garden gate waiting to greet my sister on her way home from school. Then came World War I and my father went off to Ypres as a gunner in the Royal Artillery. Once when he was home on leave he carried me on his shoulder into our garden at night to witness a zeppelin which was ablaze over London. On another occasion when London was thought to be attacked, the Martins, my mother, Barbara and I were in the basement of 103 to shelter from what we were told was an air-raid. Mrs Martin, whom I knew as Marty, was sitting on an inverted metal container and I was always remembered for remarking in a high treble voice, "Why are you rattling, Marty?" Marty was scared.

Barbara and I were very happy together. In our early years she tended to have the bright ideas, which we would both carry out. We enjoyed playing together in the garden which sloped down to a back alley. We particularly enjoyed rolling around a barrel which we found behind the house. Unfortunately one day our barrel ran over one of Mr Martin's carrots. We considered this dilemma together with the upshot that we thought the best solution to our problem would be to roll over all of Mr Martin's carrots so that he might not notice our misjudgement. To our dismay we found out later that we were in error and in disgrace. But that did not last long.

A big change in my life came when my father was promoted to become Librarian of the Plumstead Public Library, which was located at 232 Plumstead High Street in lower Plumstead. Lower Plumstead was considered a less desirable residential neighbourhood than upper Plumstead, but living at the library had many compensations. The building was handsome and solidly built, having been constructed with Andrew Carnegie Foundation money. And the librarian and his family were allotted a fine flat, which ran the length of the building on the second floor.

Plumstead High Street was a busy main street, and a number of tram and bus routes ran along it. Double-decker trams Nos. 36, 38 and 40 followed different routes up to London while a Bexley Heath tram, which was open-topped, went to the suburb of Bexley Heath. The trolley poles of these Bexley Heath trams were always jumping off the overhead wire, so that traffic would be held up until the conductor could pull down the wildly swinging pole and make a reconnection. There was also a double-decker 153 bus which went up to London, and a 99 bus which went up Bostall Hill, terminating its route in Erith. Looking out of our windows onto Plumstead High Street was a fascinating occupation for us children.

On the west side of the library building was a private street, and across this street were the Plumstead Public Baths. These comprised a number of private baths for both men and women and two fine swimming baths, First Class and Second Class. My father, after his safe return from the Front, taught me how to swim at the Plumstead Public Baths, and we often started the day with a quick dip before breakfast. In the winter the swimming baths were drained and closed over to become two large halls which were used for all kinds of assemblies and exhibitions. Ramsey McDonald addressed a political meeting in one of them as leader of the Labour Party; and my mother won a medal for bread baking, and I won a prize for model making at one of the exhibitions there.

Between the Public Baths and Plumstead High Street was a space which was used as a public market with semi-permanent stalls. Naturally this market provided us children with a constant source of interest. Two events stand out in my memory which I will relate here although they do not fit into my story chronologically. When I was about nine, I loved to wander around the market by myself when it was full of bustle and excitement. One Saturday morning, a huckster had set up an elaborate piece of apparatus which, when he turned on a switch, flashed an electric arc from the tip of a sword he held to another terminal. I was entranced. His real purpose, however, was to promote a tooth powder which he invited his audience to buy. To encourage them to do this he invited a small boy in the front row – me – to step up onto the platform of his truck and have his teeth cleaned with this most efficacious powder. This I did to the hearty applause of the crowd. My mother, when I got home and told her the story, was less impressed, but she had to laugh.

On another occasion, when I was slightly older, I was entertaining one of my school friends on the flat roof of the library building which overlooked the market. It was a dark Saturday evening near 5th November, Guy Fawkes Day, and the market thronged with shoppers. The stall immediately below us sold carpeting, rugs and linoleum. It occurred to us that it might be a good idea to brighten up the scene with a few jumping crackers we had ready for Guy Fawkes celebrations. No sooner thought than done. Suddenly there was a glorious but rather frightening chaos below us. My father, the librarian, was informed. He stormed upstairs to find the culprits. My friend was sent home in disgrace. I was sent to bed. I realize now that although I diverged from rectitude quite a bit during my pre-secondary school period I always had the full understanding and love of my parents. My father never laid a hand on me, and as I grew older my respect for my parents constantly increased.

The war was still at its height when my father was officially transferred to the Plumstead Public Library so it was agreed that my mother, who had excellent teaching qualifications, would act as librarian until my father's return from the Front. This meant that my sister and I were looked after by a "governess" while my mother worked in the library. There was a "garden" behind the library, and when we were not at school we played there with the children of the Fouracres. Mr Fouracre was the superintendent who ran the baths across the street. I put the words garden and governess in quotes because the person looking after us was certainly untrained for the job and the garden was just an unused piece of land surrounded by a high solid fence. At 11 o'clock each morning there would sound the siren of the nearby Woolwich Arsenal, which was manufacturing munitions at top speed, and this would be the signal for Barbara and me to run down our private street and wait for our governess to lower half a large, green Wellington apple on a length of cotton thread to each of us from the kitchen window of the flat upstairs.

A pleasurable memory associated with these early years was the happy relationship Barbara and I had with Mrs Ancliffe, one of the cleaning ladies at the library, who also came into our flat once a week to clean for us. Mrs Ancliffe was a proud lady; the taps in our bathroom were of brass, and when she had finished her work on them they shone brilliantly. We loved to talk to her and listen to her cackly laugh. Occasionally she would invite us children to her home in Cires Road where she would serve us canned peaches. Upstairs from the lending library there was a fine reference department and a museum of which my father was the curator. As Mrs Ancliffe was responsibile for cleaning the museum, and Barbara and I had the run of it when the museum was closed on Sundays, our discussions often centred around it. It was a hotch-potch of a museum with a multiplicity of exhibits which gave us great delight. There was for example, an array of African spears and shields, various old firearms, a canon ball which gave off a sound like thunder when rolled along the wooden parquet flooring, a wonderful collection of moths and butterflies mounted in chests of drawers, stuffed exotic birds in domed glass cases, a special display of Egyptian artefacts, ancient pottery and tear glasses in a beautiful breakfront cabinet, and much more, a pandora's box of wonderful treasures. A late addition to the museum was a huge shark's jaw, more than two feet across, with a fiercesome array of teeth, which my uncle sent us from Sydney, Australia, after he had paid us a visit at the Library. It was obviously a recent addition to the museum as it still smelt remarkably fishy.

A special exhibit which intrigued us perhaps more than anything else was a large stuffed dog in a huge glass case which was purported to have been fathered by a wolf. It looked like a very large collie. Mrs Ancliffe loved this dog. Now there was in Plumstead a group of people who were very interested in the natural history of the area. They founded the Plumstead and District Natural History Society and wanted to use the local museum as their base. With some reluctance, and under pressure from the Borough Council Library Committee, my father agreed to this measure, and in due course

5

became the unpaid secretary of the society. After some time the influence of this society became so strong that it was decided to change the nature of the museum to one which would have a natural history bias with a local background. Slowly, and then not so slowly, many of the time-honoured exhibits were disposed of and replaced by exhibits of local interest such as grasses and fungi, and examples of local cottage industry. For example, we had a glass-enclosed exhibit of local grass snakes and glow worms and I was recruited to go out into the fields and bring home small frogs for their sustenance. What to do with all those time-honoured exhibits? Some, like the butterfly and moth collection, were preserved. A few went to other museums. And to my dismay quite a few, like the collections of stuffed animals and stuffed birds, were condemned to the furnace across the road at the baths. Among the condemned items was the big dog in the glass case. Mrs Ancliffe heard of the dog's impending doom and pleaded to be allowed to keep it in her house. Her request was granted. The dog was transported to the bow window of her little house and proudly stood there for as long as I can remember. Mrs Ancliffe brushed and combed her treasure every day as carefully as she would have done any living animal.

After our move from upper to lower Plumstead, my sister and I both went to the Conway Road LCC School, a fifteen-minute walk from the library. By 1918, when the war ended and my father returned to civilian life, all our lives had become more ordered and peaceful. My sister and I both won Junior County Scholarships in the national so-called Eleven Plus Examination and as a result she went to the Plumstead County Secondary School, known as The Brown School because the school uniform was brown. I went to St Olave's Grammar School, in Tooley Street, right next door to Tower Bridge in central London. St Olave's was a school that had an Elizabethan foundation and an excellent academic reputation.

I enjoyed my nine years at St Olave's very much and played a full part in all its activities. In due course I played in the First XI at soccer and cricket, edited the school magazine, and in my final year shared the captaincy of the school with E.S Probst. I was greatly influenced by its Headmaster at the time, H.G Abel, and I am sure that without his help I would never have succeeded in being admitted to Oxford University in 1932. It was he who recommended me for a Rushbrooke Scholarship and obtained further financial help from the Thomas Wall Trust after I had been admitted to St Edmund Hall. Abel was rather an aloof man, but he made a deep impression on the school and on many individual boys like myself.

On Monday afternoons the Headmaster would take the whole sixth form for two consecutive periods of Scripture. The Sixth Form room would thus be quite full with perhaps thirty boys from the History, Classical, Science and Modern Languages Sixths. I was specializing in French and German at the time. Looking back I now realize that what was ostensibly a study of Scripture, and we did read passages from both the Old and New Testaments, was used by the headmaster as an opportunity to teach us ethics. He urged us to stay with the denomination in which we had been brought up until and unless we were convinced that there was good reason to change, and instilled into us the need to strive for excellence in whatever we did. Abel also took most of us for periods in which we studied Shakespeare's tragedies. I remember studying *Hamlet* and *Macbeth* with him, and the lasting impression these two plays made on me.

Individual encounters with the Headmaster were of course few and far between. Three stand out in my memory. Once, when I had stayed late at school to play football in the playground, I found that I had left my wristwatch in the school bathroom. On my return there it had gone. I reported the matter to the Headmaster, who was working late in his study. To my dismay he had no sympathy with me for my loss, but upbraided me for leaving the watch in the bathroom, and so tempting someone to steal it. On another occasion I reported sick to him in his room, and declared I would like to go home. He allowed me to go without demur, I think now because I was a remarkably healthy boy and was hardly ever absent on health grounds. The third occasion was the most important. Those of us who were monitors (prefects) in the Sixth Form were allowed to go out from the school grounds at lunchtime to buy sandwiches from a sandwich shop down the street. We would eat these in our Sixth Form room, and sometimes afterwards we would become a little obstreperous. At the back of the Sixth Form room, a row of handsome bookcases rising almost to the ceiling were mounted over cupboards in which we stored our gymnasium bags. These contained gym shirts and shorts and a pair of gym shoes which we would take along to the gym to change into at the appropriate time. During one lunchtime we became a little more boisterous than usual and started throwing things at one another across the room. Seeking heavier ammunition we soon turned to our gym bags, which, weighted with our gym shoes, proved to be perfect missiles. One of my shots hit the glass front of one of the bookcases and shattered it, even though I had aimed carefully at the brass bars which protected the lower shelves. Being a monitor I sought out the Headmaster immediately to report the damage. I found him conveniently coming down the stairs. He entered the Sixth Form room, looked at the damage and said "I suppose it was an accident." I answered, "No, Sir I threw it", and thereby won his respect and friendship for life. He made sure I paid for the damage myself from my own money in instalments, but I knew I had made a friend.

While I was still in the Sixth Form at St Olave's we had a visit from a distinguished Old Boy who later was to become Parliamentary Secretary to the Ministry of Education (1937–1940). His name was Kenneth Lindsay. He brought to the attention of the Sixth Formers that there was an opportunity for a selected scholar from St Olave's to migrate to Canada and be sponsored for higher Education by the Canadian Government. I remember taking this proposition home to my parents for their consideration. However, we did not pursue it. The opportunity to go to Oxford came a short time later. This was something I could accept immediately as it fulfilled my highest hopes.

I remember vividly how I learned that I had a place at Oxford. On Tuesday afternoons in the summer term, if the weather were fine, most of the boys would forsake the school building next to Tower Bridge in Tooley Street, walk to London Bridge station, and bearing cricket gear, take the train to North Dulwich where the school's playing fields were. I happened to be batting in a game near the grounds' entrance. At the end of the over, I glanced towards the pavilion and was amazed to see my mother and father standing on the boundary line. I was so astonished that I was 'out' almost immediately after that, and ran over to greet them. They brought the joyful news that I had a place at Oxford, at St Edmund Hall. I don't think I ever shared so much joy with my parents as at that time. I knew I owed my place at Oxford very largely to them and in particular to my mother.

My years at St Edmund Hall, Oxford, 1933–1935, I skipped in my original writing of *Luke's Log*, yet after completing the first draft of it I became more fully aware of their importance to my story, so an account of them is now included here. My original courses were in Modern Languages, French and German, and during my first term I was content to specialize in them. But as time went on I became more political, and in my second year switched to Modern Greats (Politics, Philosophy and Economics). The reason for this was my growing interest in politics through my friendship with Bill Nield, who had also started in Modern Languages but switched to PPE as his interest in politics grew. The Senior Common Room at St Edmund Hall were somewhat reluctant to agree to my switch as they thought that I should obtain a safe second and possibly even a first if I stayed in that discipline. I had taken French and German in the sixth form at St Olave's and that background showed up in Oxford. However, after some discussion, the Senior Common Room agreed to the proposed change, and as a result the class of my finals turned out to be a disappointing third. I should have remembered I had no liking for history at school, and history accounted for a substantial part of the PPE curriculum. In retrospect I do not regret changing courses, for I had a lot of fun through my political contacts at Oxford, who shaped my life at the university and gave me friendships which lasted a lifetime.

Bill Nield stayed on for a fourth year and took a first. He went into Government Service and finished his career as Secretary to the Government, the highest post in the Home Civil Service. When I told my mother that Bill was going to stay an extra year at Oxford, she immediately said "You can't do that!" Knowing the tremendous sacrifices she had made to get me there at all I agreed without demur.

In a sense my social life at Oxford was also divided into two parts. At first my interest in Hall soccer brought me into close contact with two other players in the Hall First XI – Gordon Fallows, a scholar and ordinand from Barrow-in-Furness, and Herbert Cook a red-head from Sheffield. A fourth member of this group was Maurice Wall. The four of us would have tea in one another's rooms every Sunday. We could obtain wonderful anchovy toast from the Buttery and pour our individual cups from a large teapot. After tea Gordon and I would go off sermon tasting to one or another of the Oxford churches. If a well-known preacher were preaching at St. Mary's we would certainly go there. One such preacher was Dean Inge, the Gloomy Dean of St Paul's Cathedral in London, a regular contributor to the national newspapers, who, one London newspaper quipped, might not be a pillar of the Church, but was certainly good for two columns of *The Times*.

I remember I had an opportunity to introduce Gordon to my family. The Hall soccer side had a number of away matches, one of which was with Alleyn's School in Dulwich, which happened to be relatively near my home, so I managed to take Gordon home for a visit. My father was a palm-reader and perhaps a little psychic. He read Gordon's palm and out of the blue declared that the young lady to whom Gordon was attached, whose name I forget, was not really suited to him and that he should not marry her. I was embarrassed and a little astounded by this, but sure enough the girl

Gordon did eventually marry was not the girl we all knew he had been engaged to but Edna who proved to be a perfect wife for a bishop. Gordon long afterwards declared that he had been greatly influenced by my father's pronouncement and was deeply grateful for being guided to avoid a marriage which he later realized would have been a mistake.

In my second year, as mentioned above, I became interested in politics and joined the Labour Club. The teas with my soccer friends became less regular. By my third year I had become thoroughly political and went into digs in Wellington Street with Bill Nield and Michael Kennan from the Hall, and George Thomson from St John's College. Bill, George and I were reading PPE, and therefore most of the guests who came to our digs had a political bias. Once Sir Stafford Cripps, a Labour Minister and father of John Cripps, who occasionally spoke at the Oxford Union, stood on our fireside rug. However, Michael, who was reading Anthropology brought relief from the political atmosphere of our lodgings by the guests he occasionally brought in for meals. Once he invited a student colleague in to lunch – Prince Kiki Niabongo from Uganda. These two were good friends who had a relationship because each of them, for different reasons, wore a gold ring on a little finger.

Most Sunday evenings Michael and I would take time off to go out to a fine dinner together in an Oxford restaurant, smoke a cigar after it (Mike's father, who had died young had left him a box of excellent Havana cigars), and then attend one of those wonderful Sunday musical concerts by eminent musicians offered free to all university undergraduates in the hall of Balliol College. You had to be wearing a gown to get in.

What happened to these friends of mine? It is interesting to look back. Maurice Wall I lost touch with entirely. Herbert Cook taught French and German in his grammar school in Sheffield and was head of the Modern Languages Department there. George

Thompson became a lecturer in Political Science at Liverpool University for a time, but then moved to Singapore to become Head of Information Services. He later became a friend of the Prime Minister, Lee Kuan Yu, and Professor of Political Science at Nanyang University. I kept in touch with him over the years though we met only once in Singapore, at a meeting I have recorded elsewhere. Bill Nield I think would have chosen to go into politics, but he had no liking for Clement Attlee the Prime Minister of that time and so stayed with the Home Civil Service to become its highest officer, Secretary to the Government, and be awarded a knighthood. I saw Bill and Gwyneth whenever I was in England after being freed from Changi Gaol.

Gordon Fallows I kept in closest touch with over the years. I visited him and his wife Edna at their parish near Coventry, just after the notorious blitz there, and also paid them a visit in Preston, Lancs, after Gordon had been appointed vicar of the prestigious Preston parish church. Later, Gordon was appointed chairman of the Board of Governors of Ripon Hall Theological College where he had been trained, and then Principal of Ripon Hall. I stayed the night with Gordon and Edna at Ripon Hall once when I was on home leave, and attended a garden party there at which several members of the House of Lords were present, for by then Gordon had been named Chaplain to the Queen. In July 1968, Gordon wrote to me informing me that he had been appointed Suffragan Bishop of Pontefract. I am sure he enjoyed writing to me, "Yours ever, Gordon Pontefract". Quite shortly afterwards he was elevated to become Bishop of Sheffield. Unhappily, however, Gordon did not enjoy his new status for long, for his health deteriorated, and he died on the morning of 17th August 1979 from a melanoma. Sadly, two of Gordon's three children, turned out to be predisposed to melanoma, and unhappily died young. I was privileged to be godfather to one of them, his son Michael.

But to return to Oxford, the period of my undergraduate days was very political and I revelled in it. My friend Bertie Nightingale, who was some seven years older than I, had presented me with a little money when he knew I was going to Oxford, and I used it to become a life member of the Oxford Union. It was a good investment for I heard a number of memorable debates there, including the one on the motion: "In no circumstances will this House fight for its king and country", which was redebated round the world. The motion was carried with acclamation at the time. It was especially memorable for a speech by one of the paper speakers, C.E.M. Joad, who was noted for being a key performer in the BBC *Brains Trust* of the day. Joad recounted a story about Lytton Strachey who was asked, "What would you do if you found someone trying to rape your sister?" Strachey replied in his high squeaky voice, "I would do my best to get in between them!" The house was in an uproar for several minutes. Harold Nicholson of *Diaries* fame tried to have the motion of that meeting expunged from the minutes at the next meeting of the Union. But he was not successful.

I spoke a few times myself in the Union debating hall, and was once a paper speaker. This meant I was one of the first four speakers who would be called upon by the President to speak on the motion before the House. In those days, all the officers of the Union wore tails for a debate, as did the paper speakers. I did not possess tails but found a friend who lent me a suit. I do not now remember the motion of that evening, but I remember I raised a laugh by noting that that day was the birthday of Lord Beaverbrook. What the relevance of this piece of information could possibly have been I cannot now remember.

I also achieved the smaller distiction of becoming president of the St Edmund Hall Debating Society. During my presidency, the debate I enjoyed most was one we had with the Oxford Home Students Women's College. The motion before the house was "Men are made of clay, and women make mugs of them". The outcome was indecisive, but we greatly enjoyed taking the ladies out to dinner to prolong our discussions. This choice of motion for debate perhaps correctly indicates that I was not averse to the company of women. In fact under the influence of my mother I had become a confirmed feminist by the time I reached Oxford, and during my second term contributed a leading article to the *University Isis Magazine* entitled "In Defence of Women". The Vice-Principal of the Hall, John Brewis, was so surprised by this that he called me to his room to find out why I had written it.

As I remember it the period 1933–1935 was very politically charged. The gate-house notice boards of Oxford colleges often displayed posters demanding "No more War!" and condemning arms manufacturers as Merchants of Death. There was a depression, and the Hunger Marchers were marching south from the northern counties. As a member of the University Labour Club I was active in assisting the feeding of the marchers as they passed through Oxford and slept on the floors of church halls on their way to London. There was also a communist club at Oxford called the October Club, of which David Floyd, who was on the same floor as I was at the Hall, was a member. He lived very simply and had a large portrait of Lenin over his mantlepiece. I was interested to note that David finished his career as correspondent to the *Daily Telegraph* in Moscow. I wonder what happened, for the *Telegraph* is a true blue right wing paper. As I never lived in England as a permanent resident after 1936 I never had an opportunity to find out.

Bill Nield became chairman of the Oxford University Labour Club, but I did not seek office in it. Nevertheless as a result of my membership I sometimes had duties to perform. For example, I had the pleasure of taking Dora Russell, a former wife of Bertrand Russell, out to coffee at the Mitre Inn, after she had been a guest speaker at the Club. As an active member of the Club I also once sought an article for a Labour Club publication from G.D.H. Cole, a don at University College and a prolific writer of left-wing political books. I remember I went with a friend and found Cole alone in his study, sitting on the floor, surrounded by books. He asked us to sit down and thereupon wrote the article we requested while we waited.

In 1935, at the end of my three years at Oxford, there was still a strong anti-war feeling in the university and I volunteered to go speaking for the League of Nations Union in the English country-side. I found I was to join three other third year students from different colleges awaiting their results. They were Giovanni Previtali, an Italian, Basil Cartland, a nephew of Barbara Cartland, the novelist, another student whose name I forget, and myself. Previtali, fair-haired and handsome, was older than the rest of us. He owned a car, a dashing Lancia tourer, and sported one of those bunny fur coats. He must have been an early starter, for he had an itinerary ready and a number of addresses in the county of Buckinghamshire where we might stay after we had delivered our speeches. We got along famously and by the time we were address-ing our second church hall meeting felt we were warming to our task. But what to do at the end of the day? Previtali had an address. We drove up an impressive drive and stopped in front of a fine house. A liveried maid answered our ring. What name should she give? "The League of Nations" we replied. There was a burst of laughter from a distant dining room, and we were invited in.

Before we rang the door-bell Previtali and Cartland had hatched up a little scheme. Cartland was dark haired and swarthy while Previtali was fair, so they agreed to switch identities if we were asked in. After we had been invited to help ourselves from cold-cuts on the side-board we sat around a large table at which four people in evening dress were already seated, two men and two women. Everyone seemed in festive mood. After a time the little deception was disclosed and everyone laughed. Then the ladies left the men to their port. Finally we rejoined the ladies and in due course we took our leave. In many ways it was a hilarious evening, but I remember feeling secretly embarrassed.

Strangely, as I write of this period, sixty-three years ago, I do not remember the church halls and other places where we delivered our speeches, but only what we did with our spare time and the wonderful hospitality we were given. Perhaps it is because that hospitality was so spontaneous and generous. The second evening of our speaking tour we finished our day in Banbury. It had grown dark, but Previtali declared he knew where we should go. We drove up to a largish house on the outskirts of town and knocked on the door. In a few moments, contact was established between Previtali and the daughter of the house who obviously had known Giovanni at Oxford. In another few minutes she had taken control of operations. Her parents, in night attire, appeared on the landing at the top of the stairs and under her instructions and with her help pushed mattresses and bedding over the bannisters to the four of us below. We made ourselves at home as requested, and quickly fell asleep on the living room carpet. Next morning, after quick showers and a good breakfast, we helped our hosts straighten things up and were soon on our way again. I wonder now whether they thought of their efforts as a unique contribution to the League of Nations.

I remember two other places where we stayed on this speaking tour. Both were rectories. The first was notable for an attractive garden in which in lovely summer weather a beautiful young girl sat in a wheel-chair. I cannot now recall the nature of her disability but it seemed to be long-standing. I remember Previtali demonstrating how it was possible to leap headfirst over a chest-high wire fence and, by curling into a ball, sustain no injury. We bought this young lady a huge box of chocolates on our departure. The atmosphere during our stay could well be described as festive. However, during this time at one point I found myself alone with the rector in his study. Suddenly he turned to me and said "Do you really believe in the League of Nations?" I remember, proudly now, suddenly becoming serious and saying "Yes, I do. Unless we all join to support it, or something like it, civilization cannot survive." The rector seemed pleased.

The last overnight stay on our League of Nations tour was also at a rectory. The rector wore a habit and seemed very severe to us. The small parish church apparently had historical connections with the United States. What exactly they were I do not now recall. The relationship seemed to me to be unimportant at the time. What struck me most, and stays in my mind even to this day, was the fact that we were required to kneel by our high chairs to say grace before breakfast.

I enjoyed our League of Nations tour, but what I now regard as a special bonus for changing my courses from Modern Languages to PPE were two external activities made available to selected PPE students who had just completed their third year. The first was a tour of British industry which included visits to various industries and a film studio in the London area, other industries in and around Birmingham and the factory of Rolls Royce in Derby. The second was a visit to Marburg University in Germany with a smaller selected group of Oxford students who were guests of the university.

The visit to Marburg University was memorable for a number of reasons. Our group comprised only seven people as I recall, and was led by R.H.S. Crossman, a don at New College. Crossman, besides being an eminent classical scholar, was also a prominent political theorist and a fluent German speaker. In 1964 he was to become Minister of Housing in Harold Wilson's Labour goverment and begin his controversial *Diaries*, published in 1975. The other six were: Lincoln Gordon, an American Rhodes Scholar from Balliol who, at the age of twenty-two, took a PhD at Oxford, and went on to teach at Harvard, become Assistant Secretary of State for Latin American Affairs, United States Ambassador to Brazil, and President of Johns Hopkins University; Josephine Burroughs, an American student who had met Crossman in Germany (she returned to Springfield, Illinois, to marry Bob Saner, a bank president, and be active in community affairs); a young Quaker Oxford woman student whose name I cannot now recall; and the three of us from the Wellington Street digs who were interested in politics – Bill Nield, George Thompson and myself.

As guests of the university all the men of our party, with the exception of our leader Crossman, were expected to participate in *fruhsport*, which meant exercises in the very early morning clad only in shorts and gym shoes. Linc Gordon politely but firmly declined to participate in these, and thereby almost caused an international incident. He redeemed himself in the eyes of his hosts, however, when we were shown over the university rifle range. Linc casually picked up a rifle and showed himself to be a crack shot.

What we did not fully realize at the time was the tremendous influence that Adolph Hitler had already exercised upon Germany. The Marburg University students, often clad partly in black and wearing black-top boots, were seemingly all pro-Hitler and not at all put out by the news we received at the university that a putsch had been carried out in Nuremburg at which Rohm, a possible rival to Hitler, had been murdered. We were conducted at night to witness duelling between students which was officially forbidden but obviously clandestinely allowed. The student opponents conducted their duels with unbaited sabres in a way which was reminiscent of duelling in the middle ages, except that the eyes and necks of the contestants were protected by goggles and a kind of thick black medical tape. Each combatant had his second, and medical students stood by to treat the wounds of the combatants. It was considered an honour for a student to sustain an angry scar on one of his cheeks.

During our stay in Marburg I made a friend of one of the senior students there who was studying English. He was retiring and aesthetic, cultured and talented. To my surprise, however, before we left he announced that he had to fight a duel. What had brought him to this pass I never discovered, but from that moment until our departure he was practising his sabre fighting every afternoon.

On our final evening there was a get-together, and on invitation we sang a few English songs. Then before the evening ended we were invited to join with the German students in singing the Horst Wessel Lied, the marching song of the new Hitler Youth. Crossman thereupon made a warm speech of thanks in German for the hospitality we had all enjoyed, but to our relief graciously declined on our behalf to join in with the singing of that particular song. We returned to England without Crossman who was staying in Germany to fulfil a speaking engagment. We understood that we would be able to hear him on the BBC on our return to England. We turned on our radios at the appointed time and listened to a speech. But the voice was not the voice of Crossman. The German news station had decided not to broadcast what he had written. Fortunately Crossman had sent a copy of his speech to England by mail so it was read by someone else at the BBC at the appropriate time.

What to do after leaving Oxford was a problem for all of us undergraduates. I took a crammer's course at Davies's in London which was designed to prepare us for various civil service examinations and interviews, which in turn might lead to an appointment in one of the Civil Services, the Home Civil Service being considered the most prestigious. I did not aspire to enter the Home Civil Service with my academic record, but I had hoped to be selected for HM Consular Service. The offer of a place in the Malayan Education Service was unexpected, but not to be turned down.

And so in 1934, at the age of twenty-two, I was selected to become an Education Officer in the Malayan Education Service. The appointment brought with it a year's post-graduate training at the University of London's Institute of Education, which was situated in institution-like buildings in Southampton Row. There were about twenty of us in the Colonial Course leading to a Diploma in Education of the University of London. Only one other student, George Tacchi, was destined for Malaya. The rest of the group were either from or bound for various Colonial Territories in Africa, Asia or the Caribbean. Among those enrolled were teachers from Kenya, a Miss Judd who had served on the staff of Achimota College, Gold Coast, a Mr Jones, who was Director of Education, Granada, and Mr Ho Seng Ong, who was taking a master's degree of the University of London, and auditing our courses. When I met Mr Ho Seng Ong subsequently in Malaya he had become principal of the large Methodist Boys' School in Kuala Lumpur. Some years later, after taking a PhD at the University of Denver, Colorado, he became Secretary General of the whole American Methodist Mission Education system in Malaya.

Our supervisor at the Institute was Brian Mumford, who had written a book on the Education system of Indonesia. We joined in with the regular students for the main methods courses, and listened to lectures on Principles of Education by Sir Percy Nunn, Director of the Institute, who had written a textbook on that subject. Our lecturers in method included: Parker, English; Hamlin, Educational Psychology; Scarfe, Geography: and Laurys, General Science. Occasionally we had visiting lecturers. Once T.S. Eliot read some of his poems to us in what seemed to me to be a strange monotone.

I enjoyed my year at the Institute. We Colonial Course students had an aura of romanticism about us, which set us apart, and although we joined the regular students for the methods courses, we had special seminars and visits arranged for us as a group. I remember particularly a visit to a school for deaf children, and one to an open-air school, where on the winter's day of our coming the only person with a cold was the headmaster. He had an open fire in his room, while everyone else was outside in the open air wearing an overcoat.

An optional course, which we were encouraged to take, was the international Scouters Woodbadge Course at Chigwell Park in Essex. I remember enjoying parts but not all of it. I was in the Woodpeckers Patrol, which included among its members a Catholic priest and a master from Epsom College. We were, I believe, the crack patrol in the competitions. What I did not like was washing in ice-cold water, and being made to sit on a log in the open air taking notes with fingers so cold they could barely hold a pencil. In a first group meeting we were solemnly told that camp time was so many minutes and so many seconds past such and such an hour. I asked a question more out of politeness than for need of an answer. But the answer when it came, "That was a stupid question!" did not encourage my cooperation. I remember restraining myself with difficulty from replying, "At least it was civil."

We were asked to state in writing that we owed a total allegiance to King and Country. These were the years of "No more War" student campaigns against the Merchants of Death, and the Hunger Marchers. As one who was actually present at the famous Oxford Union debate on the motion, "In no circumstances will this House fight for its king and country", and who had helped feed the Hunger Marchers on their way through Oxford, I expressed some reservations on this point. I was not awarded the Woodbadge.

The time came at last for our departure. We sailed from the London Docks at North Woolwich in August 1936 with the P&O ship SS *Ranpura* bound for Singapore. I realize now how sorry my parents were that I had decided to work overseas, but they knew I was keen to go, and insisted that I follow my inclination. My father, as librarian of the Plumstead Public Library in south-east London, was popular and easy-going. He was interested in the welfare of my sister Barbara and me, but it was to my mother that I owed most of what success I had achieved up to that point. It was she who had drummed into me that unless I won a Junior County Scholarship I would never get to a good secondary school. It was with her help and encouragement that I had entered St Olave's Grammar School, Tower Bridge, in 1923 with such a scholarship, and subsequently obtained a London University Matriculation Certificate at the age of fifteen, the youngest in my group. As mentioned earlier my sister Barbara also won a Junior County Scholarship.

Only much later did I fully appreciate all that I owed my mother. When I sailed on that summer's day for South East Asia with an Honours Degree in PPE from Oxford, and a Teaching Diploma (with a distinction in Teaching Practice) from the Institute of

Education, University of London, I regret that my debt to her, and indeed the unfailing support of both my parents, did not cross my mind in the excitement of the moment.

My willingness, even eagerness, to go to Malaya was closely connected with the friendship between our family and the Nightingales. Their son Bertie had joined the Malayan Civil Service a few years earlier, and while on his first home leave had fired me with the desire to see the East for myself. The link between us was that both families had attended the Viewland Road Congregational Church in Plumstead. Mr and Mrs Nightingale came with my parents to see me off at the docks, and gave me a parting gift of fifty cigarettes and some money. Strangely, although I remember the occasion well enough I cannot now picture my parents or any of those who came to see me off at the moment of that leave-taking on board.

Departure for Malaya

How different travelling to the East was in 1936 compared with doing so today. As a new member of the Malayan Education Service in my early twenties, I travelled as a first-class passenger. We dressed for dinner – black dinner-jacket or white mess with cummerband – and were summoned to our tables by a Goanese steward sounding a silver trumpet. As soon as we were out to sea we looked forward to three weeks of gracious living. Malcolm Muggeridge in his autobiography, *Chronicles of Wasted Time*, describes how on his first sea voyage to India he noticed the men becoming more aggressive and the women's accents more affected as the journey progressed. There is undoubtedly some truth in this, but it seems to me looking back that this change applied much more to those disembarking at Bombay than to those of us who were destined for Malaya.

Apart from George Tacchi and myself, there were on board a group of newly recruited Malayan Civil Service cadets, who kept together and exchanged views on their coming assignments. Among them was T.M. Hart, who attracted considerable attention from us because he was a Scottish rugby international, and had captained Scotland at cricket. There was also an attractive young woman, Philippa Perry, who was a geography specialist in the Malayan Education Service. She was returning to St George's Girls, School, Penang, after her first home leave. Philippa was enthusiastic about life in Malaya, and she allowed me to squire her around a good deal on board, partly, I realized afterwards, to keep the young Bombay bloods at bay.

Once through the Bay of Biscay and past Gibralter, the crew and the stewards changed from their blues to white drill, and George, who had been brought up in Hong Kong, taught me how to use a spoon and fork for my first curry tiffin, drawing my attention to the fact that real limes rather than slices of lemon were served with the curry. We felt then that we were really on our way.

Our next stop was Port Said, where we were entertained by Arab boys diving for coins thrown by the passengers from the deck, and by the remarkable gulli-gulli man, whose repertoire of tricks with live chicks and other conjurer's appurtenances as he sat crossed-legged on the deck won universal admiration. Small boats filled with hummocks made of camel leather and other wares clung to the ship like barnacles. A brisk trade took place by rope and basket, with much bargaining between passengers on deck and Arab traders below. Everyone paid a visit to the famous store of Simon Artz and returned to the ship laden with Turkish delight, something in leather, and maybe a pith helmet or topee, for such headgear was by no means extinct in those days.

Afterwards came the slow descent down the Suez Canal. From the deck, we waved from time to time to small groups of British soldiers working, or just sitting on the banks; watched the supercilious movements of camels; discovered the reality of mirages; or sipped exotic new drinks in velvety black nights under the starlit sky.

The fierce heat of Aden was another new experience. I remember perfumes and cameras in the shops at bargain prices in the customs-free port, the acrid smell of camels at close quarters, the refuelling of the ship from floating pontoons, and then at night chugging our way through mysteriously looming vessels back to the welcoming lights of our own ship.

Arrival at Bombay was an important event. Here the pukkah sahibs moved with arrogant confidence into their special world, exemplified in Bombay by the Taj Mahal Hotel, luxurious and exclusive. We ourselves went to Green's which at the time seemed to me to equal the Taj Mahal in elegant affluence. Philippa looked stunning in a long silk Chinese embroidered housecoat, and was the cynosure of all eyes.

Somehow we did not miss the "Bombay smarties", as we called them, after their departure. Some of them had let fall remarks about a couple we had become attached to on the games deck. He was in the Indian Civil Service, but I heard the smarties call his pretty wife a "stengah", which was pronounced "stinger". I had just learned to use this word to designate a whisky soda, the term "sa-tengah" meaning "a half" in Malay, and was puzzled and shocked that such a derogatory remark should be of a charming girl, who showed no sign of being of mixed blood to my inexperienced eye, and even if she were, what, I wondered could that possibly matter. This was my first brush with the colour prejudice found in British India.

The next port of call was Colombo. I often think when making journeys by air to places like Bangkok, which today one can reach non-stop from London, not always very comfortably, how much one misses in these modern journeys. By sea, in a span of three weeks, one had time to assimilate the change of climate and savour the character of each new port of call. There was something unforget-table and thrilling in the slow approach to Colombo harbour, from which indefinable spicy smells wafted. The harbour of Colombo is spacious, and when we arrived it was filled with shipping. We anchored a short ferry-ride from the quay and lost no time in going ashore.

There were two essential stopping places ashore in those days – the Galle Face Hotel and Mount Lavinia. The Galle Face was anoth-er shrine of the pukkah sahibs. Its most impressive feature was its battery of ceiling fans in the dining room, sweeping majestically over tables arrayed with white napery, and attended by a score or so of uniformed waiters. Its verandahs overlooked the Indian Ocean, and were fanned by a constant stiff, warm breeze. The whole hotel gave the impression of confident power.

Mount Lavinia is on a promontory a short drive along the coast from Colombo, where a hotel is perched overlooking picturesque boulders and a sandy beach. The journey to it is remarkable because the vegetation along the way, in sharp contrast to that of Bombay, is lush with different shades of green. At the Mount Lavinia Hotel we had a curry tiffin and on the return journey to the ship, stopped at a shop to consider the possible purchase of a precious stone or two, for in Colombo, we were told, if you knew what you were about, there were sapphires to be had at bargain prices.

Now we were on the last leg of our journey. I remember well sitting out on deck in the tropical night with Philippa and later watching the phosphorescence ripple back from the bows of our ship. We were looking for the flashing light of the Muka Head lighthouse and we came upon it long after midnight. But as we knew the business of seeing Penang and getting to our jobs would be exhausting, we did not wait up for landfall.

I'm sure I did well not to stay up that night, for waking in my bunk at 6am the next morning to find we were alongside the quay in Penang was an unforgettable experience. In 1936, incoming ships tied up at the quay which abuts into the town itself and by thrusting my head through the port-hole I could take in the sight, the smell and the uniqueness of Penang in one glorious moment. We had arrived.

It seems that in those days arrangements for the assignment of new staff to the Education Department were left flexible until the last possible moment. I did not know to which school I would be going until I was informed in an official cable which reached me in Colombo. I was to go to the Malay College, which was situated in the small town of Kuala Kangsar, some sixty-eight miles inland from Penang. As the day-mail train left Penang in the early morning, I had to disembark with despatch and get my luggage through customs and onto the train as quickly as possible. Philippa was disappointed that I felt compelled to move directly to my job. She had hoped to show me Penang, one of the most beautiful islands in South East Asia, before I moved on. But I was glad that I did catch that train, for I would undoubtedly have given a bad impression to the school I was destined for had I stayed a moment longer than necessary in Penang.

The capital of Penang is Georgetown, but the island is small enough for its capital to be known generally as Penang too. There is no railway on the island itself other than a funicular railway which carries passengers by cable-car to the top of its 2000-foot high hill, but it has a station where one can buy tickets and a railway ferry boat which takes passengers across to Butterworth on the mainland, where the railway line actually begins. (At time of writing, 1999, I note with a touch of sadness that the stretch of water between the island of Penang and the mainland has just been spanned by one of the longest bridges in the world.) On that morning in 1936 I eventually found myself on the day-mail Kuala Lumpur in a compartment with a "mem", who quickly discovered that I was a new arrival. She asked me many questions, some in Malay, and even checked to see whether I knew how to write the Malay word for dog, "anjing", in jawi, the Arabic script. As I had studied Malay as part of the Colonial Course at the School of Oriental Studies off Finsbury Circus under Sir Richard Winstedt, the foremost British Malay scholar of the day, I was glad to be able to satisfy her curiosity.

The railway track from Butterworth to Kuala Kangsar runs through some of the most beautiful country in Malaya. First the wide expanse of rice fields around Bukit Mertajam, with perhaps a glimpse of Kedah Peak in the distance on fine days, and then rubber plantations and rising ground to a pass near Taiping. Kuala Kangsar lies twenty-two miles further east and south past more rocky outcrops spectacularly rising several hundred feet above bright green paddy fields. At first the railway track and the road run side by side, and one can see from the railway carriage a thin stream of automobile traffic interspersed with an occasional bullock-cart, but later the road swings away to reappear only at intervals throughout the journey. At least that is how it all looked in 1936.

I shall never forget my arrival at the Kuala Kangsar railway station. The headmaster, Mr Charles Bazell, apparently had not received any firm intimation of my coming. But knowing the scheduled arrival time of the *SS Ranpura*, he had sent the college clerk, Che Hashim, in his own car, a tourer of ancient vintage even in that year, to meet the day-mail from Penang, on the off-chance that I might be on it. Che Hashim was a solemn, decorous Malay who soon had my luggage aboard, and together we were driven sedately by the Headmaster's driver to the Headmaster's house.

Kuala Kangsar is situated in the State of Perak where the Kangsar joins the much larger Perak river. "Kuala" means confluence, so the name Kuala Kangsar denotes where the Kangsar and the Perak rivers join. It is distinguished by its being the seat of the sultan of Perak. The Sultan has a fine palace in pink marble overlooking the Perak river, with its golden, onion-shaped domes gleaming in the sun. Kuala Kangsar is also where the Malay College was founded in 1905 as an elite boarding institution for the sons of the Sultan of Perak and of the other Sultans of the Federated Malay States and for the sons of the Malay nobility, the "raja-raja", country-wide. Apart from these two special features Kuala Kangsar had, and still has a well-known multi-racial school of its own, named Clifford School after Sir Hugh Clifford, one of the country's best–known Governors.

Mr Bazell was pleased with my prompt arrival. The college, was not in session at the time, but would be in a few days, and he proposed to set me to work to teach English in the Lower "Prep" School without delay. I was handed over to his senior assistant,

Dennis Ambler, with whom I was to share a bungalow, until a bungalow similar to his, but temporarily occupied by a Malay master and his family, could be prepared for me. I felt quite embarrassed to find myself the cause of a senior Malay member of staff with a rather large family being summarily transferred from the bungalow he was in to another much less attractive one. But it quickly became apparent to me that the Headmaster's ruling was absolute law and was certainly not to be challenged by a young new arrival straight off the ship.

I followed Dennis past the pillared front of the school and alongside the tennis courts and the small swimming pool. Then, as I entered his compound, I received a welcome for which I was quite unprepared. A golden-haired gibbon ape swung down from a tree, perched on my forearm, and put a long arm about my neck. This was Winnie, Dennis's pet ape, and for me the beginning of a long love-hate relationship. I quickly appreciated that Winnie was making a friendly gesture, but I was not pleased at the mushy mango stain that her right hand left on my new white drill suit.

After I had settled my luggage in my room and had a bath and a change, Dennis suggested that we visit "the Club" before dinner. The Idris Club was exclusive to expatriates – government servants, rubber planters, a few businessmen – and their wives. The only non-European members were honorary – the royal family itself, His Highness the Sultan, the Raja Muda, the heir apparent and the Raja Bendahara, the second in line to the throne. We had a drink together, and I was introduced to a few people. Then Dennis suggested that he play a hand of bridge with some friends. I readily agreed, but was so tired that I fell asleep on a settee. We finally sat down to dinner in Dennis's bungalow at around 10:30pm. I did not play bridge, and I think that first night's experience turned me against it. Throughout the whole of my twenty-one years in Malaya I was quite happy to be known as a non-player. In any case I soon learned that Dennis was an outstanding player, indeed one of the best in the country. This did nothing to encourage me to take up the game.

My first assignment, as the Headmaster had indicated, was to teach English in the junior or Prep School. The boys in this part of the Malay College were the newcomers. They were enrolled, as were all the college students, from the Federated Malay States (FMS) – Perak, Selangor, Negeri Sembilan and Pahang– and from the Unfederated Malay States (UNS) – Perlis, Kelantan, Trengganu and Johore. There were no students from the Unfederated State of Kedah, because that State preferred to send all its Malay boys to the Sultan Abdul Hamid College in its own capital city of Alor Star. The College also enrolled a few students from the neighbouring territories of Sarawak and Brunei. The common denominator was that all the College boys were ethnically Malays, and either of noble birth – the "raja-raja" as they were called– or the sons of well-placed Malay government officers. They entered Form I of the Prep School at the age of twelve or thirteen.

In 1936, the islands of Singapore and Penang, and the town of Malacca and its vicinity, were known as the Straits Settlements, and were administered separately by British Governors. Malay boys from the Straits Settlements were not eligible for admission to the Malay College, Kuala Kangsar, or the MCKK as it was called. Members of the Malayan Education Service, however, could be appointed not only to schools on the mainland of Malaya, including the Malay College, but also to schools in the Straits Settlements. Thus I found that while I had been posted to the Malay College, my friend George Tacchi had been sent to a school in Singapore. The normal posting of an "Education Officer", which we soon discovered was our official designation, was a tour of about three years, normally followed by a generous spell of home leave.

The formal class I faced on my first day as an assistant master in the Malay College were a very attractive group. The boys appeared to my western eye to be small for their age, but gentle and courteous. Each of them wore the national dress of the Malays, a loose blouse or baju, a skirt or sarong in brightly patterned cotton of ankle length, sandals, usually with rubber soles, and a songkok, the rounded black velvet cap of the Malays. They were eager to learn and I enjoyed teaching them.

As time went on my workload increased to include the older boys and other subjects, but the main thrust of my teaching programme remained the improvement of the spoken and written English of the boys in the various grades. After some time I was entrusted with the English Language and Literature courses for the Cambridge School Certificate, the qualification which was the recognized gateway to the higher levels of employment in the Government Service, and to "Higher Education", which in the Malayan context of the time meant admission to Raffles College, Singapore.

In addition to educating Malay boys up to the School Certificate level, the College had another mission, the training of Cadets for the Malayan Administrative Service, the junior arm of the Malayan Civil Service. When I first joined the staff of the College such training was done on an ad hoc basis, but when I returned to the College as Headmaster in 1953, after various other postings in the Education Department, the training was organized in a sixth form with candidates for the course being selected from all parts of the Federation.

It was the policy of the British Government to restrict entry to the Administrative Service almost exclusively to the Malays, partly because it was recognized that the Malays were the indigenous inhabitants of the country, and partly to protect them from the economically more aggressive Chinese and Indian immigrants. In general the Malay is proudly independent, and does not adapt easily to being a paid employee in any business enterprise. Largely for this reason, tin-mining was developed with imported Chinese labour, and rubber-planting with imported Indian labour. While the economy of the country depended heavily on these two industries developed under British management, the lower and intermediate branches of the Civil Service were staffed predominantly by Malays, some of whom in time became skilled administrators. Though the higher posts of the Malayan Civil Service remained in European hands until the British Government actively began to prepare the country for independence after World War II, this early training in administration ensured that when Malaya became independent in 1957 there was a cadre of administrators capable of running the country already in place.

By the time I arrived in Malaya in 1936 the country had become stratified by occupation in what was known as a plural society. The workforce of the tin-mines was largely Chinese, the management sometimes European and sometimes Chinese. The Chinese had also moved into commerce, banking, small businesses and construction. The workforce on most rubber plantations was Tamil labour under European management. "European" in Malaya in the 1930s, it should be understood, generally meant "the white man", the "orang puteh", and embraced Britons, Australians and New Zealanders. White men of other nationalities were rare.

There were some curious exceptions to these divisions, however. The Malayan Railway, apart from top management, was almost exclusively manned by Tamils at all levels, from porters to locomotive drivers and station masters. In a similar way, the majority of the labour force in the Government Postal Services was Indian. Malays tended to be employed exclusively in Government Service jobs, including the police and the army, or, at a lower level, as salaried drivers popularly known as "sais", or as office-boys known as "peon". Sikhs were often employed as night-watchmen or "jaga". They were also members of the police force; or money-lenders.

Life in Kuala Kangsar for a young bachelor "European" schoolmaster was extremely pleasant. The academic requirements were not onerous, and the opportunities for sports of all kinds were great. At Oxford I had kept wicket for the St Edmund Hall First XI at cricket, and had captained its XI at soccer, so I was immediately given coaching responsibilities at the College in both these games.

I also quickly learned some skills in field hockey and later played for Perak State in rugby, though I had never played either of these games before going to Malaya. In fact like most of my contemporaries in those days I would be playing a game of some sort almost every afternoon. If it were not a team game, then it might be tennis or some other court game. At the College there were squash courts, and even Eton fives courts, which enabled games to be played in the early mornings, or in the case of squash, by floodlights at night. I had played Eton fives at St Olave's but left my fives gloves behind in England, as I felt certain there would be no fives courts in Malaya, let alone Eton fives courts, which are quite rare even in England. I soon discovered that the MCKK courts were the only ones of their kind in the whole country. Mr Bazell was keen on fives, and every Sunday morning at 8am he would call upon three members of his staff to join him in a game. It was he who had been responsible for installing both the fives courts and the squash courts at the College.

The Sultan of Perak, Sultan Iskandah Shah, was a keen horseman and horse fancier. He kept a stable of polo ponies, and the polo ground in Kuala Kangsar was claimed to be the most beautiful in the country. Every morning at break of day His Highness could be found seated beneath his huge yellow umbrella, the symbol of Perak royalty, watching his ponies at exercise. I was told I might be allowed to join in this activity if I wished, and so I quickly learned to follow a certain routine.

To enable full advantage to be taken of the coolness of the early morning, the first classrooom period at the College took place around 7am before a break for breakfast. I would drive down to the polo ground in my car before daylight and greet His Highness in the first rays of dawn. HH would call a sais to lead up a pony. I would express my thanks in my best Malay, mount and ride off. I had no previous riding experience, and my earliest efforts were confined to the riding school compound. But later I was allotted a former racehorse called "Why worry?", who gave me some quite frightening times, as he thought the polo ground was a race track. Usually after a short ride I would thank HH again, and return to my bungalow for a quick bath and change. This would be if I did not have to teach a first period. Occasionally, however, I would take a first lesson straight after a ride, still wearing my jodhpurs.

As mentioned earlier there was another school in Kuala Kangsar called the Clifford School, which served the town and district. It differed from the Malay College in that it was a co-educational multi-racial day school. It was known as an "English" school, as English was the medium of instruction. Children came into Primary I at the age of six or seven, knowing only the elements of their mother tongue and would be taught English by the direct method. Subject to their ability being adequate, they could move up the school year by year to the School Certificate classes. A typical class in the upper school would comprise Malays, Chinese, Indians and Eurasians. There were also in the Kuala Kangsar area Malay Schools conducted in Malay, Chinese Schools conducted in Mandarin, and Indian Schools conducted in Tamil. Malay children, because of the preference given to them by the Government, had the opportunity of transferring into "English" schools through Special Malay classes, SMI and SMII, at the age of about twelve, after which they would be absorbed into the main stream of the "English" schools.

Clifford School, Kuala Kangsar, known colloquially as CSKK, with an enrolment of approximately six hundred, including about one hundred girls, had more than three times the numbers of the College. Naturally there was great rivalry between the two schools, especially in sports. The Headmaster of Clifford School, Mr Bazell's contemporary, was Bernard Preedy. His two special passions were the school's hockey team and an elaborate electric model railway, which occupied a section of the school grounds. Malaya had, and still has, an international reputation for field hockey and badminton, and Clifford School was regarded as the cradle of Perak State hockey. So great was the rivalry in hockey between the two schools that fixtures between them were restricted in some years, until finally they were eliminated. By the 1960s, because this rivalry had increased rather than diminished, no games of any kind took place between the two schools.

It happened after a few months that T.M. Hart, the international rugby and cricket player, who had been with us on board the *Ranpura*, was posted to Kuala Kangsar as Assistant District Officer. He immediately became associated with KK cricket. He helped coach the College XI, and organized an all-European KK side which played whole-day matches on Sundays against various local teams. To field such a side it was necessary for certain planters to travel long distances from their estates, and so on occasion we would have to accept a player from the other side to make up a team. Usually, however, the eleven could just be made up if local members of the Malayan Civil Service, Police, Agriculture, PWD, and Education Departments, as well as the planters, all answered the call. Tom Hart's enthusiasm was such that he appeared not only at the MCKK cricket nets, but even organized one for these KK Europeans as well.

Shortly after my arrival in KK the town was plunged into festivities connected with a royal wedding at the palace. Whether it was a Perak prince or princess involved I cannot now recall, but the lavishness of the celebrations, which continued for many days and nights, was most impressive.

The European community was generously invited to most of the festivities, and I have a vivid memory of stage dancing by a professional troupe; many displays of "ronggeng"– the traditional Malay dance in which guests are invited to join; "Wayang Kulit"–puppet shows in which traditional stories are enacted by cut-out figures whose shadows are thrown upon a translucent screen; a tea-party in the Palace gardens, at which the British Resident spoke and ice-cream flavoured with durian was served; football and hockey matches; Malay theatre shows; a polo tournament, to take part in which teams travelled from far and near; and the pièce de résistance, as far as we young Government servants were concerned, a grand ball in the great palace ballroom.

The arrangements for this kind of celebration were elegant and conducted with Malay panache. A typical touch, which was no doubt the brainchild of the horse-loving sultan, was an elephant procession, primarily for the polo-playing guests, but extended to others, which meandered through the jungle and forded the Perak River on its way to the polo ground. I remember years later thumbing through a *Country Life* magazine and being struck by what seemed to be an incongruous photograph in a magazine devoted to the English countryside. It was a string of elephants, with bulging houdahs, crossing a river. I was even more surprised to read that the river in the photograph was the Perak river at Kuala Kangsar.

The most important part of a Malay wedding is the "bersanding" in which the bride and bridegroom sit side by side on a kind of throne, staring straight ahead, with only their little fingers touching. They have been led to their positions by retainers, the bride by the women, the groom by the men, and they sit immobile. At this point in the wedding ceremony the bride and the groom are not allowed to speak or look at each other. In the case of the royal couple they sat beneath an elaborate yellow silken canopy in resplendent garments. Guests as well as relatives passed in line to sprinkle yellow rice and scented water on them in token of their good wishes for the couple's prosperity and family well-being. I remember also admiring some of the wedding gifts which were on display. Typical gifts were pillows and fans fashioned in plum-red velvet, heavily embroidered with gold thread.

When I arrived at the College, the only other European on the staff besides Dennis Ambler and the Headmaster, was Gar Woods, an Irishman from Bangor, County Down, who lived with his wife Nora on the other side of the tennis courts. Gar was a gold medalist in mathematics from Queen's College, Belfast, and an excellent teacher, though the boys found his accent difficult to understand until they became accustomed to it. Gar and Nora were kindness itself in showing me the ropes, and discussing, over innumerable cups of tea, any problems I might have. They also persuaded me to have a shot at golf and bridge. However, while I enjoyed their company immensely, I never took to either of these games.

In 1937 a young woman school teacher, a primary and handwork specialist named Jessie Hirst, was posted to Clifford School. As young, unmarried, white women were extremely rare in Malaya, I immediately struck up a friendship with her, which rapidly developed into a whirlwind romance. We went about together constantly. It ended when Jessie was transferred to Singapore, where she fell in love with the music specialist there named Glan Williams. When she found that Glan was only interested in a relationship without marriage, and that she was to be posted to Alor Star, Kedah, in the far north of the country, she sent in her resignation in disgust. It was promptly accepted by the Government. I went to see her off when she sailed from Penang for England, but we never met again.

About this time there were a number of moves and transfers which made an impact on my life. Charles Bazell retired from the service on reaching the mandatory retirement age of 55. He returned to his native Somerset and purchased two cottages next to each other in the little village of Canningtown, near Bridgwater. These he converted into a comfortable dwelling. Being a confirmed bachelor he arranged for a family to live with him on the understanding that the property would become theirs on his decease. Mrs Gibbs would look after his creature comforts, while Mr Gibbs would do the heavier work in the garden. This arrangement proved felicitous for all concerned, and Mr Bazell lived quietly in his village until he died at the age of 96. For a number of years my wife Phyllis and I sent him a bottle of sherry at Christmas, and I visited him several times during my leaves and stays in England.

Charles Bazell was headmaster of the Malay College for fifteen years, from 1923 to 1938. He was a strict disciplinarian, and in this respect carried on the tradition of Hargreaves, who had been the College's first headmaster from 1905 to 1918. Smoking, for example, was invariably punished by caning by both of these headmasters. Once Bazell found he had unjustifiably caned a boy for smoking, for the boy was proved to be innocent. He said he was sorry, but that it was a good lesson for the boy because it showed how unjust the world could be. This remark was typical of Bazell, who claimed to be a stoic, and set up Kipling as his hero. He suffered greatly from arthritis, but never let this disability keep him from his work. He was also something of a misogynist, except with respect to the headmistress of the Raffles Girls School in Singapore, Miss Richardson, whom he greatly admired. I remember reporting to him that I intended to marry Jessie Hirst. He was not encouraging. "God help you!" was his comment. He was a great believer in the prefect system, and the prefects, especially the head-boy, were given considerable responsibility and power. Once a week he gave them cakes and tea in his bungalow. These teas were highly prized, as the cakes were of excellent quality, sent specially by train from Penang.

In 1938 Bazell was replaced as headmaster by H.R. Carey, who had served as an assistant master at the college from 1924 to 1928. Carey was a great athlete. Besides being a prominent polo player he had run for Cambridge University, played soccer, rugby and cricket for the State of Perak, and hockey for the Federated Malay States. Sometimes he would supervise the playing fields and observe the various games on horseback. He was a good headmaster who gave the school prestige and style. Among the changes he introduced was a new house system. Instead of the house names Heads, Wheels and Rookies, based on the names of house masters of the past, four new houses were established named after the four rulers of the Federated Malay States at the time of the foundation of the college in 1905. These were Ahmad (Pahang), Idris (Perak), Mohamed Shah (Negeri Sembilan) and Sulaiman (Selangor). The representative colours of these rulers black, white–yellow and red– became the four colours of the college flag and crest. Carey also brought the curriculum up to date, introducing the Cambridge Junior Certificate, and improving the course of the probationers for the Administrative Service, who now proceeded to Raffles College, Singapore, after one year at the College.

Carey had hardly settled in before a new member of staff arrived. This was C.W. (Bill) Jackman, a hockey blue from Lincoln College, Oxford, who was about my age, and quickly became one of my best friends. It was understood that his fiancee would be coming out to marry him as soon as possible. Within a short time this was arranged, and I had the pleasure of being Bill's best man. Bill and Peggy were married in the tiny Church of the Resurrection in Kuala Kangsar, and the reception was held in the Headmaster's house.

The next change was that Gar Woods was transferred to the Penang Free School, and the Woods' bungalow was taken by the new maths master, F.C.W. Edge and his wife Margaret. Clifford and Margaret had known each other in Tsingtau, China, and had been married there.

Bill's life was complicated by the fact that Peggy was convalescing from tuberculosis. For this reason the Jackmans installed an air-conditioner in their bedroom at a time when such appliances were rare and regarded as luxuries. Bill's father had been a parish priest in Kent and a canon of Canterbury Cathedral, so Bill naturally became a pillar of the Church of the Resurrection. This little Anglican church, built of wood, which could accommodate no more than about fifty people, was serviced by All Saints Church in the larger community of Taiping.

The Malays are a Muslim people. Under the treaty which the Sultans signed with the British it was agreed that the British would rule and protect the country, but would in no way interfere with the country's religion or customs. As far as the Malay College was concerned this meant that time was set aside for religious teaching by Malay teachers, and that the boys observed the law and the customs of Islam, including in particular praying five times a day, fasting during the month of Ramadan and attending mosque on Fridays. There were few Christians in Kuala Kangsar, and among the Christians few church-goers. In the larger towns, however, there was a small but quite a strong representation of Christianity. There were Catholic churches and their schools and convents, and American Methodist churches and their schools, which catered mainly for non-Malay children. In Kuala Kangsar there were none of these. This little Anglican church, therefore, standing a stone's throw from the town mosque which adjoined the College, was an anomaly.

One of the attractions of living in Kuala Kangsar was the existence of two beautiful jungle pools, which were ideal for picnic parties. The one at Menggelunchur, about three miles from Padang Rengas, was reached after about an hour's trek from the main road into the jungle. Menggelunchur means "sliding place". It consisted of a smooth rock sloping sharply downwards some 100 feet, with a thin trickle of water running down its smooth surface into a small pool about two feet deep. The water gushed out from both sides of the pool and became a small torrent plunging into the jungle. On one side of the sliding place was a long wire leading from the bottom of the slide to the top. This was to assist the sliders to the take-off point. Each slider would sit on a betelnut palm leaf or "upeh", and launch him or herself down the slide. Sometimes there would be a pile-up in the pool, but I never saw anyone seriously hurt. A few of the more adventurous tried coming down the slide standing up on the "upeh", but without much success. I remember Menggelunchur well because it was there that I first saw Carey. Standing there in his swimming trunks he looked a magnificent specimen of a man.

The jungle pool at Kenas was equally attractive, but in a different way. It was also situated in deep jungle, but was part of an irrigation system, so the water was deep and clear, ideally suited for swimming and picnicing. Our bottles of drink were anchored below the surface so that when we were ready for them they would be ice-cold. The pool was surrounded by high trees in dense jungle, and the boulders along the banks for some reason attracted hundreds of butterflies, many astonishingly large and brilliant in colour. It was an idyllic spot. In a letter to my mother written in October 1941, I wrote:

"This afternoon Margaret, Clifford and I went to Kenas for a quiet bathe. It was lovely – the water cold as ice, the sun as warm as toast. We had tongue and tomato sandwiches, apples and bananas, boiled eggs, pilchards, brown bread and butter, milk and ginger beer. It was very amusing watching an ant, an inch long, dragging off the veretbral column of a big pilchard. Later we watched a large fly being caught by a huge spider with a thorax the size of a thimble. Or so we thought at first. But then the "fly" climbed on the spider's back, bit him, and killed him. Then it just rubbed its hands and face, and to our immense astonishment calmly dragged the spider off. It must have been ten times its own weight."

Winnie

When I settled into Dennis's bungalow I had perforce to become better acquainted with Winnie the gibbon ape, who had greeted me on my first day in Kuala Kangsar. She was a beautiful animal, with long golden hair and an appealing face. Dennis doted on her. She was perfectly free, spending her time swinging from tree to tree in the compound, or sleeping under the bungalow roof. The college bungalows, like those of all Government servants, were provided by the Government. They had been built by the Public Works Department (PWD) and were of standard designs, each design varying according to an officer's grade. Basically they were constructed of wood, but were raised on stone pillars in an attempt to control the predations of termites or white ants. Dennis's bungalow consisted of a dining room, two bedrooms, each with its own bathroom leading down from it, a spare room and a wide verandah running round the whole building, except where the bathrooms interrupted it. In one place, near where a flight of steps led up to the entrance, the verandah widened to provide a living-room space under a ceiling fan. The roof sloped down over the verandah with a wide overhang to provide shade and to keep out the monsoon rains. The windows of the rooms had wooden shutters. All segments of the verandah were provided with blinds, made of lengths of split bamboo tied together with cord, which could be lowered as required to keep out sun or rain. At the rear of the building, steps to ground level led under a covered way to the kitchen and servants' quarters.

I soon discovered that Dennis's bungalow differed from others in one significant way. It had been adapted to cope with Winnie. As she liked to swing on anything swingable, the electric lights had no hanging flex, and bulbs were screwed directly into the ceiling. Dennis's bedroom, moreover, was Winnie-proofed in that it was provided with a spring-loaded door made with panels of mosquito-proof wire-netting. His verandah was similarly enclosed. My bedroom was less well protected. True, the good PWD had provided a solid teak frame from which a mosquito-net could be hung. But this was suspended from the ceiling by four chains, which Winnie found very interesting, especially when my mosquito-net had been let down, and I was inside it lying on the bed.

She particularly enjoyed descending in the very early morning from her own sleeping quarters in the roof, and swooping onto my mosquito-net frame, from where shortly afterwards her long arm would trail downwards to start all kinds of mischief.

Winnie had a character all her own. In some ways she resembled a retarded child. She demanded attention, and when she got it could be affectionate and endearing. If she were thwarted, however, she would retaliate by interfering in whatever was going on. Normally her requirements were simple. She would lie on her back on the floor and put up the sole of a foot to be tickled, first one and then the other. If you tired of this operation and stopped, she would pull at your hand to get you to resume. She had no regular feeding times. In any case she lived by the principle that stolen food is best. From time to time there would be a commotion in the kitchen and Winnie would emerge at the run with some stolen tit-bit held high above her head. Round the table she would go, pulling down a chair or two in her stride to impede the cook, and perhaps the gardener as well, who would be in hot pursuit. They never caught her. Sometimes the stolen object was not edible, but something which had taken her fancy, like a pen or a spectacles case. Then it would be necessary to station someone to watch her, so that the article could be recovered when she tired of it. She usually dropped it from wherever she had retreated to after a few minutes, provided our interest in it did not remain obvious.

Winnie loved dogs but teased them mercilessly. The Woods had a large Alsatian named Satan who would come and bark at her, while she taunted him from the verandah rail. In any encounter she usually managed to jump on and off his back and pull his tail. Satan quite enjoyed these meetings, but never came anywhere near catching her. Winnie had a fine voice, and when in the mood would throw back her head, round her mouth in a perfect O, and whoop up the scale in a crescendo of sound. Nothing would stop her when she was in full cry, and at these times her face expressed an uninhibited ecstasy.

Because of our special relationship to Winnie it was possible for Dennis or me to catch her in the act of misbehaving. As her arms were long and slender it was easy to pin them behind her back by the elbows for a second or two. She would then gibber with rage. As soon as she was released she would give her captor a sharp nip and dart to freedom. Those were the only times when she would bite us, but it was different with the postman or messengers. With them she had a bad reputation and they came prepared to defend themselves.

Winnie was generally well disposed towards invited visitors, but as she retired early she would not be seen at dinner time. However, she loved to be present at luncheon or tea. Mr Bazell was not one of Winnie's admirers, and he had tried to persuade Dennis to get rid of her. It was one of those strange situations one finds in a school. Bazell, the hard-liner on so many things allowing Dennis his senior assistant to keep Winnie. One day Bazell was invited to lunch, and there as usual was Winnie delicately sitting on the punkah, as it swung gently over the dining-room table. To be taking a meal beneath a majestically swinging punkah used to represent the acme of comfort in the tropics. The ceiling fan, which within a few years was to supersede it, somehow does not produce a motion of air nearly as satisfying.

Bazell became aware of Winnie's presence. He knew of her thieving habits where food was concerned. His eyes moved from the punkah to his plate. He pressed his fork into a juicy meatball topped with a little salad. "Here", he said, holding up his fork, "is something Winnie is not going to get." It was an ill-chosen time to make such a remark, for at that moment Winnie's long right arm drifted down like a veil and gracefully whipped the morsel from the end of his fork. Bazell's mouth remained open.

Tea in the presence of Winnie would be a more successful meal as far as guests were concerned. Friends liked to take tea with us, because often Winnie would be swinging around in the garden in an entertaining way, and sooner or later would elect to join us. She would be given a banana or allowed to acquire a piece of cake or a biscuit. and it was amusing to see her bear her prize away. Her drinking habits were most lady-like, for she dipped the back of her long fingers into the liquid she was offered, and then sucked the fur delicately, repeating the operation until her thirst was quenched.

One of the pleasures of living in Kuala Kangsar was receiving visits from the "barang" man. "Barang" in Malay meant "thing" or, colloquially, "property" or "luggage". The barang man was usually a Chinese or Javanese itinerant merchant, who would arrive on his bicycle with a huge bundle wrapped in cloth on its carrier. Inside the bundle would be a wonderful array of bric-a-brac, which, with very little encouragement from anyone in the bungalow, he would spread out over the verandah and offer for sale. He would sit cross-legged, surrounded by Chinese embroidered cloth or pottery, carvings in ivory, kris (ceremonial daggers of the Malays and Javanese), Indian brassware, or Javanese heads carved in teak, and we would enjoy the game of haggling over the prices. On these occasions Winnie could be a menace, and we never invited a barang man in unless she were out of sight.

One day an old Malay woman arrived around teatime, carrying a tray fitted with compartments in which were displayed a variety of semi-precious stones nestling in cotton wool. We were pleased to inspect her wares. Suddenly Winnie appeared, swinging down from the roof onto the verandah balustrade. In a flash she snatched a selection of gems in a series of lightning moves. Her long arm swung from tray to mouth three or four times before she could be stopped. It was an expensive afternoon for us, as there was no hope of recovering what she had swallowed. The old woman retired bewildered, but not dissatisfied with her afternoon's "sales".

There was no doubt that Winnie preferred men and was jealous of women. Whenever she found me talking to a woman she would show her disapproval by tugging on my arm and trying to divert attention to herself. Once, when Dennis was on leave, I returned from a trip of several days to find a woman friend of his on the verandah. She was the wife of an Inspector of Schools, a great friend of Dennis's, and had called in on her way to Taiping. She had found the house empty except for the servants and Winnie, who was nervous and antagonistic. When I appeared, Winnie, starved of her normal companionship, was most demonstrative. She clung to me passionately, making little whoops of joy. The visitor was impressed. I was embarrassed but flattered.

A characteristic of Winnie was her ubiquitousness. If she were interested in a proceeding there was little one could do to prevent her from satisfying her curiosity to the full. Even Dennis, protected in his bedroom from Winnie's incursions as he was, was surprised one day to find she had managed to penetrate his innermost stronghold. I have mentioned the predations of white ants which the pillars supporting the bungalow were supposed to control. They did so up to a point, but termites love to eat anything made of wood or wood products, so they would build tubes of mud, which hardened into tunnels, up the pillars under the house, and so into the planks of the floor. Although white-ant searchers inspected PWD houses at regular intervals, and would be rewarded by payment of an extra dollar over and above their regular pay for each termite queen found, they sometimes arrived too late to prevent extensive damage.

So it was that, Dennis resting on his bed one afternoon, heard a scratching noise above his head. On looking up he saw to his amazement the face of Winnie peering at him through the wooden partition which separated him from the spare room. She had heard the termites at work, picked away at the point where the noises came from, and discovered that there was no wood between the two layers of paint in several of the planks that separated the two rooms. In no time she had torn the flakes of paint away and was into forbidden territory. Dennis found later that before climbing up into the partition, the termites had eaten through a corner of the spare room floor, and burrowed through a pile of books standing there.

Winnie's curiosity also took her into bathrooms, whenever she had the chance. One of our friends complained; "I don't mind her watching me" he said, "but when she makes off with the toilet roll that really is too much."

I did not own a car when I first arrived in Malaya, but after several months of struggling without one, I bought a second-hand "Standard" saloon. It had a sunshine roof made of waterproofed canvas, of which I was rather proud. It was my custom to park this car under the largest tree in my compound, a huge mango tree which gave good shade. It was also a favourite haunt of Winnie's though the mangoes the tree bore were small and sour. One day, in a gesture of exuberance, she dropped from twenty feet or more onto to the roof of the car and went right through it. I had a long correspondence with the manager of my insurance company in Ipoh about compensation for this. In the end the company paid up, and I had the roof repaired under my accident policy, as the damage was construed to be an "act of God". This, however, was only so, as the manager pointed out to me over a drink at the Idris Club, because Winnie was actually owned by Dennis. Had she been my ape no payment would have been due, as it would have been my business to keep her under control.

Dennis left the College about the time of Bazell's retirement, to become headmaster of the Kuala Pilah English School in the State of Pahang. It was then that a decision had to be taken about Winnie. Dennis did not wish to take her with him, and I, when it came to the point, did not wish to assume sole responsibility for her, as complaints about her behaviour, and in particular her aptitude to bite visitors, were on the increase. So Winnie was sent to a wealthy animal fancier in Calcutta. She departed in a huge barred crate with every comfort. I regret to add that she did not live very long in her new habitat. I suspect she missed an environment ideally suited to her own particular brand of mischief.

A Jungle Trip

One of the first English women I met in Malaya outside of Kuala
Kangsar was Celia Taylor, who was a Domestic Science (Home
Economics) teacher living in Taiping twenty-two miles away to the
north. In April 1939 she invited me and several other of her friends
to join her over the Easter weekend on a trip to the northern corner of Perak, where she was going to inspect the work being done
in a remote Malay village girls' school. The special attraction of this
trip was that we were going there with the help of three elephants,
and returning by rafting down the Perak river on a bamboo raft.
Our party, besides, Celia comprised Phyllis, the wife of a Telok
Anson Education Officer, Tony who worked for a Taiping commercial firm, Bill Jackman and me from the Malay College, the Malay
Visiting Teacher from Grik, whose job covered the Upper Perak
District, three Malays in charge of the elephants, and three members of the hill jungle tribes of Malaya known as Sakais. The
clothing of the Sakais consisted of a string round the waist, and
they carried blowpipes with a sheaf of poisoned darts which they
demonstrated for us on several occasions.

Two of the elephants were provided by the Government, and the
third smaller elephant was hired at the rate of $2.50 (Malayan) a
day. When one considers that the exchange rate for the Malayan
dollar at that time was about eight Malayan dollars to the English
pound it is clear that our trip, though it might be extraordinary,
was not going to be expensive. We soon discovered, however, that
our progress would be far from speedy. First, we had to be introduced to the elephants, and we turned in early on the advice of the
chief elephant driver or "gembala". Second, we had not bargained
for the time it would take to load the elephants, nor for the fact

that after travelling for half a day they require half a day to rest and eat. We found that we had to cross numerous small bridges, and that the elephants had to move at a laboriously slow pace because the bridges could not support their weight. They often used their front knees on a particularly steep bank. On the first morning we had to traverse a small suspension bridge over a deep ravine. It comprised a single line of planks and two hawsers which were secured to trees on either bank, and it swayed precariously so that no more than two of us could cross at a time.

About three in the afternoon we reached our halting bungalows in a tiny clearing on the bank of the river. These were three simple huts all of the same pattern. Each one of them consisted of two wooden walled rooms with corrugated iron roof , two windows and a door, and were connected to one another by a wooden or bamboo platform ten to twelve feet wide. The whole structure was about twelve to fifteen feet from the ground and was raised on strong wooden piles, enabling the elephants to be loaded or unloaded straight from the platform. There were no bathrooms and no furniture except for a large sand tray and some bricks on the platform on which we did all our cooking. The huts were extremely hot in the afternoon, pleasantly cool at night and really cold in the early morning. We waited until our elephants arrived, and soon had a saucepan of water boiling for a welcome cup of tea. Then we changed into our bathing gear and took a dip in the river. Shortly afterwards we were joined by the elephants who enjoyed themselves immensely. They lay on their sides in the water and were scrubbed by their gembalas with coconut fibre brushes. We turned in early – the two women in one room and the three men in the other, sharing the two mosquito nets.

The next morning we made an early start. The men went on ahead while the two women decided to try taking a ride on the back of one of the elephants They found this an interesting experience. The ride was slow and uncomfortable. The elephants' feet sank deep into the mud and made a great squelching noise when they were pulled out. They noted that their elephant was careful to put its feet into the holes left by the elephant in front of it. They rode only for four or five miles, but it took all of three hours. The last part of this ride took them down a steep and slippery ravine to a shallow part of the river. Here the elephants enjoyed sluicing themselves with their trunks but they had been trained not to squirt on their passengers so the ladies remained dry.

That night we camped in Kuala Temengor (Kuala means confluence) where the smaller river Temengor joins the larger Perak river. It was here that we saw the Sakais carrying water in long hollow sections of bamboo. The partitions inside the bamboo are removed except at the end of a fifteen-foot section so that the hollowed-out part can hold nearly two gallons of water, which can thus be conveniently carried on the shoulder. A Sakai village consisting of only four or five houses built entirely of clean new bamboo stood not far away.

One of the advantages the women had enjoyed by riding on the elephants was that they had escaped the leeches, which are always troublesome in the Malayan jungle. Anyone walking through the jungle cannot escape them. They attach themselves to a person's clothing as he or she walks by, and only drop off when they are gorged with blood. De-leeching is best accomplished by applying a glowing cigarette butt to the end of the leech, but it is always an unpleasant business. Celia wore her jodhpurs for the journey and found them much more satisfactory than skirts. The men wore shorts, which provided no protection, but allowed them to see how they wore faring against the leeches, and did not hinder the process of de-leeching.

The second night we stayed in a hut similar to the one we used on our first night, turning in early after a refreshing mug of hot Ovaltine. In the morning Celia set off before the rest of us because she wanted to reach early the small Malay school she intended to inspect, so that the girls could be brought back in the afternoon to meet her. She had dressed in a skirt that morning because in those days it would not have been appropriate for a European woman teacher to have appeared at a girls' school wearing jodhpurs.

The school turned out to be quite small with only about eighty pupils. The visitors book showed that no European had visited the place for eight years. The Malay Visiting Teacher went up from Grik once a year, and the Malay Assistant District Officer paid an occasional visit, but apparently Celia was the first white person that most of the pupils had ever seen. Her first task was to conduct a hygiene inspection and look at the children's work. After this the children were sent home. Then with the help of the Malay Visiting Teacher Celia concentrated on stocktaking and an inspection of buildings and furniture, the school compound and toilet facilities.

I remember Bill and I arrived after all this work had been accomplished, but we had been caught in a tropical downpour and were soaked to the skin. All of us were revived, however, by cups of tea provided by the headmaster. Tea served on such occasions as these was always made with condensed milk, but we found it extremely refreshing. While Celia finished her work Bill and I repaired the school clock with a penknife and a little machine oil. Late in the afternoon we started back for the river, where we found four stalwart Malays putting the finishing touches to the raft we were to use for our return journey the next day. Travelling down-stream it was confidently expected that we would reach Grik in one day.

When planning the week's meals Celia had expected to get a curry and rice at Temengor prepared by the teachers, but the school was so far from our hut, and she had kept the teachers working so late that in the end we prepared a small meal ourselves using up the odds and ends of food we had left, thinking that they would not come so late in the dark. But they did come, having killed, plucked and cooked at least one chicken and bringing with them a lavish supply of curry and rice. As we had all dined rather well we piled our plates with the food and transferred it to the bedroom promising to eat it later. But the teachers did sit down and share our tea, and we talked well into the night eating up odds and ends of food when we felt so inclined.

We had started out on 9th April and according to plan we were preparing to return by raft down the river on Thursday 13th. Most of our "barang" (the convenient Malay word for baggage of all sorts) had to be packed to go back to Grik on the elephants, a three-day journey, and we spent some time deciding what to take on the raft and what to leave for the elephants. Our Sakai friends were extremely sceptical about our raft for we had to get twelve people on it in addition to our luggage. The raft was eleven to twelve feet in length and about five feet wide, and made entirely of lengths of bamboo about as thick as a man's arm expertly lashed together with rotan thonging, not a nail anywhere. In the centre was a platform about one foot high and six to seven feet long, which covered the full width of the raft. Over this platform support- ed by bamboo poles was an attap (palm leaf) roof, which provided excellent shelter against sun or rain. Our baggage was lashed firm- ly to the platform, leaving enough room for us passengers to sit reasonably comfortably facing fore or aft.

Our crew navigated this frail-looking craft through some very dif- ficult reaches of the river. Two stood at the front of the raft using two long bamboo paddles, each with a short bamboo blade at the end fixed in position on pronged sticks, so that the paddles could swing from side to side. Another crew member with a similar pad- dle stood at the back of the raft, and a fourth held a long pole with which to fend us off from rocks or other obstacles. The floor of the platform was made of split bamboo lashed to the floor poles in such a way as to make a really flat surface, smooth and quite com- fortable to sit on even without cushions.

We were ready to set off by 7.30am. We paid off the Sakais, tipped the gembalas, who were later paid by the government, and left our luggage in their care. We also paid a sad farewell to our elephants of whom we had become quite fond, and also to the large crowd of Malay adults and children from the village to whom we must have presented an unusual sight. It was a particularly beautiful Malayan morning, so we made full use of our cameras. Before we left we were carefully instructed on how to throw ourselves from one side of the raft to the other in case the raft started to roll, to prevent us from capsizing. How we managed to proceed at all was a source of wonder to us, because sometimes we floated in as little as four inches of water. But bamboos are amazingly light, and being hollow, very buoyant.

Barely five minutes after we had started we came to our first rapid – Jeram Dare (Jeram meaning rapid), and here we experienced quite a terrifying rocking. Waves of water washed over us and our crew hurled themselves from side to side so violently that one of them fell into the river. This seemed to cause our crew merriment rather than dismay, so we were greatly relieved. The raft soon righted itself and from then on we never rocked so violently again, though we passed through many worse rapids. Fortunately we had kept our cameras dry by hanging them up in pouches out of danger. A little later we came across a tree fallen across the river leaving us little room to pass, so the crew got off the raft and pushed us over the shallows. All morning we drifted or glided slowly down the Temengor river. The swish of the paddles, the calling of the monkeys or jungle birds, the occasional cry of a Sakai and the music of the river over the stones were the only sounds we heard. Our oarsmen knew every bend, rock and pool, and they were skilful navigators.

At about 1pm we shot out from the Temengor river into the much larger Perak river at Kuala Temengor, and soon came to a solid two miles of rapids which were very exciting as the water was swifter and deeper. We decided to take a swim and we had a fine time diving off the raft and sometimes being towed by it. At one place we saw some wild otters and occasionally large fish. There were many birds among which the kingfisher stood out dramatically because of its brilliant plumage. We were told the names of each rapid and how many people had been killed on the most dangerous of them – Jeram Berusa.

When we reached Basir, where we had spent our first night, we stopped for a while and said goodbye to our Malay guide who had joined us there. As we got nearer Grik we left the rapids and the river widened and flowed more slowly. Our crew had to paddle otherwise we would have still been on the river by nightfall. We reached Grik about 6.30pm, sooner than we had expected, but we had not realized we were some two miles from the town and had no transport to meet us. I therefore borrowed a bicycle and rode into town to fetch my car and alert the sais of Tony's and Celia's cars to bring them to where they were.

On arrival at the rest house we had some more tea, and Celia called on the ADO to thank him for all his help. We paid our raft crew (their wages came to $9, while that magnificent raft cost $6), made arrangements to have our barang sent on when it arrived, and bade everyone farewell. We departed in our various cars about 8.30pm. Celia was indeed relieved to have her driver to drive her home, for the road from Grik to Taiping measures ninety miles and crosses literally hundreds of small bridges, besides being one of the most tortuous and lonely roads in the whole country. When she later reported her safe arrival she also mentioned that she had been surprised by a black panther bounding across the road in the light of her headlamps. Phyllis came back to Kuala Kangsar with Bill and me. She stayed the night with us before returning to her home in Telok Anson, another thirty miles or so, the next day.

As the government kindly paid for two of the elephants and the raft the whole trip was extraordinarily cheap, working out at about $15 Malayan per head, including a night at the rest house, food, tips and everything. We all agreed at the time that it was the best trip we had ever made.

NB

The above report is a precis I made from Celia's own report. I had been speaking fairly regularly with her by telephone across the Atlantic (she is now Celia Barkway aged 90 and I aged 87), and we had spoken of the elephant trip which I knew she had written up in instalments in the *British Overseas Pensioners Magazine* published by the British Overseas Pensioners Association. Celia mailed me a copy of this article and kindly gave me permission to publish the above, my own shortened version of it, in this book. Her article ran to nine single-spacing type written pages.

War

While we expatriates in Malaya were living in a relatively carefree world, the clouds of war were gathering in Europe. We were insulated from the tensions of the time because the radio news did not seem to touch us, and letters between England and Malaya, transported by Imperial Airways, were often delayed. I felt fortunate to be fully occupied and anyone who has worked in a boarding school will know that the activities connected with it inevitably make the job a full-time occupation. My College activities – teaching, playing and supervising games, organizing extra-curricular activities such as debating and theatre, and general supervisory duties – took most of my time. But time had also to be made for the study of the Malay language, which was essential if an officer wished to make progress in the Service. One had to pass the Government Malay Language Examinations, Parts I and II, within a two-year time limit, if one did not wish to be blocked by a salary barrier. Part III, an advanced level, was optional, and carried with it a $1000 (Malayan) bonus if completed within a certain period. I managed to pass all three levels by 1940, but took Part III too late to collect the bonus.

I also enjoyed playing games outside the College precincts, especially those Sunday cricket matches on the town padang, and rugby for the State of Perak. This last activity entailed occasional travel to Selangor, Negeri Sembilan and Penang. The Saturday game would be followed by a rugby dinner in the major local club, and in Penang by a swim and often a water-polo match on the following Sunday morning at the Penang Swimming Club.

On 3rd September 1939 Britain declared war on Germany. The effect on the expatriates in Malaya was at first not great. Though most of us young men expatriates applied to join one or another of

59

the armed services, we were informed that our war-time duty was to keep Malaya running as usual. Most of us were members of the Federated Malay States Volunteer Force (FMSVF), a kind of territorial reserve, which could be mobilized at any time. But many of us did not take it very seriously. I was a private in a machine-gun company. As I had an interest in flying, however, and had even started to learn to fly at the Ipoh Flying Club, I applied to join the RAF Empire Training Scheme, for which training was being conducted in Canada. I felt very pleased when I passed the stringent medical examination for pilots, and was told to stand by for eventual release from the FMSVF to enable me to proceed with the Air Force training. However, events moved too fast for me to be recruited, as I shall explain later. Before I could report for duty, I was to meet my future wife in Taiping, and be required to take home leave.

In the days before the war Taiping was the capital of the State of Perak, although it was and still is smaller than Ipoh, the largest town in the State, which is situated some thirty-one miles to the south of Kuala Kangsar. It had no doubt been chosen partly because of its scenic beauty. The town nestles at the foot of Taiping Hill, then known as Maxwell's Hill, which rises sharply to nearly 3000 feet, and between the criss-cross of the town's streets and the hill were the beautiful Taiping Gardens, a splendid artificial lake, a golf course, and the New Club. Here in Taiping the British Residency was located. There were also in close proximity the Taiping Gaol and the Taiping Museum. Taiping was, in addition, a garrison town. A battalion of the Burma Rifles had been stationed there. By the time I arrived in Kuala Kangsar, however, their place had been taken by a battalion of the Dogra Regiment from India.

It was in Taiping that I first met Phyllis Sharpington, who was also a member of the Malayan Education Service. She had been transferred to Taiping from Singapore in 1939 to run the Primary School of the King Edward VII (English) School, and to train primary school teachers for the State. We met at a dance at the New Club, and immediately felt a mutual attraction. I learned that she was a Londoner like myself, and had come out to Malaya on the P&O ship *Stratheden*. War on Germany had been declared by Great Britain just as the ship was passing through the Straits of Gibraltar, and the *Stratheden* was in fact the last ship to pass through the Suez Canal before it was closed for the duration of the war.

For the next few months Phyllis and I saw much of each other, and each of us travelled the twenty-two miles between Taiping and Kuala Kangsar many times. We also spent a wonderful holiday in a government bungalow three thousand feet up Maxwell's Hill with our New Zealand friends Eve and Les Russell. Les was an Education Officer in the Taiping Office. At this point I was informed I had to take leave, as I had already been more than four years in Malaya without it.

I was advised to take my leave in Australia, as other government servants were doing at this time, on account of the war and the hazards to shipping in the North Atlantic. I discovered, however, that there was a possibility of getting to England by a ship leaving Penang in December 1940. This was the SS *Anchises* of the Blue Funnel Line, a ten thousand tonner with a cargo of rubber in her hold, and space for about one hundred passengers. I had no hesitation in deciding to sail with her, as I had not seen my parents for four years.

I had a wonderful send-off at the Kuala Kangsar railway station. Just about the whole school turned out to see me board the train, and wave and cheer me out of sight. In fact, however, my departure by train was an innocent deception. I had planned with Phyllis that she should come to Penang to see me off, and help me buy presents for the family, my mother, father and sister; and to do this she had offered to drive me the fifty or so miles from Taiping to Penang in her car. So it seemed a good idea to use my railway ticket, provided by the Government, only as far as Taiping, in order not to disappoint the College boys, who wanted to give me a good send-off, or to publicize too much the progress of our attachment. In the event, a friend of Margaret Edge was on the train and saw what happened, so our little secret was not a secret for long.

We spent a whole day in Penang revelling in the pleasures of buying Chinese embroideries, hand-decorated table linen, small carvings in ivory, Japanese lacquer work and Kelantan silver, almost filling a suitcase with presents. By the time we finally said goodbye we knew we were deeply in love and had a mutual understanding that we might marry on my return from leave.

I was pleased to find that my old friend Bill Nightingale was also travelling on the *Anchises*. We had discussed the question of insuring our luggage, but we found the rates so exorbitant that we decided that we would do nothing about it. That the rates were so high was a sobering thought. In the dining room I sat at a table with Bill and another MCS man named Skip Harris; two men from the Malayan Police Department, John Parker, a former ADC to the Governor, and an officer named Woosey; and Tommy Thomson, a rubber planter with American Plantations.

Although it was clear that the ship would be in serious danger on the last stretch of her voyage, the spirits of the passengers during their first few weeks at sea were high. There were deck games or makeshift cricket in the well-deck by day, and dancing at night. After a time, a sports and entertainment committee was appointed. Skip Harris was elected president, and I was its honorary secretary. Besides the usual deck sports and competitions we arranged quizzes, team games and a treasure hunt by couples, for which the final test was to bring to the judges' table the elusive ship's cat.

Our first port of call was Durban, for as Suez was closed we were obliged to travel round the Cape of Good Hope. We found that because of the fuel shortages the ship would have to substitute coal for oil, so that we spent several days in Durban loading up with coal. As much of the coal had to be stowed on deck, some of the younger passengers lent a hand with shovels. This work, in which I participated, however, did not prevent us enjoying what the city had to offer in the way of entertainment. With some of my friends I visited a nightclub and took a rickshaw ride, pulled by a magnificent Zulu, who on a downward slope so balanced himself between the shafts of his rickshaw that he made giant strides, and travelled at an amazing speed. There was no hint of subservience in his bearing, so that I felt nothing but exhilaration from the ride.

Capetown was different. There was something magic about Table Mountain which affected the whole city. The countryside was bountiful, the fruit and flowers spectacular. I shall never forget the flower market, ablaze with colour, on my way to the museum, which was housed in a fine building in the Dutch style, nor the rollers from the Indian Ocean curving up the beach at Muizenberg a few miles up the coast. It was a dream-like place, made more so by the backdrop of the war, except that its beauty was for me marred from the start by the attitude of the Whites towards the Africans. Apartheid was ugly at first sight and experience of it only made me feel its injustice and danger more deeply.

Our emotions in Capetown were coloured by our situation. Once round the Cape we would be in waters that could be hostile. So we were in swinging mood, enjoying the moment to the full. I remember especially a restaurant in which we chose our steaks for grilling, and sat in a balcony beneath a dome which somehow had been opened to reveal a starlit sky. A large band was giving a stirring performance of "Let us begin the beguine". The war seemed very far away.

After we had resumed our journey there was time to take stock. We had lost some South African passengers, including the South African Commercial Attache from Shanghai, who had been one of our liveliest companions, and we took on board a few new passengers. Among these was Jean Sherring, an English doctor who had brought out to Capetown some English children from parts of the country which had suffered most heavily from the German bombing, and was now returning to England. She soon became one of my inner circle of friends,- to join Bill Nightingale and Major and Mrs Dobbs from Hong Kong.

After Capetown the seriousness of our situation was reflected by several new developments. A complete blackout of the ship was ordered at all times. The ship pursued a pre-determined zig-zag course, so that it would present a difficult target for submarines, and some of the younger men passengers were invited to train as alternates to the ship's crew to man the four-inch naval gun and the two hotchkiss anti-aircraft guns mounted on the stern of the ship. I was pleased to join this passenger team.

The journey up the west coast of Africa was uneventful. We anchored briefly off Takoradi on the Gold Coast, and finally slipped through a boom into the great harbour of Freetown in Sierra Leone. I had no idea how important a port Freetown was during the war. When we arrived, there were scores of ships at anchor. Many of them were waiting to join a convoy for the last dangerous run through the Atlantic. We the passengers were not told of the risks at the time, but we learned afterwards that enemy planes flew regularly out of Dakar, Senegal, to report to the German High Command on the movements of shipping leaving Freetown, for Dakar was in the hands of Vichy France.

We arrived in Freetown harbour on the 10th February 1941 and remained there for five days, waiting to learn whether we would be attached to a convoy, or whether we should make the journey alone. My recollections of this stopover in Freetown are few, but vivid. We took a drink in the City Hotel, which we were told had provided the authentic background for Graham Greene's *Heart of the Matter*. We visited the modest cathedral, and marvelled at the memorial plaques on the walls, for it seemed that few of those who died there had attained an age much beyond thirty-five, the toll of malaria and other tropical diseases had been so great. We were also surprised by the local golf course, the greens of which were of baked mud rather than of grass. In the town the vultures flopped ominously from rooftop to rooftop, while the little African boys begged cheekily for money. I took a long run along a sandy beach in my swimming trunks, feeling gloriously fit.

In the end it was decided that we should travel alone, and we slipped through the boom at dusk for the last part of the journey. All passengers were thereafter obliged to carry their life-jackets with them at all times. During daylight hours it was four hours on and four hours off for us on the gun watch. We slept in our clothes, ready to rush out onto the deck in an emergency. As we moved north the weather became colder and the seas heavier. I put on as many layers of clothes as I could, and was glad of the sea-boots and sou'wester that I had been lent by the crew. Joan Dobbs was also kind enough to lend me her fur-lined gloves.

On one of our watches we passed a waterlogged lifeboat and as time went on there were other signs of disaster at sea–a raft, an oar, a wide spill of oil. We were beginning to think that our luck might hold, however, and that we might be able to run safely into some British port, when on the morning of the 27th February at about 9 o'clock, as I was sleeping during my four hours off, I was awakened by the sound of gun-fire and a tremendous crash and thud, which jerked me out of my bunk and had me pulling on my sea-boots all in one motion. I ran out on deck and along towards our gun astern as quickly as I could, just in time to see a plane circling out of range to make a second run across us. So it was a plane and not a submarine that had attacked. The aircraft, thin and long like a pencil, seemed to line up for its second run in a leisurely fashion, and then it was flying over us again, its machine-guns blazing. We saw its bombs falling, but by some miracle they did not hit us, plunging harmlessly into the sea on either side of the ship. The plane flew off and did not return, leaving us to take stock of the situation. The heavy machine-gun shells had spattered the deck, but surprisingly no-one was hurt. However, one of the first string of bombs had exploded below the water-line amidships on the port side. The ship's plates had been stove in and the Anchises was shipping water heavily.

The passengers were ordered to stand by the lifeboats and be ready to abandon ship, and when it was found that the ship was list-ing badly, the captain ordered the passengers to take to the boats. We had practised our lifeboat drill regularly and there was no panic in this operation. The sea was quite calm. We pulled away from the ship and waited to see what would happen. I noted that in our lifeboat there were about twenty-five people, but the only two I knew well were Major Dobbs and his wife Joan, who sat together in the stern. The only crew members with us were one of the purser's staff, a number of stewards, and some Chinese stokers who had come up from their stoking duties woefully poorly clad for the bitterly cold weather. I was in the bow of the lifeboat at the farthest point for-ward. And so we waited. There we sat hour after hour watching our ship settling slowly in the water as we drifted farther from her. We tried to see what had happened to the other lifeboats, but from where we were we could see only two or three.

Before very long evening and darkness were upon us, and as it became darker, so the sea became more turbulent. Suddenly it began to rain. A wind whipped across the crests of the seas. Our boat was tossed around like a cork. We began to ship water. Lightning flashed and the thunder cracked quickly after it. The rain turned to hail. At first the oars we found were put out in an effort to keep the boat straight. But the stewards and stokers were in no shape to use them effectively. One by one the oars were torn from the grasp of those who tried to row, until I found that my oar up in the bow was the only one in action. My hands also soon became incapable of gripping an oar, but it was possible for me to hook my oar under my arms, and pull when the seas seemed to want to push the boat sideways and capsize her. The oar was never out of the water, but a heave at the right moment at the bow had considerable leverage, and helped to keep the boat cutting into the seas rather than meeting them broad-side and so shipping masses of water.

As my back was towards the frothing peaks I was given encouragement by Joan Dobbs, who would scream "Pull" when she thought a particular swirling crest needed a special effort. This went on for some time until a corpulent steward in the middle of the boat shouted: "Shut up you old bitch!" My feeling was simple astonishment at this outburst from a ship's steward to a first-class passenger, especially as Joan was doing her best and was a gentle, gracious person still in her thirties. I received no further encouragement.

After this episode there followed a nightmare of pulling and baling. Because of the cold and lack of balers very few could lend a hand with baling out the sea-water, which threatened to make us completely waterlogged. But at last the storm subsided somewhat, and we felt we might stay afloat after all. Slowly we realized that we had lasted through the night and would at least have a dawn to help us. When dawn came we found ourselves alone. No *Anchises*, no other lifeboat in sight. Somebody had found a can of condensed milk, and had driven two holes in its lid. It was passed round, and those who could took a short pull of condensed milk. It was a wonderful reviver. But many by this time were hunched in semi-consciousness, unable to move or speak.

I realized then how fortunate I was to have been chosen for the gun crew, for I was dressed for just such an emergency as this. I had five or six layers of clothing on and long thick seaman's stockings to go with those sea-boots. Moreover, because I was "on the gun crew" I had been given a capok-filled life-jacket such as were provided for the crew, rather than the cork-filled type supplied to the passengers. The cork-filled life-jacket, which is now obsolete, impeded movement and could quickly make one raw under the chin. My capok-filled life-jacket protected my chest when I pulled on my oar and helped to keep me warm.

Our spirits were rather low at this point. We were alone in the North Atlantic in February, cold and wet. The seas were still running high. There were still threatening clouds. Each of us

67

pondered about our chances of being sighted, let alone rescued. Hours passed and hardly a word was spoken. A piece of chocolate came my way and was gratefully accepted. Then suddenly, at about 2pm somebody thought he heard a plane and there was an eager searching of the skies by all who were able to do so. And then someone spotted a plane in the distance. Our disappointment when it disappeared was profound. But to our relief it came in sight again after some minutes, and finally it bore down upon us. Friend or foe we wondered briefly, but soon all doubts were dispelled when we recognized a Sunderland Short flying boat. It flew low over us and dropped a smoke-bomb into the sea. The pilot waved, circled around us once and was gone. There was quite a long wait after that, but our black despair was gone, as we felt certain now that we would not be abandoned. Then a different plane appeared, which we identified between us as a Lockhead Hudson. It flew towards us and retraced its flight-path several times as though it were guiding a vessel beneath it.

This indeed proved to be the case. After what seemed an endless wait, momentarily, when we were on a crest, we spotted what seemed to be a pathetically small ship sitting very low in the water. We saw it again shortly afterwards when we and the ship rose to high points on the seas together. Then we were lost again in the troughs of mountainous seas. At last the corvette, for such the ship proved to be, came close and hailed us through a loud-hailer. They would throw us two lines and pull us alongside, a voice shouted. Shortly afterwards the lines were propelled through the air and we managed to make them fast at bow and stern. There followed what we learned afterwards was the most dangerous part of the operation. Slowly the lifeboat was winched alongside the corvette until it was bashing against its side. Then, under the directions of the loud-hailer, we propped up the passengers one by one in a kneeling position on the seats running round the side of the boat, and the sailors pulled them individually over the rail when the sea lifted the lifeboat up.

One of the crew and I were the last to leave the waterlogged boat, which was then cut free. I remember being grabbed by half a dozen arms and hauled with great difficulty over the ship's rail. My six foot one inch frame and its many layers of sodden clothes must have weighed enormously heavy, let alone the sea-boots filled with sea-water. As I sploshed full-length onto the deck a sailor muttered, "Up for'ard, mate", for with my sou, wester and oilskins I was taken to be a member of the *Anchises* crew. So "mate" staggered up for'ard.

There with the stokers and stewards I was relieved of my wet clothes and given a blanket, which I found out later gave me a fine ringworm. Our clothes we understood were to be taken to the boiler-room to dry. Within a short time a cry went up: Cover up, cover up. Woman doctor coming!" A fine time for such niceties, I thought. And then to my surprise and delight appeared Jean Sherring in a raincoat. It transpired that Jean's lifeboat and three others had also been located by the corvette with the assistance of the aircraft, and that the passengers rescued from them were being accommodated with the passengers rescued from our lifeboat in more prestigious parts of the ship. We were the last of the five boats to be picked up by the corvette that day. Bill Nightingale's boat was missing, and we understood that the aircraft were going to continue to search for it until nightfall.

Jean, as a medical doctor, was making a round to see what help she could give to those who had been injured or were suffering from severe exposure. She had won great kudos, she told us long afterwards, by assisting a Chinese stoker who had his jaw locked open as a result of exposure. She had never had to deal with such a case before, but knew what had to be done. So with a towel wrapped round her thumbs she pressed with them on the hinge of the jaw inside the man's mouth. There was a click and the jaw slipped back into place. Jean's reputation was made. She also reported that only after completing her rounds did she realize that every time she leant forward over a patient the raincoat she was wearing parted gently at her back in a most revealing way, as the raincoat was her only garment. So much for covering up. I learned that Joan Dobbs was in good shape, but that her husband, the major, was a hospital case. Our rescue ship, the *Kingcup*, a corvette of the "flower" class, was one of those vessels provided by the United States under lease-lend. We were filled with euphoric relief and gratitude to all concerned.

I don't know how long it took the *Kingcup* to reach Gourock on the coast of Scotland, sailing at its maximum sixteen knots. We had been bombed, I understand, some hundred and twenty miles north-west of Ireland. The exact location I found out later was 55 14 N: 13 17 W. We were certainly dealt with expeditiously on arrival. An immigration official inspected my soggy passport matter-of-factly. "A bit damp," he said. Most of those rescued boarded a train on which space had been reserved to take them to Glasgow, where they received an outfit of clothes. Joan Dobbs, Jean and I missed this rehabilitation assistance because Major Dobbs had been taken straight to hospital, and we wanted to keep close to him. We went to the hotel at the sea front. Jean and Joan were found accommodation, but there was no room for me. Ship survivors in Gourock were commonplace, so no special sympathy was evoked by our situation. Nevertheless, everywhere we were given every assistance possible. A business man said I could have his room, he could stay "elsewhere". The manager of the hotel "lent" me a suit, a shirt and some underwear. We were touched by the sustained practical kindness everyone showed to us. I telephoned my father and mother that I was alive and on my way home. Joan, Jean and I, a motley trio, went to visit Major Dobbs in hospital. We were assured that he would recover. A representative of the Holt company, the owners of the *Anchises*, was present. He offered funds for any immediate expenses and was kindness itself. Jean and I in borrowed clothes, and I still in sea-boots, sallied into the town, exchanged some still damp travellers cheques, and bought some clothes.

I made my way alone to Glasgow to take the train to London. In Glasgow I went into a shop to buy a packet of razor blades, but was allowed to buy only one blade, as they were rationed. The train travelled through the night in a complete blackout. I was met at Euston station by my sister Barbara accompanied by a friend of the family, Arthur Dawson. With the dimmest of dim lights Arthur drove us across London to where my parents lived.

As mentioned earlier, my father was the librarian of the Plumstead Public Library in south-east London, and he and my mother and sister lived in a spacious flat above the library building. It was one of those libraries built with Carnegie funds and was therefore solidly constructed with the best materials available. Because of its centrality and solid construction its basement had been designated as a wartime shelter. On a bad bombing night several hundred people would take shelter there. My father was Warden-in-Charge, and because of his warm good nature and cheerfulness he was very popular with the regulars. My mother and sister preferred to take shelter in a single-storey brick building on a plot of ground behind the library, which was used for stores and as a staff-room. It was not as safe as the basement perhaps, but its facilities for making tea made up for that.

Some of the worst bombing of London had already taken place and my family had in some measure become inured to it. When the sirens with their haunting, pulsating wail, announced the approach of German planes up the Thames Valley, they gathered whatever was necessary for a night in the shelter, and stoically made their way to it. I was much more scared than they were when this happened on my first night home, especially when the bombs were near enough for us to hear the swoosh of their descent, and the sickening scrunch and earth shudder as they hit the ground or a building.

On my second night home I helped my father put out an incendiary bomb in the yard of our shelter. It was shaped like a round stick about one and a half inches in diameter and a yard long, with a finned tail-piece. The nose of the bomb was incandescent and gave out intense heat capable of burning through anything combustible. "Our" bomb smacked into the concrete of the shelter's yard, chipping a lump out of it and leaving a black burn mark about two feet across. We rushed out with our bucket of sand and pokers and quickly had it smothered. Incendiaries were dropped in batches so that they lit up the sky and set fire to the roofs of buildings, lighting up targets for the German bombers. For this reason there were fire wardens for every street in London, chosen from the occupants of the houses. Their duty was to watch out for incendiaries, particularly at night, and call out the volunteer fire-watchers whenever and wherever necessary.

On another evening during a raid my father was asked by a street warden to check our living room in the flat upstairs, as it appeared from the street that someone had left on a light, which was visible from the road. My father and I immediately went up to investigate. We opened the living room door, and indeed there was a light in the room. An incendiary bomb had poked its incandescent nose through the ceiling, lighting up the room as though by flood-lighting. My father rushed out for a bucket of sand, while I turned back the carpet. We poked down the bomb with a broom handle, and caught it in the bucket. Fortunately for us the Germans had not yet introduced anti-personnel warheads to their incendiaries; otherwise our dealing with incendiary bombs might not have been so successful.

My sister was working for the Inland Revenue (Income Tax) Service in an office near Finsbury Circus in north-west London. Warnings and daylight raids became so frequent that, in the end, when the sirens sounded, the workers there stayed fatalistically at their desks rather than make the long journey downstairs to the shelters below ground level. There were frequent breakdowns in the London transport system, and the suburban electric train she took was often delayed through damage to the track. Sometimes buses were provided to take the place of the trains. On a typical day she would return home just before 8pm in the blackout. "Business as usual" was the slogan, "London can take it!" And it did.

After feeling thoroughly united with my family I paid a visit to Phyllis's sister, Elsie, and her husband, Ronald Melville, in Twickenham. Ronald was a senior botanist at Kew Gardens and had made a name for himself through developing the rosehip as a source of Vitamin C, which was in short supply under rationing. His PhD had been obtained through researches on the growth and cultivation of the tomato, and his practical help and advice with regard to tomato growing were much in demand in the area. On the evening of my arrival, there was an air-raid warning and I spent several hours in the Melville's simple air-raid shelter in their garden. It was waterlogged, and Ronald and I took turns at pumping it dry. Phyllis's school friend Kathleen Long joined us later, and I gave what news I could of Phyllis. It was pathetically small, and therefore I am sure rather disappointing to all three of them.

From conversations I had had in Scotland, and from information I gleaned later from other sources, I learned what had actually happened to the *Anchises*. She had been sinking sufficiently slowly for the master of the ship, Captain J.W James, to hope to get her towed to safety. In order to do this he kept back some of the crew to close certain bulkheads and stand by to receive assistance. However, by nightfall Captain James decided that the ship could not be saved. He could do nothing in the dark because the seas were dangerously high, and the ship could not show a light. Nevertheless, the radio, which, I had been told by the second wireless officer, had been out of action, was made serviceable again through a spare battery and the first wireless officer had sat up the whole night sending out and receiving messages. As soon as it was light enough the master decided to transfer the remainder of the ship's company to the corvette by means of the last remaining serviceable lifeboat. But the seas were so high the bows of the corvette crushed the lifeboat, which was awkwardly placed for launching, killing the master, a seaman and the ship's baker. Shortly after this catastrophe the *Anchises* herself sank.

The lifeboats which were launched in calm water all stayed afloat, although I believe there was at least one fatality from exposure in each of them with the exception of ours. I believe we may have avoided deaths from exposure by not using a large tarpaulin provided in the lifeboat. In boats where this was spread out it was impossible to see what was going on under it, and some people just slipped unnoticed into the unbailed bilge water and died.

I have said that the lifeboats launched in calm water all survived. But that did not seem to be the case at the time. After my return home my parents quickly passed on the glad news to the Nightingales, and they of course immediately asked me what had happened to Bill. I did not know. Apparently the boat in which Bill had been had not been picked up. I knew no more than that. The days of waiting lengthened into weeks. It was difficult to speak to the Nightingales as their hope and ours began to fade. Then suddenly they told us over the phone, for they lived some distance from us in Croydon, Surrey, the incredible news that Bill had indeed been picked up, and was in a hospital in Londonderry, suffering from frostbite.. We were overjoyed.

Bill's lifeboat had been separated from the ship by the storm as ours had been and had travelled under sail to such an extent that it had not been spotted by the aircraft. There had been twenty passengers and crew in the boat to begin with, but as one day passed into another, exposure took its toll, and people drifted into unconsciousness and died. The survivors pushed the bodies into the sea. After six days only fourteen people were left including Bill Nightingale and Barbara Mitchell-Heggs, a nursing sister. Their food was exhausted, but they had managed to collect some hail for drinking water. One day they thought they saw several naval vessels on the horizon, and within a short time a destroyer swung round in their direction. It steamed up close to them, and Bill held out Barbara's long hair as a signal of distress. Somewhat ingenuously, it seemed to them a voice bawled out through a loud-hailer, "Do you want to be picked up?" With all the urgency they could command they indicated that they did. A network of ropes was thrown out over the destroyer's side and they were lifted aboard without the ship coming to a full stop.

They discovered that their rescue ship was a destroyer, the SS *Assinaboine,* a part of the Canadian fleet on manoeures. As the Canadians had experience with frostbite, they were in good hands, though two more of the boat's complement subsequently died in hospital. However, because the destroyer was on active duty, it could not send any signal to its home base. In fact, the Canadian ships were on their way south to take part in a naval battle. As gun-fire burst over their heads, Bill and Barbara thought how frustrating it would be if they were to be wiped out in a destroyer which had rescued them from almost certain death. Fortunately that did not happen and they were delivered to Londonderry some three weeks after the *Anchises* was sunk. All survivors were suffering from frostbite: one, Smith, had several toes off, another, Crowsdale, had both feet off, with his hands probably to follow. One Chinese got out of bed and put his feet into boiling water and was expected to lose them both. Both Bill and Barbara were immediately hospi-talized and Bill did not return to duty for a whole year.

In Malaya, news of the sinking of the *Anchises* was heard in a German radio broadcast. The Edges remembered hearing it with dismay. But I quickly sent cables to Carey and to Phyllis to inform them of my safe arrival, so they were not kept in suspense very long. Since no news of shipping movements was allowed in a message, I cabled to Phyllis, "Arrived safely lost luggage calling Twickenham love Luke". I knew she would remember that suitcase full of presents.

My leave in England passed like a dream. I remember meeting with Marjorie Bliss, a physiotherapist, a little younger than I, who worked at Guy's Hospital, to whom I had been deeply attached dur-ing the year I had been at the Institute of Education. While I had been in Malaya she had married a dentist named Graham. We had dinner at Odonino's and went to a show at the Victoria Palace, where a chorus girl stepped down from the stage, and perched briefly on my knee as part of the show. I did not trust myself to meet Marjorie a second time and wrote her a letter saying that as she was married to Graham, and I was returning to Malaya, we should not meet again.

I also had a couple of meetings with Mina Bugler, whom I had first met in Bridport, Dorset, when I was a "pioneer" at my School Camp at West Bay. She had become a nurse on the staff of Sir Harold Geddes, the plastic surgeon, and worked at a hospital in Basingstoke where miracles of plastic surgery were being performed on service and civilian casualties. That is where I went to see her, for we had enjoyed meeting each other from time to time over the years. It was a day or two before I was due to return to Malaya. We had met before in London, when she was visiting a sick brother in the Brook Hospital near my home. We had been out late, and she had missed the last train back to Basingstoke. So I had taken her home to the flat and introduced her to the family. She had stayed the night in my sister's room, dear B., and in the wee hours of the morning I had borrowed Arthur Dawson's car, for we had no car of our own, and drove her up to Paddington, so that she could catch the "milk train" back to Basingstoke, and be in time to report for duty. I somehow needed to see these young women from my past. I think now I was subconsciously testing my affection for Phyllis. At least that was part of it.

Shortly before I went to Basingstoke, Jean Sherring had invited me to her home in Odiham, Hampshire, where she lived with her mother in an attractive house. Mrs Sherring, a distinguished lady, was the widow of a High Court judge in the Indian Civil Service. Jean drove me around Odiham, while she carried on with her "locum" doctor's job. It was a strange but delightful interlude in a turbulent period.

All too soon it was time to return to Malaya. Our departure was to be from Glasgow and after rather sad farewells at home, I made my way there by train. Our ship, the *Ulysses* was another of the Blue Funnel ships named after Greek heroes, but this time we were destined to travel in convoy. We set off in a group of some twenty ships, and found that after a week under a heavy naval escort we were off Halifax, Nova Scotia. Only certain privileged people seemed able to get ashore there and we were soon on our way again, heading south to Capetown.

I do not recall much about this return voyage, except that it took ten weeks, and that the people on board were a remarkable cross-section of humanity. The ship's company included a few professionals like myself, with jobs to return to, but a large proportion of the passengers were either servicemen proceeding on active duty, or service wives joining or returning to their husbands in India, Ceylon or Malaya. By the time the ship had been three weeks at sea all kinds of liaisons had developed between men and women, whose spouses were elsewhere. It was a voyage filled with strange relationships and intrigues, thrown into relief by the dangers of war.

A ship at sea is always a small world sequestered, so that passengers who are traveling alone feel free to experiment a little with their affections. There is usually no one to chide or remind them of their responsibilities, and there is a deadline vaguely ahead, that will, they fondly hope, permit an escape from precipitate commitments without scars, into a smooth restoration of the status quo ante. In a voyage of ten weeks duration, amid the uncertainties of war, the conditions are extremely propitious for wild and extraordinary love affairs. The ship's officers on the bridge of the *Ulysses*, like the chorus of a Greek play, watched romances wax and wane on the deck below them, while the players played their parts and waited with apprehension or relief for their exits.

I did not emerge from that voyage uninvolved or entirely unscathed myself, but I was restored and inspired by what happened in Penang. We did not expect any special arrangements for our arrival, because of the restraints of wartime security. Nevertheless, as we approached the harbour at Penang, we were surprised by the lack of activity on the quay, which we were slowly approaching. Hardly anyone to help us tie up alongside, or so it seemed. And then I saw a single figure standing, waiting in isolation. Could it be a woman? And if so how had she managed to cut through all the restrictive red tape? And then in a flash I realized it was Phyllis. It was a great moment. No other passenger was met by anyone.

There can be few places in the world more romantic than the narrow lawn by the sea wall of the E&O (Eastern and Oriental) Hotel in Penang, when the air is balmy, and the moon shining clearly through the palm trees. It was here that Phyllis and I discussed what we should do. We were in love, but with our future so uncertain we were hesitant about marriage. The atmosphere was heavy with rumour and tension. Some kind of an insect bit Phyllis as she rested her hand on the sea wall. It seemed a little ominous. We held each other tight as I comforted her.

Back in Kuala Kangsar it was suggested that I take a commission in the Malay Regiment instead of joining the Royal Air Force, but after some hesitation I decided to reaffirm my application to join the Empire Training Scheme and I made a special trip to Singapore in order to do this. There I was told I must wait at least until mid-January before leaving for the next course in Canada. So with my belongings half-packed and a growing restlessness, I tried to settle down to teaching again. In a letter to my parents, dated 30th October 1941, I wrote:

"As I look from the verandah I can see a squirrel running along the branch of a big tree, green rambutans and green mangoes weighing down heavily, my own row of hybiscuses which I planted three years ago, now five feet high and flowering luxuriantly, the rose of Sharon behind me bursting with buds, and over the hedge in Clifford's garden, another squirrel nibbling his way deep into a jack fruit, with darting jerks of his tail. It is a lovely peaceful scene, if your heart is at peace, but an exquisite exasperation in time of war. Yesterday Ah Tee Shew, my "house-boy", gave me the only piece of advice he has offered in five years. When I said I was not going to Singapore to work with the flying ships until January now, he said, "Good. Why go at all? Nobody else is going." It is true. Very few are doing anything more than talk.

The letter I was replying to had a news item in it which intrigued me greatly. Bill Nightingale and Jean Sherring had married. I was surprised because I had no inkling of any such romance when I was in England, and I knew that Bill had been actively courting my sister Barbara, until she decided that she did not wish to marry him. My comments home were:

"I was astonished by the Walter–Jean business. Bill was sometimes called Walter, and then not so astounded. At least now I cannot by any stretch of the imagination feel an atom of self-reproach. It will be an interesting match. I certainly wish them well. I think it will be good for Walter to be married."

Fortunately I had plenty to do. Carey and his wife were on leave in Australia, and were due back on 27 November. Although R.P.S. Walker, principal of the Sultan Idris Training College, was acting administrative head of the Malay College as well as being principal of SITC (as the SITC had temporarily moved up from Tajong Malim to Bukit Chandan in Kuala Kangsar), I was responsible for the day-to-day running of the school.

One day Che Ariffin, a senior staff member, told me he had heard on his radio the shattering news that the battleships *Repulse* and *Prince of Wales* had been sunk by the Japanese in the Pacific. We were stunned by this news, as we had set great store on the protection these ships had been expected to provide.

Shortly after this Carey returned to Kuala Kangsar to discover to his astonishment that the Japanese had already infiltrated the country as far as Grik, a small village in the north-west corner of the State of Perak. He obtained permission to send the boys home and they departed in small groups during the next two days and nights. When he found that he still had with him the boys from the east coast States, Kelantan and Trengganu, he asked the Sultan (Yang di-Pertuan Besar) of Negeri Sembilan by telephone if he would look after them, as Kelantan and Trengannu were already regarded as a battle zone by this time. The Yang di-Pertuan without hesitation agreed to receive them, and send them home to their parents.

With the departure of the boys I found myself attached to the District Officer of Kuala Kangsar, A.C. Jomoran, as by then I had resigned from the FMSVF (Volunteers) to join the RAF, and so had no service commitment. It was at this point that Phyllis and I decided that we should get married. We managed it just in time. Padre Clarke kindly agreed to conduct the service in All Saints, Church, Taiping. There were only five of us in the church– our witnesses, Eve Russell and Ruth McLeod, both New Zealanders, Padre Clarke, the priest, Phyllis and I. Eve lent us her wedding ring with which to perform the ceremony. Cars zoomed past the church as we spoke our vows, for all European civilians were beginning to evacuate the town. It was only as I was signing the register that I realized I was being married on my birthday, 16th December.

Later I was to learn that the Japanese had landed in Kelantan, the most northerly state in Malaya, on 8th December 1941, the same day as they had bombed Pearl Harbor, though because of the international date line it was 7th December there.

After the wedding Phyllis returned briefly to her house in Taiping to pack a small bag and then move south: I returned to KK, where Jomoran ordered me to take a despatch that very night to the officer in charge of a company of Argyle and Sutherland Highlanders, who were already in contact with the Japanese at Grik. Grik is a small township some sixty miles north of Kuala Kangsar and the narrow road to it seems to wind interminably through the jungle, crossing scores of small bridges on the way. Driving there at night is a scary business. I took three armed Malay Volunteers with me in my car, and drove as fast as safety would allow. We arrived at the outskirts of the village without mishap. Shortly afterwards we were flagged down by British troops, and I was escorted under guard to the officer in command of the outpost. The young Scottish captain was quite suspicious at first, and questioned me closely before he was prepared to receive my message. Eventually he did so, and my party and I were allowed to return to KK.

On 19th December 1941 I moved into Jomoran's house on the hill overlooking the Perak river, as my own bungalow had been taken over by the military. By the 22nd there were only nine European civilians left in the town. One of my first duties was to work with Carey to distribute the rice that was stored in the godowns (warehouses) near the railway station. The idea was that it would be better in the troubled times ahead for the local population to have the rice rather than the Japanese invaders. Each family was allowed one sack and they dragged the sacks away and onto bicycles with much noise and gesticulation. Two regular soldiers stood by with tommy-guns to see that order was maintained. Although the inhabitants of KK were frightened and bewildered rather than riotous, the distribution had to be abandoned in the end because the crowd became uncontrollable.

Finally, the only Europeans remaining in KK. were Jomoran, the DO, Walker, the Principal of SITC, the Chief of Police, and myself. The cars of the DO and Walker had already been requisitioned by the Army, so my little Standard had to serve the four of us. As I drove the DO round a curve up to his house in those final days, we were smashed into by a military truck. I rounded on the driver. An Indian Army officer leapt from the cabin of the truck. "Do you know who you are talking to?" he shouted. "A bloody bad driver!" I retorted, and drove on. I was amazed to hear myself swear, for it was the last thing I thought I would do. Jomoran remained silent, but as we turned into the porch of his house, he remarked that he thought my wheels had been over the white line. When I inspected the bashed-in side of my new Standard, I could hardly believe that. But I suspect that he was right.

The Japanese continued to advance down the Grik road, and it soon became clear that the little band of civilians could not remain much longer in KK. The DO thereupon made an official call on the Sultan of Perak and handed to him his sword of office. The Sultan bowed, and said "I understand your position. In exchange for your sword I give you my Bentley. When you return, as I know you will, we will exchange again." Shortly after this the DO instructed me to make my way to Ipoh. My bashed-in Standard was one of the last cars to cross the Iskandar Bridge spanning the Perak river, before the bridge was blown up by British sappers.

In Ipoh I billeted in a communal house, and helped with the civilian attempts at food rationing. This was made difficult by the Japanese bombing of the town. The bombs were small, but the raids seemed incessant, so I spent a good deal of time ducking down in monsoon drains. On the second day, while I was taking a snack at the house, two men came running in soaked from head to foot in gasoline. A petrol tank had been destroyed by the bombing, or perhaps by our own scorched earth policy, I did not know, and the fuel had drenched them. But miraculously it had not caught fire. They tore off their clothes outside the house, and rushed in to shower as quickly as they could.

As the situation worsened it looked as though I should be captured as a civilian if I stayed much longer in Ipoh. In the event I was glad to be ordered to move south so that I could regain service status. I was well pleased with this development because I knew that Phyllis had gone to Kuala Lumpur, and that she would be cared for by the British Resident of Selangor, Reginald Jarrett. And that is where I found her. The British Resident and his wife had remained in their official residence, a most beautiful mansion called "Carcosa", next to the Lake Gardens. They welcomed me warmly, and suddenly Phyllis and I realized that we would be spending Christmas together. Phyllis had rescued my best suit and her own black evening dress, so on Christmas Eve we sat with the Jarretts in the splendid dining room of that regal house, and solemnly toasted the King and the Sultan of Selangor in champagne. Then we heard the King's Christmas broadcast speech, and Phyllis and I retired early, for this was in fact our wedding night.

On Boxing Day it had been agreed that I should go on to Port Dickson, the headquarters of the FMSVF, to re-enlist as a Volunteer, and that Phyllis would move down to Singapore and stay with friends. So Phyllis and I went down into town to complete a few business arrangements. Suddenly we found ourselves in a rather bad air-raid, in which the Japanese planes seemed to fly very low and do just as they pleased. We lay on our faces in a small dugout in front of the Selanger Club. Bombs fell near the Club and on to the Chartered Bank building, one on each side of us and only about fifty yards away. When we eventually emerged we found that Phyllis's Wolesley had been machine-gunned and had bullet holes through its hood. My car fortunately was being serviced at the time, and so was not damaged by the raid. So we left KL and drove down to Seremban on the way to Port Dickson, I driving in front in the bashed-in Standard, and Phyllis behind in the machine-gunned Wolesley, carrying between us everything we possessed in the world. It was mostly canned food.

We had tea in Seremban and, as it was too late for me to report in Port Dickson that night, we stayed in a small hotel on the coast called the "Si Rusa Inn". There were no lights, so we dined by moonlight on the lawn beside the beach. And in the early morning, before the sun was fully up, we swam in the warm sea in the buff, because no-one was about, and we certainly had no swimsuits. The monkeys came down to the water's edge, and in a kind of ecstatic peace we watched the sun come up behind the coconut palms.

Then we re-arranged our worldly possessions. This time everything went into Phyllis's car, except my basic clothes which went into mine, and I set off to report to the FMSVF and re-enlist. In a matter of an hour or so I had picked up a few khaki shirts, boots, a "tin" hat, a revolver, a rifle and a bayonet, and become private 7869, No 2 Platoon, A(S) Company, 4th Pahang Battalion. As the Volunteers would be regrouping in Kuala Lumpur, and my re-enlistment had taken less time than I had expected, Phyllis and I still had a little time longer together. So there was one more night of extended honeymoon in Seremban, where Phyllis had found a room for both of us in a friend's house. Next morning Phyllis parted with her car. She handed it over to a transport officer in exchange for a little piece of paper, to avoid having it requisitioned later. We said goodbye, and she headed for Singapore with the Standard. Thereafter the Volunteers would have to provide transport for me.

Looking back at my period of active service, I realize how unglamorous and unheroic it was. I remember thinking sadly of the Empire Training Scheme for air pilots, about which I had received a telegram informing me that my assignment to it had regretfully to be cancelled because of the Japanese invasion of Malaya. Nothing could be lower than a private in the Volunteers, I thought, and the fact that the OC of the Pahang Battalion was Somerville, the Forest Officer of Taiping, and that his captain was none other than Dennis Ambler, now a resident of Pahang, did little to comfort me.

From my letters to Phyllis of this time I note that by 10th January 1942 I had been up into Kelantan taking up various gun positions, but without actually contacting the Japanese. After a time it became clear that our troops were retreating down the peninsula, and that we, No 2 Platoon of A(S) Company, 4th Pahang Battalion, were among those expected to provide cover for the sappers, who were to blow up railway bridges in a staged withdrawal. Our Vickers machine-guns were specially equipped for jungle work, each gun being carried in a wicker contraption mounted on a single wheel.

One man pulled on the shafts in front of it, and a second pushed and guided it in the shafts behind. It took considerable strength and staying power to manoeuvre this unusual gun-carriage along uneven jungle paths and railway tracks. One night we walked out of a situation with full equipment and guns, travelling non-stop 3am.to 12 noon the following day.

Yet curiously it seems we were still able to write letters, and were even instructed to advise our wives in Singapore to evacuate from the city as soon as they could. For the most part our letters were received. Phyllis, who had billeted with her friends the Roses, was reluctant to leave. She had a job in a convalescent home for wounded soldiers and was very hopeful that I would get some leave, and be able to visit her. After taking up various positions for a battle that never materialized, and camping in the jungle or in rubber estates, one night we drove in trucks to the FMSVF headquarters in St Patrick's School, Singapore. It was a welcome end to stinking clothes and mosquito - infested nights and to my great joy I was allowed leave to go into Singapore and meet with Phyllis again. That night was precious, even though we spent much of our time in an air-raid shelter. It was the last time I was to see Phyllis for nearly four years.

The next morning I returned to the FMSVF headquarters. It was my hope that Phyllis would be able to get away from Singapore, for although I had thought, with many others, that Singapore was a fortress that would not fall easily, I now realized that no major effort was being made to save it, and that it was unlikely that I would have any news of Phyllis for many months.

Almost as soon as I returned to camp I fell sick with malaria. The cities and towns of Malaya in the late 1930s were singularly free from malaria, and I had lived in Kuala Kangsar entirely free of it, without taking prophylactics. To sleep in the open in the jungle or on rubber estates without a mosquito net, however, as after enlistment we had of necessity to do, had been asking for trouble. I was promptly sent off to hospital. I remember two things about that first hospital. One was that a nurse took off my soaking pyjamas, when I groaned in the middle of the night after a violent bout of the shivers, and put me in dry ones. I blessed her for it. The second was the inability of a volunteer nurse to shake down the mercury in her clinical thermometer, when she made her rounds to take our temperatures. There were plenty of volunteers to help her to do that. She was charming and she amused us by carrying her tin hat around with her wherever she went. Poor girl, the tin hat did not do her much good, for one morning as she entered the building, she took the full blast of a bomb and was killed.

After a short stay at the first hospital, I was moved with a number of other patients to the Gillman Barracks Hospital to the south of the island. We soon became aware that this hospital was likely to be captured, for mortar bombs were falling in the courtyards, and those who had to move between certain blocks of the buildings had to make a dash for it. One morning a hospital official spoke privately to a few of us who were walking patients, and suggested that we might like to move under our own steam to the General Hospital in Singapore itself, as he feared the Japanese would over-run the hospital we were in in a very short time. I decided to follow this suggestion, and with two others set off on foot to Singapore. Someone offered me a revolver, but I did not accept it, as the three of us felt we would fare best by going to the General Hospital as transferring walking patients.

Along the road we were overtaken by an army truck. The driver told us he was on his way to the General Hospital. He would return for us, he said, after he had delivered some wounded there. The wounded were British soldiers who had shot one another by mistake across a street while they were on patrol. The truck did not return, but we knew the way we had to go, so we pressed on despite a feeling of light-headedness due to our weakness. We reached the General Hospital at last after passing a petrol pump spectacularly ablaze.

The scene that met our eyes made Gillman Barracks Hospital appear serenely at peace by comparison, for the General Hospital was filled with casualties, both military and civilian, from the Japanese bombing of Singapore. The wards were overflowing. Men and women with terrible wounds lay on stretchers along the corridors or on the floor, the civilians often surrounded by anxious members of their families. I understood that Margaret Edge had become a nurse at the General, so I quickly sought her out. Barely looking up from her work, she told me that Clifford had just joined her, and that if I felt strong enough I should report to the matron and offer to help. I found Clifford and went with him to the matron's office, where we were immediately asked to help carry out the dead. Under the direction of a senior sister, the pair of us were given a stretcher and shown where the dead were. We carried out bodies to a huge communal grave in front of the hospital, piling the corpses one on top of the other and shovelling a little lime over each one. A chaplain beside the communal grave was saying a brief prayer for each of the dead, and collecting the identity tags from the necks of military personnel. I recognized this priest as John Hayter, Assistant to the Bishop of Singapore, Bishop Wilson. John Hayter had been one of my team-mates in the St Edmund Hall soccer side in 1935. The sister took us to one bedside. "He had gangrene, poor lad," she said of the dead soldier. "Take out the whole mattress as well as the body. It is dangerous to touch him."

We worked until dusk, and then, as night fell we were told that Singapore would be taken over by the Japanese officially on the following day. An eerie quiet permeated the whole hospital. A semi-official message was circulated to those of us who were Volunteers to the effect that if we tried to escape at this point we would not be regarded as deserters. I weighed my chances. Knowing no reasonable escape route to explore, and remembering the trigger happy soldiers we had met on the road, I decided to stay in the hospital and see what the dawn would bring.

The matron invited Clifford and me to sleep in the nurses wing, and we dragged mattresses onto the floor there. I had my pajamas in the small army haversack I had brought with me from the other hospital. So I put them on and prepared to sleep, as I was desperately tired. Clifford and Margaret had other mattresses in a far corner of the hall. A nurse friend of Margaret's, apprehensive at the prospect of internment, had been drinking steadily from a bottle of Drambuie at the end of her day. She dragged a mattress alongside mine, and made overtures of friendship. At another time and in another place it would have been a tempting moment, but with my heart full of memories of Phyllis I had no difficulty in withstanding such blandishments. The sleep of complete exhaustion quickly followed.

The next morning was indeed capitulation. There were quick farewells between husbands and wives among the expatriates. The Volunteers with other military personnel were assembled on the padang in front of the Cricket Club and marched the sixteen miles to Changi, which had long been the military area of Singapore. We learned later that non-military personnel, including women and children, were taken to a camp on Sime Road, near the centre of the island, where they were interned.

The Japanese quickly established their principle of using POW officers to take command of other-rank POWs. Our officers had been instructed to order us to destroy or hand in any Malayan currency we might possess, in accordance with the denial to the enemy precept. I had very little, and forget now whether I complied with this order. It seemed ill-advised in the event, as Malayan money continued to be legal tender for some time.

My feelings as we marched through the streets of Singapore were part shame, but mostly incredulity that I should be captured by a people whom up until then I had known only as shopkeepers and hairdressers. The Japanese had been the professional photographers of pre-occupation Malaya, and there was usually a Japanese photographer's shop in any medium-sized town.

It is now assumed that many of these photographers formed an effective fifth column during the immediate pre-invasion period. There were also Japanese purveyors of Japanese goods – cheap crockery, laquer-ware and glass. The "Japanese shop" in each of the larger towns was in fact an excellent repository of sundries and gifts, which was always well patronized by the European community.

But most memorable to me were the hairdressers. I have never had a better haircut before or since those days than one which could be obtained for (One Malayan Dollar) in a Japanese hairdresser's salon. The haircut was always skillfully and speedily executed. However, that was not the most satisfactory aspect of one's visit. It was the massage after the cutting that was so satisfying. The hairdresser was a skilled masseur. Back would go the barber's chair and after a steaming hot towel had enveloped one's face and head for a moment or two, the wizardry would follow. A faraway look would come into those black eyes, and then would begin the pummelling, thumping, and stroking of head, neck, arms and shoulders, which made one feel so relaxed that one was sorry when it stopped. And it was all part of the haircut. No extra charge.

The shambling Japanese soldiers with their soft-peaked caps did not look like barbers, nor did they look like conquering heroes. They were the first Japanese soldiers we had seen close to, however, and their unimpressive appearance merely added to our shame. The populace followed our march with blank stares. They seemed to share our humiliation and were shocked into silence.

In Changi we were billeted in barracks formerly occupied by garrison troops, but in quite different circumstances. Each man was allotted a small floor-space and had to manage with that. As time went on we settled down. Kitchens and medical facilities were set up, latrines were dug, tasks were assigned, activities were organized. It seemed to us at first that life as a POW might not be so bad. The Japanese left us alone. Our officers were billeted in a separate part of the camp, and we saw little of them. There were opportunities to attend lectures– some by professors of the university, who had become Volunteers rather than internees. For the time being we Volunteers, having been consolidated from various regional Volunteer units, seemed to be kept segregated from the regular troops. I found Gar Woods from a Penang unit as a sergeant cook in one of the cook-houses. There were Les Russell and Tom White from the Education Department in Taiping, and a new Education officer I had heard about, Hamish Tod, who had been posted to Singapore about the same time as Bill Jackman had been posted to the Malay College. Hamish Tod had started to give a series of lectures on ancient history and attending one out of curiosity, I found him to be a most entertaining and articulate speaker. We met after the lecture. I introduced myself and congratulated him, and we became fast friends.

In those days of upheaval and change we did not stop to ask what had happened to friends and colleagues other than those with whom we had been captured. Bill Jackman, I learned later, had been on leave in Kashmir with his wife Peggy when Japan came into the war. The ship which was bringing him back to Malaya was sunk by the Japanese. Bill clung to a table in the ocean until he was picked up. We who were delivered to Changi learned all this years later because Bill had a commission in the Volunteers and so was billeted with other officers. In due course he was drafted with his officers' group to work on the railway like the rest of us.

In those early days we had the advantage of certain little supplements we brought in with us. For example, Clifford Edge and I shared a two-pound can of IXL Australian apricot jam, which we had bought between us. There were also possibilities for making black market purchases. Some POWs, at great personal risk, were slipping under the barbed wire perimeter of the camp at night, and buying canned food from local Chinese vendors with money they had brought in with them. They resold these purchases inside the camp at an exorbitant profit. Canned cheese was a particularly desirable item, as a thin slice could be taken with any rice meal. A special treat, reminiscent of the *Anchises* shipwreck, was a can of sweetened condensed milk. One could take a swig through one of two holes bored into the top of the can. The holes could them be carefully plugged until the next time. Used sparingly in this way such a can could last one or two weeks.

The most useful item most of us took into POW camp was a watch. The Japanese guards were always interested in watches, and to display one at any time would immediately attract a guard's attention. It seemed curious to us that the guards did not simply confiscate our watches, but this apparently was not their code, and an individual guard would quickly make a cash offer for a watch. By chance I had two watches with me when Singapore capitulated – both Movado's. I liked my own model so much that I had bought a lady's Movado for Phyllis in Singapore some time before the Fall, but I had never had an opportunity to give it to her. The funds derived from the sale of these two watches to Japanese guards in Singapore gave a significant lift to my diet. The dollars were spent mostly on cans of cheese and condensed milk, though on a few rare occasions I remember buying a black-market can of "M & V" – meat and veg. I cannot remember any POW owning a watch after about a year of captivity.

There was one "fatigue" I particularly enjoyed. A party of about fifteen men would be detailed to bring salt water for the cook-house. This would be done by using a large tank resembling a petrol tank mounted on a motorless truck. The truck would be dragged to the beach by two long ropes pulled by the men, and the tank filled with salt water through a man-hole in its top. The filling was done by a human chain passing buckets of sea-water from the sea to the tank. After the tank was filled we were allowed to take a dip in the briny before we returned to the camp dragging the full tank. Apparently rice cooked well in sea–water, which provided the necessary salt flavouring.

My bedspace at this time was on the first–floor verandah at a corner of a barracks building. It was dusty and draughty, and one day I realized I had become a victum of one of the most prevalent diseases in the camp, dysentery. I soon became so weak that I had to be carried off on a stretcher by two hospital orderlies. By then I was in such dire straits that I had to get them to stop several times on the way to allow me to crawl to a hedge to relieve myself. The hospital, which was about half a mile from the barracks, had a special dysentery ward. Merely to think of the place fills me with nausea even to this day. All but the weakest of patients were expected to leave their beds and get to the jambans in a corridor at the end of the ward without assistance. The jambans were tall metal canisters which must have been used as containers for some kind of liquid. The water closets, if there had ever been any, were no longer in use. A limited supply of cotton waste was provided instead of toilet paper. The stench was indescribable. I was conscious that a number of patients did not leave their beds alive. One strong-looking fellow died of a heart attack on his umpteenth journey to the jambans.

The doctors who worked in that ward were brave men, for they had no proper drugs, and they seemed to fall sick with the disease themselves before very long. I became delirious and was making no progress, when the doctor I knew best said he would take drastic measures to cure me. He thereupon gave me a course of very heavy doses of Epsom salts. The result was that after another week I tottered back to my barracks a bearded skeleton, but with my bowels more or less under control. I then received a gift from a fellow POW named Thompson, which I shall always remember with special gratitude. It was a tablet of Cashmere Bouquet soap.I had a shower with it, and felt a new man.

Shortly after my return from hospital it was announced that some of us, and more particularly those who had been sick and were convalescing, would be sent to an island off Singapore, where conditions would be particularly propitious for complete recovery. A selected group of us were thereupon taken by truck and boat to the small island of Blakang Mati, which rather ominously means "behind the dead". While we were moving into a barracks building there, we saw a group of about thirty POWs marching by. They were tall and sunburned, and seemed to be returning from a work party. Their khaki shirts were draped over their backs. Their khaki shorts were ringed with sweat at the waist. On their heads were battered felt hats, which we recognized as "comfort" hats – the hats which were sent out for POWs by the Red Cross. These hats were among the few supplies which actually reached some POWs. An exchange of greetings elucidated that these men were an Australian contingent; that they had been brought to the island to work; and that the Japanese military on the island were a tough lot known as the Miki Boutei.

We quickly found this to be true. When the medical officer in charge of us courageously explained to the Japanese commander through an interpreter that most of us had been seriously sick and could not work, the Japanese officer was furious. He had us all out on the parade ground, drew his sword, and invited anyone who was unwilling to work to step forward. There was no doubt in any of our minds that this wild-looking officer intended to behead any one of us who showed the slightest resistance. Everyone was thoroughly scared, and no one moved.

Then began a new phase in my POW life. We soon learned to assemble in the early morning for "Tengko", the body count, and then set off with a few Japanese guards on a work party. We would cross on a kind of ferry to Singapore, and then move down to the docks or the railway station in trucks to move drums of gasoline or bombs out of "tongkang" or barges onto the quays, or out of trucks into railway wagons. Sometimes this process was reversed, and we would be loading "tongkang" or trucks with bombs or drums of gasoline. At first we were so weak that the Japanese were dissatisfied with our work most of the time, and we were constantly abused. But the stronger men helped the weaker, and little by little we struggled to a level of skill which at least enabled most of us to get through the day without being beaten up by those in charge of us. The Geneva Convention strictly forbids prisoners of war being used as labour in the war effort of their captors, but this certainly did not deter the Japanese from using us for this purpose.

The bombs were of varying size up to 1000 kilograms, and were packed in individual boxes. The war-head end of the bomb was by far the heavier, and therefore the stronger men would usually struggle with that end. POWs who tended habitually to seize the lighter fin-tail end were not popular. The understood rule was well put by the Aussies—"You can bludge [go slow] on the Nips as much as you like, but you don't bludge on your mates."

As far as drums of oil were concerned, we usually had to deal with the sixty-five-gallon drums, painted a dull pinky red, which had two heavy rims around them to make them easier to roll. To get these drums off the trucks we would drop them onto two or three old truck tyres. Getting them onto the light barges called "tongkang" needed a little more sophistication. We became quite adept at guiding them lengthways down the quay steps in a slithering slide, and then levering them over the side of the "tongkang". The drums played havoc with the concrete steps, breaking great chunks out of their edges, but the guards did not seem to mind unduly, and we certainly did not.

Passing through Singapore streets to our places of work was an interesting experience. The faces of the local population who were mostly Chinese were curious and expressionless, but frequently we met with gestures of sympathy. The Japanese paid us a few cents a day for working, and with this money we were sometimes able to buy from hawkers little titbits, or "ikan bilis" (a kind of tiny white-bait about an inch and a half long, dried in the sun) to supplement our rice and vegetable. Specially sort after were little sachets of flavouring, usually made up of "blachan" with a little ground-up red chilli, which were sold by children or hawkers. "Blachan" is a powerful flavouring made from crushed fermented shrimp. It has an appalling smell, but gives a welcome piquancy to the blandness of rice. The 3/4 inch wide, three–or four inch long sachets were made from the thin individual leaves of the coconut palm frond, and their contents were held in place by a piece of the hard vein of the frond threaded through the leaf. On a few occasions, at the railway station, we were able to buy "poughs" (to rhyme with boughs). A pough is a white dough-like ball with some kind of sweetmeat in the middle of it. These were regarded as a special treat.

One day the Japanese required us to fill out a form showing what occupation we followed in private life. We thought this an ingenuous exercise on the part of the Japanese, and an imaginative one for us. I put myself down as a house painter, an innocuous calling I thought, unlikely to assist the Japanese war machine in any way. Several of my friends also proclaimed themselves to be house painters. Among them were Les Russell, my Taiping friend, and Percy Ayliffe, who in private life ran an electrical supply company in Singapore. Within a short time we found that our talents were to be put to good use. We "painter-man" (no plural), as the Japanese called us, were given the task of servicing the small boats which plied between Blakang Mati and the main island of Singapore, with special emphasis on scraping and painting their hulls. Sometimes we were left to ourselves for hours at a time, scraping the barnacles off boats in dry dock, but quite often I found myself assigned to work alone with a Japanese carpenter named Nagarasan. Nagara had a notorious reputation. He was short and nubbly with a violent temper. He knew no English, but if any one working with him did not understand what he wanted, he became angry at once and would beat his unfortunate helper mercilessly.

I knew that the man who had worked for Nagara before me had been put into hospital as a result of a blow he had received from him, so I went to my assignment with considerable trepidation. Fortunately I had learned a few words of Japanese from the Syonen Shimbun, which had replaced the Singapore Straits Times, and quickly added to my vocabulary the names of the carpenter's tools. This saved me from many blows, and the blows Nagara did deliver tended to be aimed at the old khaki topee I had picked up in one of the derelict store rooms. I wore it constantly as its shape and construction provided admirable head protection.

From our point of view the Japanese guards seemed to be moody and unpredictable, though they had some traits which I suppose may be regarded as universally human. They appreciated any attempt we might make to speak their language, and they loved their children. One of the first questions we would be asked by a new guard would be "You: how many children?" "Boy? Girl?" etc. One day I had a relapse of my malaria and was ordered to bed in barracks. To my great astonishment Nagarasan came to visit me, bearing a bottle of orange-crush as a gift, and squatting by my bedside in almost schoolboy-like embarrassment. When I returned to work, however, there was no change for the better in his behaviour, and I continued to need the protection of my topee.

Before I returned to work, however, I was confined to barracks for some days. After the Miki Boutei had made their point that a certain quantum of work had to be accomplished each day, they did not interfere with any reasonable sick leave approved by our medical officer. During my time off duty I prepared a special meal each evening for the six or seven of my friends who ate round a trestle table on the ground floor verandah. It was possible to light a fire behind the barracks, fry curry powder and a few tiny purple onions in red palm oil, and transform that ikan belis into something quite appetizing. My friends therefore thoroughly approved of my sick leave, and were solicitous that I should not return to work too soon. There was also a tiny selection of books in the barracks and when I was not cooking, I read for the first time Boswell's "Life of Johnson". I remember that short period as one of pure pleasure. I did not believe that we would be prisoners for very long; I had no real responsibilities; and I was enjoying my book.

Sitting round that table for the evening meal we would exchange items of news from our day. One evening Les Russell came in hugely pleased. A high-ranking Japanese officer had chosen to use the boat Les was working on. As usual the appearance of a Japanese officer had thrown all Japanese other ranks into a flurry of confusion and subservience. Our youngest guard, known to us as "the boy", who enjoyed lording it over us, was part of the crew. He was not really bad-natured, we thought, but stupid. When the boat reached its destination off one of the smaller fortified islands near Blankang Mati, the officer ordered the anchor to be dropped. The anchor in this case was a large stone to which a long coil of rope had been secured. "The boy" hastened to comply. Over the side went the stone, and the rope slithered after it. But unfortunately the other end was not fastened to the boat. While the officer yelled his fury, Les had secretly rejoiced in the general discomforture.

Every day while working on the quay two of us would be chosen to go up to the Japanese cook-house, which was on the summit of a small hill, to fetch the Japanese "mishi" – their midday meal. This would consist of up to ten or so billy-cans full of rice and stew or pieces of meat. These cans would be threaded on a bamboo pole, and carried on the shoulders of the two of us.

A guard would accompany this small expedition. If the guard were "the boy" we would see to it that he led the way down the hill. Then the POW at the rear end of the pole would dip his hand into the billy-can of stew nearest him, and take an extra ration. Halfway down the hill, ostensibly to share the weight equally, the bearers would exchange ends. Thus each man could have a go at getting his fingers into the Japanese stew pot. About once a week the guards got a kind of stew which they did not like much. On such days we did not bother to steal, because we knew they would leave some nearly full billy-cans for us.

Very occasionally a party of us would be detailed to work in the Japanese cook-house. This we regarded as a challenge, for depending on circumstances, we would try to smuggle out anything we could lay our hands on. We all had our own army haversacks containing our meagre midday meal. These had to be left outside the cook-house. The game was to get whatever we could into those haversacks without being caught. Being caught meant a bashing. The culprit would be made to stand to attention while the guard would swing his fists with all his might at the culprit's head.

Our most intrepid swiper was Bruce Andrews, a tough New Zealander, who would sometimes walk away with something quite large, such as a kerosene can full of red palm oil, as though he were doing so on instructions. One day a sharp-eyed guard spotted him popping something into a haversack and let out a bellow. But Bruce quickly mingled with a crowd of POWs cleaning vegetables round a large tank. The guard, not to be out-done, lined us all up for identification. However, Bruce had quietly slipped off his shirt, hat and glasses, and looked a different man in the line-up. As the haversacks somehow had been emptied before they could be inspected, the guard snarled and raged, but could not find a victim to bash.

Another episode which sticks in my memory is when two of us were separated from the rest of our party to accompany a Japanese for what we understood was a special duty. We were ordered to lift a sixty-five–gallon drum of gasoline out of a small boat onto a jetty by means of a hand-operated crane. When we both put our full strength onto the winding handles on either side of the cable spindle, the drum of gasoline came up quite readily. When the drum reached a certain height a ratchet was supposed to engage and hold it while we swung it round onto the quay. Unfortunately, after we had gone through these motions the ratchet did not hold. The handles spun out of our grasp, and the drum of gasoline crashed onto the deck of the boat and into the water. It sank shimmering out of sight.

Now, we thought, we are for it. A major bashing or something much worse. But here the law of Japanese unpredictability worked out well for us. The guard looked round carefully, grunted, and marched us back to join our group without a word. We wondered afterwards whether that drum had been destined for strictly military purposes. The accounting process was certainly rather flexible.

By this time the question of food had begun to play a large part in our thinking, and we were at pains to see how best to spend the cents we earned each working day. Our staples, apart from rice, vegetables and sundried fish or ikan belis, which were provided by the Japanese, were coconut oil, red palm oil if available, blachan, tiny purple onions and pineapples. Sugar was hard to come by, and some enterprising POWs who had managed to bring in some sacc harine with them sold sweetened water by the bottle. Coconut oil has a harsh flavour, which kicks the back of the throat. Its sharpness, we discovered, could be tempered by putting a few grains of cooked rice into the bottom of the bottle. The pineapples were good, but I soon became wary of them. Unless they were very ripe, and the spines which penetrated the fruit were cut out with the greatest care, they were liable to cause enteritis. I felt I had had enough of that already.

A banner day in our Blakang Mati lives was when we were told there would be a distribution of cheese. We could hardly believe it. Apparently the Japanese, who do not like cheese, had decided that the Singapore Cold Storage Company, which had been the city's main purveyor of European foods, should no longer carry it. A clearance of stocks had therefore been ordered. As the local Chinese population had no liking for cheese either, it was decided to dispose of it to the POWs. We each received a fairly handsome ration, about half a pound, and revelled in it. We did not see fresh cheese again until we were repatriated.

A feature of our Blakang Mati life which encouraged us was that we were receiving letters from our loved ones during our stay there. The sending of these letters was limited to one "next-of-kin" source, which in my case meant Phyllis. The letters were air-letters which had been sent to Tokyo, then photocopied and reduced in size before being sent on to Malaya. From their content we deduced that the time between their composition and their receipt was several months. In this way I learned that Phyllis had managed to reach England, where she returned to teaching in London schools.

However, after quite a short time the Colonial Office asked her to assume responsibility for a school in Tabora, Tanganyika, and it was from there that her letters came. I received fifteen letters from her in all, and I often marvelled at her news and her love when she received hardly anything from me in exchange. During my whole POW period I was allowed to send just three postcards, all from Singapore, each one with a limited number of hand-printed words, and a censored content merely indicating that I was well. Fortunately we were also allowed to send our love. It was a most difficult,testing time for Phyllis, for the long waits between postcards left her in doubt as to whether I had survived or not. There was also a long wait after the capitulation of the Japanese, to the point that Phyllis's friends were fearful of meeting her because she had had no word from me. News that I was alive came only in a telegram from Colombo when I was on my way home on a repatriation troop-ship. But her story is worthy of a separate recounting later.

After some months in Blankang Mati we began to hear rumours that POWs from the main camp were being sent in groups "up-country" for reasons unknown. It was believed that we might join them. The groups committed to this operation were called "Forces". The first "Force" to go presumably could have been "A Force", but I have never heard details of any of these "Forces" other than "F" and "H". The one which we were scheduled to join was "F Force". I was preparing to depart with Les Russell and most of my other friends, when I had another bout of malaria, and was obliged to stay behind. On this account I was assigned to "H Force" instead.

Only long afterwards did I hear some details of the fate of "F Force" from an account written by my friend Hamish Tod, who survived being a part of it. Two other close friends and colleagues of mine, who were also in the Malayan Education Department, Les Russell and George Tacchi, I am sad to say, did not. They were among the thousands who died in camps along the infamous –Thai Burma Railway.

According to Hamish Tod's account, "written after repatriation in September 1945", the Japanese had demanded 7000 men from the POW Command, half of whom were British and half Australian. The men of this draft "left Singapore in April 1943 in thirteen trains on consecutive days". They detrained, after three days and four nights, in Bampong, a small town some fifty miles west of Bangkok. They then marched in appalling conditions to appoint- ed camps, where they were forced to construct a stretch of road and railway to link up with a railway nearing completion, which stretched south from Rangoon. The aim of the Japanese was to complete the railway by September 1943, in order to make their push at Imphal in the spring of 1944. Out of the roughly 3500 British POWs in "F Force" some 60 to 65 per cent died in the series of camps along the road. The Australian casualties were lower, but ran around 40 per cent. The casualties of "H Force" were lower than those of "F Force", among the British about 50 per cent.

Of course, when we set off on "H Force" we had no idea what was in store for us, but it turned out we followed the pattern set by "F Force". Most of us selected a special friend to work with on the jour- ney. I had such a friend in Roy Williams, a New Zealander Volunteer, who had lived in Taiping and been Chief Electrical Engineer of Anglo Oriental, a large Malayan tin-mining concern. We found an ammunition box with rope handles which we deter- mined to fill with useful items such as local peanuts and red palm oil, and carry between us in addition to our kit. Most men had a kit- bag, one or two haversacks, and some sort of a bed-roll. Hamish, I found later had had a similar idea to ours, he and his friend had taken a discarded stretcher with them. Neither their stretcher nor our ammunition box, alas, lasted very long.

The journey north from Singapore was an ordeal. We were herd- ed into covered railway trucks, twenty-seven men to a truck. Each wagon being made of steel, became like an oven in the hot sun by day, but its temperature dropped sharply after dark, so that we found ourselves shivering soon after the sun went down. We had only our packs to sit on, and because there was so little room we slept on top of one another at night. We suffered greatly from thirst, and the lack of sanitation. Once a day we were allowed to climb down from the train and relieve ourselves along the railway track. Our food for the first thirty-six hours was rice and a thin vegetable soup. Later dried salted fish was added, which intensified our thirst. On the first night we kept up our spirits by singing against the noise of the train.

We passed Kuala Kangsar in the middle of the morning. The train slowed down to a walking pace, and we crowded round the open door of the truck as we had done when passing through other stations earlier. There were a few people on the station platform, but not enough to suggest that they knew a special train would be passing through. The last time that I had been there had been when I was distributing rice from the station godown. It was then that I spotted the shocked face of Singaram, one of the Malay College Tamil gardeners, who did work for us at the house sometimes. I made a sign of recognition to him. But he, poor man was so shaken he could only stare at me agonizingly.

Looking back with hind-sight at this situation I have sometimes asked myself why I did not make a dash for freedom in territory familiar to me. However, none of us really gave this possibility serious consideration at the time. Apart from the armed guards watching the train carefully at all times, I believe our attitude towards the local people was too paternalistic for us to be prepared to expose them to danger, while the possibility of joining up with the communists in the jungle seemed politically undesirable to many of us, quite apart from the difficulty of making contact with them.

At Ipoh we actually halted, I remember, because the locomotive filled up with water there, and some of us managed to fill our water bottles from the dripping hose. It was really the first time that I had had an opportunity to inspect the station at close quarters, for we always went to Ipoh by car. I thought wistfully of the Ipoh Club and those memorable rugby and cricket matches on the Ipoh Padang, and felt relieved that up by the water hydrant there was no one to witness our humiliation.

The journey from Singapore through the whole length of the peninsula to Padang Besar, which is the border town between Malaya and Thailand, is around five hundred miles, and the distance from Padang Besar through the Isthmus of Kra to Bampong is roughly the same distance. I suspect that we Volunteers were able to endure the journey north in these degrading conditions a little more readily than the regular soldiers because of our knowledge of the country, and a deep belief that we would be freed in the end. We did not realize that our situation was to become progressively worse.

After more than three days of suffering, varying in degree according to the physical resistance of each individual, all of us approached the border with a measure of curiosity, because although many of us Volunteers had been as far north as Alor Star in Kedah before, no one, in our truck certainly, had ever entered Thailand by rail. We found that the border demarcation was not merely political. Thailand had a number of characteristics which made it very different from Malaya. First, the country seemed to spread wide and flat before us without much change except for scattered clumps of coconut palms. There were no well-kept rubber and coconut plantations as in Malaya. The villages were poorly kept and, although the water-buffaloes looked healthy enough, there were many mangy, half-starved pariah dogs mingling with the scraggly poultry. Drainage and sanitation seemed more primitive than in Malaya, the movements of people less purposeful, attitudes more permissive, the pace of life slower. The Thais are of Mongolian stock with a historical tradition of freedom, Buddhists with a peaceful, passive acceptance of life and death. The peoples of Malaya, reflecting the disciplines of the Muslim religion and the experience of colonization, appeared as a more ordered society with a higher standard of sanitation and public health.

The journey north from Padang Besar seemed to emphasize these differences. As we moved further into Thailand, which we spoke of then as Siam, we noticed different smells, a sparser vegetation and a drier dustier atmosphere. The straggling villages seemed drab compared with those we had left in Malaya. In Malaya the heavy humidity screened the fiercest rays of the sun, and left roads free of dust, but in Thailand the sun shone with a more glaring heat, and white dust would be kicked up on the roadways except when it was laid by rain.

Then at last the news passed from truck to truck that we were approaching the junction of Bampong, where we would detrain. We struggled with the task of collecting our belongings in the confusion of the truck, and felt our spirits rise, as we were told we would move to a camp for that night, a short distance from the town. After four days of cramped confinement and acute discomfort we looked forward to the change.

We were soon standing in five columns along the station platform on the orders of the Japanese guards, who shouted their commands in angry bursts, often ending their harangue with what sounded to us like a complaining nasal bellow. Here we were counted and recounted, and informed that we would have to leave right there on the platform any gear that we could not carry ourselves, for from now on we would be marching. The things we left would be brought to us later they said. Having already been deceived by the promise of a convalescent camp at Blakang Mati, we were highly skeptical of this being so, and in fact all those who left gear on that station platform never saw it again.

Then we set off through the main street of Bampong in a straggling line of twos and threes. Roy and I were not prepared to leave our ammunition-box behind, and we determined to struggle with it to wherever the camp might be. The Thais looked at us from their houses and their coffee-shops impassively, their faces expressionless, though sometimes I thought touched with pity, or incredulity that we "Europeans" had sunk so low. But the Chinese were openly friendly. They seemed to regard us as comrades who had suffered misfortune in the fight against the common enemy Japan. Defying the guards, who in any case could not effectively supervise the long drawn-out line of men, they handed us bananas and drinks. One or two even made the Churchill "V" for victory sign. These gestures of friendship were heartening in a grim time.

Although we had been told that it was only a short distance to this first camp, it was a struggle for us to reach it with our heavy kit, and we had no way of knowing just how far the "short distance" would be. The line of men became longer and more scattered, as there must have been some three hundred men in our trainload. Roy and I, still carrying our ammunition box between us, became separated from the rest. Then suddenly a Thai darted out from the side of the road, snatched Roy's "comfort" hat from his head, and ran off with it. Roy treasured that hat. He let his side of the ammunition box drop, chased the thief, and recovered the hat. We were surprised at first that any Thai would think one of our old hats worth stealing, but later we were to become aware of the extreme shortage of clothing in many parts of the country.

The camp, when we finally reached it, was hardly worthy of the name. It consisted of three or four hundred-metre long huts, built of bamboo and roofed with attap, of a kind some of us were to remember vividly for life. The cook-house was primitive in the extreme, consisting of large open pans or kualis set over stones on the ground, and covered with a flimsy attap roof. Sacks of rice and skips of vegetables stood nearby. We were separated from the road by a high palisade, near which was an open trench latrine, which permeated the whole camp with a noisome stench. I have never been so nauseated by a latrine. Within the trench and around its edges was a solid sea of writhing whitish maggots. Water had to be carried across the road from the Japanese camp, and it was then, as we passed the pallisade, that we became aware that the Thais were interested in acquiring any of our clothes, wretched though they were, and that a black market in POW possessions had already been established through earlier POW contingents passing through. We were warned not to let any of our kit out of sight as it would be stolen, and indeed I heard of several POWs losing their haversacks at night while they were using them as pillows. I myself had the unusual experience of having a Thai bargaining for my shorts while I sat on the latrine.

Anyone caught black–marketeering could reckon on at least a bashing, but the possibilities were so plentiful, especially at dusk, and the need so great, that few POWs refrained from parting with a few items from their kit for Thai money, as there was no shortage of food in southern Thailand, and money could buy it. It was at Bampong that I bought my first duck egg, already cooked, and felt so strengthened by it, that I bought several more for the journey we knew lay ahead of us.

The Japanese had installed an advance party of cooks and an officer interpreter, all POWs, in the Bampong camp, so from them we had an inkling of what lay ahead. We would stay one night only in Bampong, and then march off in the evening of the following day for fifteen miles at a stretch, bivouacking when necessary. We would march to various camps. Rumour had it that the farthest might be nearly two hundred miles north, almost to the Burma border.

Bampong was so uninviting, leaving it did not seem a special hardship. Our departure followed the pattern we had heard about. But first we were informed that we would have to leave behind anything we could not carry on our backs, for our backs would be the only means of transporting our belongings from then on. As the

POW officer of the advance party confirmed this, each of us had to make an agonizing reassessment of his kit for the second time. In the case of Roy and myself this meant the abandonment of our ammunition box, and some quick black-market dealing. In fact before the line-up in preparation for our march, there was a quiet frenzy of black-market buying and selling.

I suppose it was decided that we should travel in the dark because of the cooler night air, and also probably because the Japanese needed our labour urgently higher up the road. We were told we would start to move as soon as we had finished our evening meal. But that proved to be not soon enough for the Japanese, who impatiently forced us to gobble the poor meal the POW cooks had prepared for us. And so with much shouting and the usual display of plaintive, aggressive bluster from our guards, we were harried into "tengko", the line-up for counting, and as usual were counted several times. Then, as darkness fell, bamboo torches were lit and we set off into the night.

Of all the marches I made in Thailand this first was one of the most memorable, and one of the most miserable, for within a short time the torches went out, darkness enveloped us, and the rain began to fall. It was not just rain, but monsoon rain of such intensity that within minutes our path was a quagmire, and our progress slowed pathetically. Yet we had to press on, as there was nothing else to do. I kept the man ahead of me in view and Roy was at my heels. Soon we were slipping and stumbling, and our clothes and kit were covered in mud. All semblance of marching disappeared. We had started to sing when we set out, but the rain soon silenced our voices, leaving each man to his own thoughts and the noises of the tropical night.

By early morning the rain had stopped, and in the first rays of light we came upon a Thai village, which we were given to understand was only a short distance from the staging camp. Here we were able to slake our thirst with hot sweet coffee, and buy a banana or two from wayside hawkers squatting by the road. We also found to our astonishment that there were trishaw men ready to pedal us and our kit over the last stretch for a few of the ticals we had acquired from our earlier trading. Then at last we found the camp. Some of the early arrivals were lying on the ground, sprawling in exhaustion. Further off the road were a few buildings looking more like cattle pens than a camp, and nearby, still in the camp area, were scattered portable Thai cooking stalls which offered a variety of savoury dishes, featuring eggs, meat, dried fish and vegetables, some of which were being cooked before our eyes in those open kuali cooking pans. I bought a mango here, one of the most delicious I have ever tasted. We had no way of knowing that we would never attain anything near this level of feeding again in the camps higher up the road.

In Bampong we had been informed we were to rest and then move on to Kanchanaburi, (or Kanburi as it was called by the local people), which is about thirty miles further north. The difficulty was how to rest and where. A sick parade was called, mainly to allow first-aid to be given to blistered feet. A few men had feet which were so raw that they could not join us when we moved on. In the end the rest we managed to take consisted of cat naps snatched while we lay on the ground with our kit. It was so inadequate that when we set off again for Kanburi we were still bone weary, longing for a deep sleep. The march to Kanburi was a special kind of nightmare. I felt myself moving like a zombie with heavy eyes and numbed senses. Once I awoke alone in the mud, stiff and sore, but managed to struggle back into the main stream of battered men. In this wild country it would have been quite easy to move away from the route and escape from the crowd, but the Japanese did not worry about that possibility, because there was nowhere for us to head. We heard of attempts to escape being made, but I do not know of any POW who succeeded in escaping from Thailand. There was nowhere to flee to. Moreover, our surroundings grew progressively more discouraging. The farther north we went, the wilder and more relentless the country seemed to become. There were clumps of bamboo in profusion, but virtually no life-sustaining plants or animals.

We arrived at Kanburi about mid-morning in complete disarray. A British officer, who served both as reception officer and interpreter, warned us that, although we were exhausted, the Japanese expected work from each one of us, and that unless we worked we would not be fed. We were to sleep where we could under the trees. We might beg or buy water from the Thais and we would be moving on again after one or two days. Once more there was a sick parade conducted by a British Army doctor, but we soon learned that only the completely incapacitated would be allowed to remain in Kanburi, and that their future would be uncertain. We were immediately set to work on various fatigues – digging trenches for latrines, carrying water, carting bags of rice or skips of vegetables. Later in the day we were marched in groups for a mile or so to wash ourselves in the mighty Mekong river. We passed some ramshackle Thai houses, where the children played in the dust and mongrel dogs barked at us. But we were delighted to find at last enough water to cover our stinking, sweaty bodies, though the satisfaction of bathing was mitigated by the muddy banks which prevented us from reaching dry land again completely clean.

After a few days of this routine we found that the Japanese intended to send us on the next segment of our journey by goods train, as a railway link between Kanburi and Tarso, about forty miles farther on, had already been constructed. This time we were to travel in open trucks filled with logs, which we assumed would be used to fire the locomotives. We were to clamber on top of the logs and make ourselves as comfortable as possible.

The actual procedure for our departure followed a pattern which had now become familiar. A time was set for us to be ready, which was much earlier than the actual departure time would be. As expected there were several laborious countings at "tengko", a barrage of blustering shouts to get us onto the train and a long wait once we were aboard before any movement took place. But finally, around midday, we did start to move at a laboriously slow rate. Sometimes the train stopped, and we would try to crowd round the locomotive to catch tepid water from its pistons, we were so thirsty. At other times, when it started up a gradient, the locomotive would puff clouds of black smoke into the air and wood sparks would fly. These sparks became a real hazard, and quite a number of us who were on the foremost trucks of the train had great holes burned in our clothes.

One section of this journey particularly stands out in my mind. To our general consternation we found that the train had to climb round a cliff for several hundred yards by means of a viaduct, on the outer side of which was an awesome chasm dropping several hundred feet into the valley of the Kwai river. The viaduct was a makeshift affair built of railway ties over a scaffolding of logs clamped together by huge steel staples, apparently hammered in by sledge-hammer. Committing the train and its contents to this precarious ascent seemed to us to be a most dangerous undertaking, especially as we had noticed our locomotive labouring stentoriously over much gentler slopes. In fact the train took several runs at this crazily perching curve, and only managed to skirt the cliff at the third attempt. We were all extremely relieved when the single track plunged into the jungle once more.

I feel I should interject at this point that I am writing about events that happened forty years ago. Our arrival in Tarso, and the various marches further north do not now stand out distinctly in my mind. Hamish Tod in his account of "F Force", written in September 1945, describes in some detail eight marches from Tarso to Mikki, one hundred thirty miles further north, where there were a number of POW camps servicing the railway, the last being three kilometres from the Burma border. The men of "H Force" force were also dispersed in a number of camps north of Tarso, but not as far north as those of "F Force". However, though I cannot now give time and place with any assurance of accuracy, I can recall with great clarity certain places, people and events of this period as though the time were yesterday.

After leaving Tarso we moved to camps where we actually set to work to build the railway. In the next few months I learned with my fellow POWs how to fell virgin jungle, and dynamite rock. I carried sticks of dynamite on my back along jungle paths; hammered metre-long steel drills into rock by sledge-hammer; set rails on the "sleeper" ties and nailed them into position; carved out cuttings through and round mountains; and helped to build and repair those flimsy bridges and viaducts which crossed and recrossed the seemingly endless ravines.

In one camp near Konyu a small group of us were in the charge of a Dutch officer. Our job was to carry sacks of rice and sugar on our backs up a steep path from the river to a store. It was gruelling work. Our guards were Korean, and although they had no love for their Japanese masters, they turned out to be slave drivers. At night they were drunk on saki, and our Dutch commander ordered us to keep quiet in our tents without lights lest they should feel inclined to consider themselves provoked. In this camp, which is the only one I can remember where canvas tents were provided, I had been elevated to act as interpreter on account of my slight competence with Japanese. It was a thankless task, because it was the instinct of the Korean guards, trained as they were in the Japanese Bushido tradition, to take it out on the nearest scapegoat if something were deemed to have gone wrong. I was lucky in this particular job, for though I was shouted at and abused many times, I was beaten up only once.

In these work camps one quickly learned some guidelines for survival. It was important to keep going at a steady pace, so as not to attract a guard's attention to oneself. Above all it was important to have a close friend. Roy and I were always close to each other, ready to supply help or protection whenever it was needed. We were the last to leave one camp, swinging all our belongings on a bamboo pole balanced on our shoulders. But that was a camp from which we were heading south, so though we thought wryly of our abandoned ammunition box at that time, we were not unhappy. As we

made our way along a sparse jungle road, we met an elephant dragging a huge tree trunk at the bidding of a tiny Thai who sat on the
elephant's head, with his bare feet behind the great beast's ears. At
that moment we felt suddenly elated by the strangeness and beauty of the scene.

I remember meeting Pete Byrne for the first time. I knew from
his friends that he was a Volunteer, a tin-miner who had worked on
an off-shore mine. He was a tall South African with a very dark skin
and blue eyes. We had reached one of those staging camps north
of Tarso, and had been ordered to cut bamboo to build ourselves
night shelters. Cutting bamboo is a skilled business, but it can be
accomplished effectively by a team of four or five men with a rope
and a machete, or "parang" as it is called in Malay. One man severs
a pole of suitable thickness at the base of the clump. The rope is
tied around it just above the cut, and the team then drag it free for
trimming, for bamboo shoots are packed tightly at their base. Some
of the stems have a diameter near their roots of three or more inches, and rise to a height of over thirty feet. But there is danger in
the lovely, graceful bamboo. It is covered with sharp spines in unexpected places, which can quickly cut into arms and legs. We were
soon to find out that the wounds inflicted by them often developed
into tropical ulcers.

I had returned from such a foray, and was pausing in the shaping
of a bamboo pole, when Pete approached, and said with a grin:
"Would you like a shave, Ken?" In Blakang Mati one of the men
had a cut-throat razor, and performed this service for all of us at
convenient times, for a consideration. But such a facility I did not
expect to find in Thailand. I sat down on a boulder, and Pete produced soap, brush and a cut-throat razor from his haversack, and
gave me a shave I shall never forget. It was the beginning of a long-
standing friendship. Pete was a wonder with a sledge-hammer. He
was indeed the only Volunteer who could swing the hammer in a
smooth wide arc behind his shoulders, and bring it down unerring-
ly on the drill. When he was in action, I had no fear of holding the

drill, and it had to be held, for when first applied to the rock it stood a full metre up from the rock's surface.

Another scene I can conjure up at will is within another camp, one struck by cholera. No Japanese guard would come near, because we were in a "cordon sanitaire". At first men were dying within forty-eight hours from constant acute diarrhea and dehydration, but after a time our doctors were able to save some lives by introducing a saline solution into the bloodstream of patients in a primitive hospital we had there. We learned to overcome our fear of the disease by being made to understand that cholera infection comes via the mouth, and therefore scrupulous care regarding what passed our lips could protect us from infection. In practical terms this meant that all our food had to be thoroughly cooked, all drinking water boiled, and all utensils sterilized. When we lined up for meals we dipped our billy-cans, knives and spoons through a series of containers full of boiling water, before receiving our ration of cooked rice and cooked dried fish. After being sterilized, the food, and everything we used, also had to be vigorously protected against the ever present attention of flies. Living within a "cordon sanitaire" did not save those who were considered fit enough from working on the railway, however. The only difference was that in the camp the guards did not themselves check the sick at close quarters in order to make up their quotas.

Being in a "cordon sanitaire" in Thailand brought home to me our isolation. No–one near us cared whether we lived or died. It was then that I found that a field mouse had bored a hole into my haversack, which I had been using as a pillow, and helped himself to a few of my carefully saved peanuts. I was delighted. I felt a kinship with the mouse, and begrudged him nothing. His thievery was a salute to life, which I reciprocated.

At another camp I was a member of an emergency team to keep a section of the line in working order. This resulted in our being summoned at any hour of the day or night, because the track and the rolling stock were so inferior that breakdowns were constant.

One night we were called out in the monsoon rains to get a loco-motive back on the rails by the light of hurricane lamps. Huge jacks had been brought up from somewhere by the time we arrived. We had to provide the manpower to use them. We struggled in the tor-rential rain and darkness, and by soon after dawn the train was ready to resume its journey.

I have the impression that our section of "H Force" completed its sector of the railroad earlier than some others, and that for this rea-son we eventually headed south for Kanburi, without getting anywhere near the link with the line in Burma, as "F Force" had done. We knew there was a hiatus of some sort, because we were told that there were opportunities for some of us to become truck drivers and move further up the line. As truck or "lorry" drivers as we called them, were reputed to receive better treatment from the Japanese than other POWs, Roy and I gave this proposition very serious consideration. In the end we decided not to volunteer, and we did not come to regret our decision, as shortly afterwards we began to make our way by slow stages back to Kanburi.

Our fortunes with regard to food varied from camp to camp. At worst, in a remote camp, it was just rice with a little dried fish. Vegetables generally seemed to be in short supply for no apparent reason. For weeks we longed for a little meat of any kind, and then one day in another solitary camp, a few head of cattle appeared from somewhere and were summarily slaughtered. Then there was an abundance of meat for a short time. Too much meat in fact; and then absolutely none again. In Kanburi, on our return there, we sometimes had stew with a modicum of beef or pork in it. I remem-ber being astonished at relishing a piece of pork fat in the stew, which in normal circumstances I would have found repugnant. The body had been deprived of fats for a long time, and one's taste reacted accordingly.

By the time we arrived in Kanburi for the second time it appeared to have grown considerably, and to have become a hospital base for the whole POW operation. I arrived there as a member of a rather small contingent, and after seeking treatment for malaria, for without proper treatment I had suffered numerous relapses in various camps up-country, I became a hospital orderly. This was partly due to my acquaintance with Jack Wood, whom I had come to know while recovering from dysentery in Changi. He was a pharmacist in private life, and had come to Malaya as a sergeant with a medical unit of the 18th Division – just in time to be taken prisoner.

One of my tasks as a medical orderly was to help with the distribution of food to the immobile sick in the one hundred metre–long huts, the like of which we had first come across in Bampong. The rations of rice and vegetable which were our staples were often supplanted by duck eggs, which could be purchased from the local Thais. The immobile sick would acquire their eggs through friends or other intermediaries. They could usually be obtained from the villagers if one had the funds. A Thai baht was worth about 21 cents and would purchase two duck eggs. It was often my job to collect these eggs from patients in a large vegetable skip. The skip would be immersed in a huge kuali or circular pan of boiling water for an appropriate time, and then I would have to return the cooked eggs to their owners. In the early days of this operation, patients would write their names in pencil on their eggs, and hope to have returned the same eggs they handed in. But there were so many eggs to be cooked that this proved to be quite impractical, and there were many complaints from patients that the cooked egg they got back was smaller than the one they had handed in.

One of my patients for whom I cooked duck eggs was a slender, dark young man covered from head to foot with septic scabies. He told me he feared for his hands, for he was an artist. At the time I had no way of knowing what quality of artist he might be. But later I had the pleasure of working with him in theatre and other cultural activities. His name was Ronald Searle.

The patients in Kanburi hospital were from many units – British, Australian and Dutch. They suffered from a wide range of diseases, the most prevalent being malaria, beri-beri, dysentery, tropical ulcers and septic scabies. Some suffered simply from extreme weakness due to malnutrition. Malnutrition and the lack of adequate medical supplies in fact resulted in many needless deaths. There was never enough quinine or other drugs to control malaria, for example. Once I had the unhappy experience of watching a patient die from cerebral malaria, which can develop from a PT?. infection. He was an engaging London taxi-driver named Singer, with a great fund of stories. He died after a series of uncontrollable fits. Most men suffered from beri-beri to some extent. Beri-beri is due to lack of Vitamin B in the diet. Had the rice we were provided with by the Japanese as rations been unpolished instead of polished, most of the beri-beri could have been avoided. Beri-beri could be either the "dry" variety which affected the heart, or more usually the "wet", which produced oedema in various forms. Most of us at one time or another could press the flesh over the shin bone, and leave a dent there. The oedema most commonly occurred in the region of the ankles, but I have seen cases in which the whole body swelled to such an abnormal size that its weight almost doubled. Unless the patient in this predicament could somehow halt and reverse the propensity of the body to produce and secrete fluid, his heart would be unable to bear the burden, and he would die. After repatriation we heard how certain internees in Changi Gaol who had been suffering from diabetes had died because their meagre supply of insulin ran out and could not or would not be replenished by the Japanese. It was a similar situation with our beri-beri patients. Small doses of Vitamin B given in time would undoubtedly have saved their lives.

Dysentery, both amoebic and bacillary, was extremely widespread and, because of the poor sanitary conditions and lack of water, was difficult to combat. Tropical ulcers, usually on the legs, developed from quite small wounds, often, as I explained earlier, from cuts made by the sharp points of bamboo. Because of the poor condition of the patient, these wounds would grow quickly into ulcers an inch or more in diameter. Treatment was drastic – scraping out with a spoon, and sprinkling with idioform powder as long as the supply lasted. In extreme cases amputation would be necessary.

There was in Kanburi a well-known Australian surgeon named Fagan, who was greatly respected. His surgery was a bamboo shelter, adjacent to the jungle, screened by mosquito–netting to keep out the flies. I was once a minor assistant of his at a leg amputation in this shelter, which also served as his operating theatre. While I was in Kanburi they brought in some men who had attempted to escape, but had turned back in desperation. They were too far gone to be attended to in the surgery. I watched the surgeon clip off the gangrenous toes of one of the survivors, as he lay stretched on the platform of his hut late at night.

One of the hardships of life in Kanburi was the shortage of water for washing, and because of this I learned to bathe in a pineapple-can of water. One of the results of this lack of water, coupled with poor food, was septic scabies. Treatment for scabies was the application of sulphur mixed with coconut oil. We ran a scabies centre for walking patients, in which the men would stand naked in the sun, and anoint themselves from head to foot with coconut oil mixed with powdered flowers of sulphur.

Such were the conditions in Kanburi, and the state of health of the men congregated there, that inevitably many died. Each morning there were likely to be several corpses laid out under the eaves of the huts ready for the burial party. Because so many men were near death, those who were regarded as incurable were put in a special "death hut" so that the less sick might have a better chance of survival.

One night I heard a young man named Bernstein sing in the hundred–metre hut in which I had my bedspace. He had a good tenor voice and he sang halfway down the hut beneath a slightly swinging hurricane lamp. The gangway down the middle of the hut was five or six feet wide, and on either side of it ran the long platforms of split bamboo on which the men slept, or tried to sleep, under a motley array of mosquito–nets. The sick men could see very little through the netting, though some of them had oil lamps of their own of various kinds, but they appreciated the songs.

Jack Wood was something of an impresario in this setting, and it was he who had encouraged Bernstein to sing such songs as the "Indian Love Call". He suggested I might like to help enliven the bleak atmosphere of the hut by doing something with Bernstein. This led to a trio of songsters made up of Bernstein, Sprod, a young Australian newspaper cartoonist, and myself. We were rather short on repertoire, and after singing "Santa Lucia" in harmony and a few other favourites, we embarked on a number of Jewish compositions, which Bernstein taught us, he alone of the trio being Jewish. The words were in Hebrew, and the songs religious in nature, but in the circumstances nobody had any objections. The haunting melodies were in fact very well received. To vary the entertainment Jack and I did a comedy turn, in which I was the foil to his stories. One night a man died in the middle of our act just behind us, but in the darkness only his immediate neighbours were aware of it, and his body was taken outside very inconspicuously.

I noticed in my rounds that the spirits of patients varied enormously. Some managed to joke though pitifully weak or in pain, while others tended to withdraw into themselves and grow listless. These were the ones who were likely to die unless the will to live could somehow be rekindled in them. I remember one young man from the 19th Division, a well-educated architect, who seemed to be going rapidly downhill. He suffered badly from enteritis, but then we all suffered from enteritis in varying degrees. One day one of the Japanese guards discovered he was an architect, and got him to sketch out and plan a barber's saloon for him. It was not the most dazzling project for a young man who had won a prize to study architecture in Greece, but it changed him completely. The light came back into his eyes. He had a reason to live.

Roy by this time was a patient in a different hut from mine, suffering from dry beri-beri. I went to see him at night, taking with me little extras in the way of food, which were often vital to a man's recovery. Next to him was a young regular with a large lump the size of a small football on the side of his abdomen. The hut orderly looked after him tenderly, but confided to me that the young man had no hope of surviving. Facilities for an operation of the kind he needed were non-existent in the camp, and in any case he was too weak to undergo surgery. We shared what we had with him and he died the next day.

I discovered that in the Kanburi camp there was another Malayan Education Officer, whose name, A.C Prigge, I knew, but whom I had not met. I set out to find him, and discovered that he was an extreme septic scabies case. He was in constant pain from the sores on his face and body, and was obviously in need of proper intensive care. I made him as comfortable as I could, but I did not like the look in his eyes, and he did not touch the boiled duck egg I had brought him. He died before I had an opportunity of returning to see him again.

Looking back I am sure that attitude of mind played a large part in determining who survived and who succumbed in those terrible times. In order to survive in the most extreme adversity a man needed to have a reason to live – a faith, a family, a hope, plus a little loving care from others. But he also needed luck. I have seen strong, motivated men swiftly killed by dysentery or cholera. In addition, the persistence of diseases like dysentery and septic scabies tended to erode not only a man's courage, but also his self-respect. Sometimes I could read in a man's eyes that despite all our efforts, limited as they were, he had lost his self-respect and given up. Only a small miracle could save him then.

On the other hand there were remarkable cases of recovery, of men who refused to die, men who had survived leg amputations in most primitive conditions, or come back from being apparently hopeless cases to comparative health. One such case is that of Ian Paterson, a Volunteer sergeant who was a senior officer in the Malayan Mines Department. He wrote to me forty years after we had suffered together in Thailand, having discovered my address in some Malayan journal, to recall that he had been inspired by a talk

I had given one night in Kanburi. We tried to organize talks of different kinds to keep up morale, and I had told the story of my shipwreck with the 'Anchises'. He recalled that I had said it seemed important not to allow oneself to sink into a torpor, and that thought had helped him to overcome his drift into indifference and resignation because of his unremitting dysentery.

Exactly how long I stayed in Kanchonburi I cannot remember, nor can I now visualize the journey back to Malaya, but it seemed that by a certain date the usefulness of many of us in Kanchonburi was considered by the Japanese to have ended, and we were therefore to be dumped back in Singapore where we came from. We were surprised, however, to find ourselves sent to Sime Road Camp in the middle of Singapore Island rather than to Changi. We arrived there just before Christmas in December 1943.

"Sime Road" was a sprawling hotch-potch of a former military camp with huts of reasonable construction, scattered widely over an undulating piece of countryside. Here we settled down to a comparatively peaceful life with work now directed towards self-sufficiency. Special skills were utilized wherever possible – welders started to make food containers from metal office cabinets, gardeners produced vegetables, rubber craftsmen made sandals from raw, smoked sheet rubber or truck tyres, wood-cutters sawed wood and winched out rubber tree stumps to provide firewood for the cook-houses. Everyone had a job of some kind.

I remember my stay in Sime Road as a follow-up on my Kanchonburi entertainment activities. There was a remnant of a British theatre group alive, and I threw in my lot with them. The Japanese at this point left us pretty well to our own devices and as a result we set up a theatre in one of the longer huts. There was a small stage at one end and a seating capacity on benches for about three hundred. I doubt whether the Japanese knew anything about that theatre, for everything was conducted under cover, or even whether they would have cared, had they discovered what was going on. Once we got started we laid on a current production every night for one week, while we rehearsed for the next production in the afternoons. Through Jack Wood I met the professional actor in charge of the British theatre group, and was cast for a number of parts. I played Captain Osborne in Sheridan's Journey's End, Godolphin in Bird in Hand, the Genie in a home-made pantomime, and the murderer in a play called Rope. I also, most ambitiously, played Scrooge in a monologue, and read the prologue to Shaw's Arms and the Man. It was here that I met up with Ronald Searle again. He began to take charge of the decor for the sets, and we played opposite each other in Bird in Hand. I found this new assignment within the camp exciting and satisfying.

Another activity I found myself engaged in was also a spill-over from what I had been doing up-country. From my experience as a hospital orderly with some responsibilities for feeding the sick, I became interested in the possibilities of camp cooking, and was given the job of monitoring the various cook-houses in Sime Road for the purpose of improving our own. All groups received basic rations in proportion to their number, but much could be done to make the food more palatable by using ingenuity and seasonings. In general the Dutch, who comprised Hollanders from Holland, mostly officers, and Dutch of mixed blood from Indonesia, were much more adept and ingenious at making the most of the food-stuffs available. The aim of our cook-house was to emulate the best. It was in Sime Road that we first became acquainted with what we called "doovers" (perhaps a corruption of "hors d'oeuvres"). These were a sort of pasty made from a pastry of ground tapioca flour wrapped round whatever there might be available in the way of flavoured protein or vegetable – dried fish, ikan belis, Ceylon spinach, purple onions, curry, blachan. Special days such as Sundays were highlighted by the main meal providing more than one doover per man. Rice, the staple of staples, was always ladled out by measure under the watchful eye of a sergeant, and "seconds" were rigidly controlled by a "back-up roster". We became connoisseurs of rice and keen critics of how it was cooked.

In Sime Road we had time again to think about other things than mere survival and food, though some men arrived in Sime Road camp so debilitated that they could not live through another illness. Among these was Tom White, like Les Russell also a member of the Education Department in Taiping. He was pitifully weak and thin after his return from Thailand, and died after a brief fight against a new bout of dysentery. He was buried in a corner of the camp grounds and I was a member of the burial party. By this time we knew that the internees, the civilians who had been taken prisoner, were interned in Changi Gaol and a message was somehow conveyed to Tom's wife in the gaol that he was dead.

In Sime Road I had a much closer relationship with a fellow Volunteer and Oxonian, Geoffrey Mowat, whom I had known as an MCS (Malayan Civil Service) officer. We had met briefly in Kanburi, and we were both quite strongly influenced by one of the Sime Road chaplains, Padre Cordingly, whose peace-time parish was in Leckhampton, Gloucestershire. Geof was so deeply affected that he decided he would give up the Civil Service if he were eventually released, and become a priest in the Anglican Church; and in fact this is what he did, though not immediately after his release.

Through Geof I met a number of Dutch officers, whose English was always excellent. In particular there was Oswald Godin, who claimed to have powers of healing. Godin was certainly a remarkable man with considerable charisma, and we spent much time in the evenings in his tiny room discussing religion, listening to his interpretation of Christianity, particularly the Epistles of St Paul, and observing his holistic methods of healing. Godin's immediate Dutch officer friends included a giant of a man named Aitkin, who had won the Diamond Skulls at Henley one year in the 1920s, and one who had held high office in the transportation system of Batavia (now Jakarta). A particular Dutch friend of mine, not in the group, was Van der Vecht, a botany specialist from the Botanical Institute at Buitenzorg (now Bogor), whose special interest was pests of the coconut palm.

I think most of us would have been happy to remain in Sime Road if we had to stay in a camp, but this was not to be. After only a few months we learned that all POWs were to be sent to Changi Gaol, while the internees were to be transferred from the gaol to the Sime Road camp. The switch had to be arranged so that the POWs and internees moved simultaneously. As a result some of us had fleeting glimpses of some of the internees when the transfer was made.

When we first moved into the gaol, on 4th May 1944, I was in a group allocated to what had been one of the working halls of the prison. Once again we were given floor–space, each man having just enough room to unroll his bedding. The gaol had been built to accommodate five to six hundred prisoners. Now nearly three thousand men were squeezed inside. Here in "D" Block, as it was called, I met up again with Hamish Tod, and he and I had bed spaces next to each other. Roy, because of his professional ability as an electrical engineer, lived in a cubby-hole under a stairway, where he had access to a limited supply of tools and equipment.

The routine of our lives in the gaol was to some extent similar to that of our earliest days in Changi Barracks. One big difference, however, was that there was "tengko" every morning and evening in the perimeter road, just inside the twenty foot–high wall of the prison, though later this applied only to working parties moving outside the gaol. The large working parties which went outside were now almost exclusively for wood collecting, which included grubbing out the stumps of rubber trees by pulley and tackle. We piled the cut wood onto engineless trucks, and dragged the trucks to the cook-house by ropes. There the wood fatigue cut it into pieces small enough to feed into the cook-house furnace, which fired a boiler. The boiler provided steam for all the cooking inside the gaol.

The largest working parties inside the gaol were those of the gardeners, who cultivated vegetables in the space inside the walls of the prison. Quick-growing vegetables such as Ceylon spinach, which can be easily propagated, were the ones most commonly planted. Part of the gardeners' duty was to provide the young plants with fertilizer. They did this by collecting the men's urine from the special urine containers, also made from filing cabinets, which were set out at night in each prison bay. A mixture of eight parts of water to one of urine was then poured around the vegetables each morning.

Not all the men brought back to Singapore could be accommodated inside the gaol itself, and as time went on other units drafted back from Thailand were quartered in various kinds of huts in the area around it, so that by the time the last of the working groups had been redrafted to Singapore, there were an estimated ten thousand men in and around the gaol. All the officers were billeted outside, separate from the other ranks, and we saw nothing of them.

Naturally it took some time for cultural and recreational activities to get started. "Housie-housie", today more commonly known as "Bingo", seemed to be extremely popular, and "housie-housie" evenings for those who wanted them were quite frequent. The internees had had a number of contacts with the town, and as a result there was in the gaol the nucleus of a library, which was run by two Australians:– Alex Downer, whom I had known in Sime Road – he subsequently became a Minister in the Australian Government, Ambassador to London, and his country's Foreign Secretary – and his constant companion, an Australian lawyer.

In Sime Road I had also become friends with the camp interpreter, Captain Wait, who had been a missionary working in Japan, and with his help, and the co- operation of a number of others, a series of lectures was organized. Wait himself spoke on Japan, the classics master from Eton College spoke on the Roman Empire, and I gave a talk on "Education and preparation for life", in which I offered suggestions for bridging the gap between school and "work", in practical and what I hoped were imaginative ways. For those fortunate enough to gain admission to a University I strongly recommended a "sandwich year" between school and college in some entirely different environment. I forget the other lectures and titles, but Ronald Searle produced advertising posters for most of them. I still own the tattered remains of several such posters.

During this period I participated in various working parties, outside the gaol collecting wood and inside working on the gardens. One day, when I was on a wood collecting party, it became known that I spoke a little Japanese and so I was attached to the Japanese guard. I tried to persuade him to get us some coconuts from a local Chinese to supplement the men's midday meal. This produced an interesting encounter. The guard and I were invited into the Chinese farmer's shack, and he plied us with local brandy. I drank out of politeness, and to forward our objective. The guard indicated his wishes by drawing characters with a stick on the ground – characters which the farmer understood although he knew no Japanese, because there are basic similarities between written Japanese and written Chinese characters although the spoken languages are quite different. The result of this excursion was a better lunch for the party, but at "tengko" that night I was retching horribly as a result of the raw brandy, and needed to be shielded as much as possible by my friends who had me sandwiched in the back row.

Partly to escape the attention of the guard on subsequent days, I applied for permission to work in two areas which were difficult to obtain access to – the cook-house, and the theatre. By gaining entry into both of these my life in the gaol was revolutionized. It was Geof Mowat who suggested that I try to get into the cook-house, for he had managed to move in there some time before I did. He worked in the tea section, producing hot tea in great steam canldrons for up to five thousand men at a time. So I approached Frank, the sergeant in charge of the cook-house, and was delighted to be accepted into the corps of two hundred "cooks".

The cook-house was a self-contained unit comprising a huge main hall, two storeys high, equipped with stone-topped serving and cutting tables, and a number of rooms surrounding it, some of which were fitted with immense steam cookers about five feet high, riveted into the floor. One of the longer rooms contained a row of about a dozen long white enamelled bathtubs, which were used for serving the rice, or mixing vegetables into it by means of wooden paddles. Upstairs round the perimeter of the hall ran a barred walkway, behind which were individual cells. Each cell contained a raised concrete slab for a bed and, in one corner, an oriental type–flush toilet, only slightly raised above the level of the floor. A small barred window looked out into a courtyard. I shared one of these cells with Geof. We took turns to sleep on the slab, because sleeping in one of the narrow slots on either side of it was like going to sleep in a coffin.

My first assignment was to the washing-up room, which was where all the cooking utensils and distribution containers were washed and cleaned. It was a room full of steam and noise. The floor was always awash and to cope with the work one needed to be strong and resilient. After a meal, the cooking pans and distribution containers, each of which could hold about twelve gallons of rice or liquid, would get pushed into the washing up room on trolleys, and the shift on duty would set about cleaning them with hose-pipe, brushes and wood-ash. My partner on my shift was a middle-aged Australian, who told me he had been the champion tie, or railway sleeper, cutter of Australia in his younger days. He was an excellent worker, and I enjoyed working with him.

Geof and I, it appeared, were the only Volunteers in the cook-house. I was rather pleased that this was so, because in general the Volunteers tended to keep to themselves, while the men in the cook-house presented a much more varied cross-section of humanity. Frank himself came from a family which ran a baking business. He had a good head for organization. Among the others were sheep-shearers and circus performers from Australia, a Dutch pro-

126

fessional all-in wrestler, a boxing coach, two ex-Palestinian army sergeants, several bus operators, a waiter from the Imperial Hotel, Blackpool, a young Dutch dancer, a long-distance truck-driver, who became the cook-house barber and about half a dozen professional butchers. The talents of these latter were largely wasted until the Japanese realized that defeat was imminent, after which meat suddenly became a part of our diet. Shortly before the official takeover of the prison, I remember looking down on the cutting tables through the bars upstairs and seeing the butchers vie with one another to show how well they could carve up a side of beef.

After some time I graduated from the washing-up room to the distribution section, which was responsible for loading the containers full of rice or tea onto the trolleys, and seeing that they were handed over to the correct recipients, who arrived at appointed times from the four corners of the gaol. One day Geof and I discovered that it was possible to climb through a hole in the wall above the walkway, which had been made by the previous occupants of the cook-house, and so reach the slightly sloping roof of the gaol. We found the air up on the roof much cooler than in our cell, and as there were no mosquitoes up there either, from that time on we always chose the roof for sleeping except when it rained.

Captain Takahashi, the Japanese commander of the gaol, as Ronald Searle's book, "To the Kwai and Back reveals", was himself an artist and a reasonable man. He had no objection to the POWs doing what they could to help themselves, provided their actions did not run counter to the orders of his superiors, or jeopardize the security of the prison. As far as theatre was concerned he agreed to one theatre being created for the whole camp, and entertainment in it could be provided by one theatre unit, which would be formed by an amalgamation of three existing theatre groups, two British and one Australian.

Accordingly quite a large stage was allowed to be built by POW engineers and carpenters, and lighting, as elaborate as limited resources would permit, was installed by POW electricians. Benches to seat nine hundred men were constructed in an auditorium open to the sky, so that if a show ran for a week, as it normally did, most men in the camp would have the opportunity of seeing it. In fact entertainment was so precious that there was rarely an empty seat. There was one upright piano in the camp and a few wind instruments. One man had built for himself a doublebass out of boxes. European civilians had left a small assortment of men's clothing in buildings close to the gaol, and a wide selection of women's clothing had been left by the military nurses who had departed from Changi in haste. These clothes became the property of the theatre, and were put in the care of a specially appointed wardrobemaster, the former tailor from the "Prince of Wales" battleship.

On the British side there were strengths in production and direction. Major D'Arcy who had lost a leg and an eye under artillery fire, had professional experience in production in a London West End theatre. He had great charm and a sense of authority, which seemed to challenge the players, and put quality into any production he directed. The black patch over his lost eye and his crutches made him a rather romantic figure. He had a penchant for Noel Coward and even played the lead in a Coward play despite his physical handicaps. Ronald Searle now came into his own as the guiding genius for stage décor, and the quality and imaginativeness of the sets improved steadily. Bill Williams was a solid standby on the musical side. He could sing the popular songs of the day, accompanying himself on the piano. One evening when the musical numbers were flowing freely, he belted out a song which touched a chord in his audience; "There'll be blue birds over / the white cliffs of Dover / tomorrow when the world is free". Unfortunately, there was also an attentive Japanese spectator in the auditorium that evening, who stood up with a yell, stormed backstage, and closed the show. We had no theatre for several weeks after that.

From the Australian group there were a number of professional actors, and several who played female roles to perfection. Once when we had Japanese officer guests in the front row, they rushed backstage to check that our women were not the real thing. Harry was an Australian circus clown, whose mocking shout "We'll never get off the island!" became a catch phrase throughout the camp. Sid Piddington, a member of the Magic Circle, had a repertoire of conjuring and magic that held his audiences spellbound. He worked with a young colleague, Russell Braddon, who after the war wrote a book on the capitulation of Singapore called "The Naked Island", which started him on his career as a writer.

Piddington developed a thought-reading act with Braddon which was very effective. He once gave a demonstration to a group of players who were on stage between rehearsals. Braddon sat blindfolded with his back to the audience. Piddington started his show by waving a variety of coloured scarves in the air and calling upon Braddon to indicate which colour was being shown. To do this Piddington would hand Braddon a slate, and ask him to write down the colour on it. Braddon was always correct. Next the names of a number of unrelated objects would be written on the blackboard. Piddington would point to several of them in turn under the direction of the audience, and Braddon, still blindfolded, would write down the right ones as required. Finally each of the players in the small audience was invited to hand in a book he had been asked to bring with him. There were twelve books. Piddington called for a number – one to twelve. Someone called out "Seven". He took up the seventh book from the top of the pile. "There are three hundred and twelve pages in this book," he announced. "Please choose a number 1 to 312." Someone chose 216. "On page 216 there are twenty-nine lines. Please choose a line, 1 to 29." Line 14 was chosen. Piddington got someone to write it on the blackboard. Then he handed the slate to Braddon and, sure enough, after some short time for rumination, Braddon wrote the line correctly on the slate. Magic!

On another occasion I was asked to take part in a similar demonstration by writing a name and address on a piece of paper, which I then handed to Piddington. In due course Braddon correctly produced the name and address on his slate. I was greatly puzzled at the time as to how this was done. Thinking over the circumstances, however, I concluded that Piddington had handed a pellet of paper to the blind-folded Braddon, when he passed the slate to him, and that on the pellet was written the name and address. I recalled that as I wrote, Piddington was looking over my shoulder, and could have copied what I had written on a small pad in his pocket. The writing could then have been screwed up into a ball, and passed to Braddon with the slate, unobserved by the audience. This had to be the way it was done, I thought, as the name and address I had written were entirely imaginary. The actual sleight of hand was so good in this and other parts of the act, that some of the audience were more than half convinced that genuine thought transference was involved. I mention this because after the war, Piddington, with his wife as his partner, were top of the bill at the Palladium in London with a thought-transference act, and later went one better by demonstrating thought transference between one of them in the Tower of London and the other in a helicopter. How any message was conveyed I do not know, but I am quite sure no genuine thought transference was ever involved.

My entry into the gaol theatre group came in an unexpected fashion. I had been introduced to Major D'Arcy by an acquaintance of Sime Road days, when the Major was working on the cast of Autumn Crocus, the new company's most ambitious undertaking up to that time. The innkeeper, a young Dutchman, and the heroine had been chosen. D'Arcy was looking for someone who could speak German and sing for the part of Herr Feldman. I immediately said that I could do both these things and would be pleased to be given a trial. So from a chance conversation I found myself a member of the Changi Gaol Company. I worked in the cook-house by day, was given time off for rehearsals, and played in the theatre at night.

In preparation for the Herr Feldman part I had my hair cut square in a German crop by the camp Barber, and added embonpoint for on-stage appearances by stuffing a cushion down my shorts. I sang a duet with my "wife", who was another Dutchman, and mixed my remarks in German with English spoken with a thick gutteral accent. Searle had excelled himself with the decor for this play. For the love scene on the mountain side he had painted a fine curtain backdrop, and for the inn itself we had a rustic staircase descending from the catwalk high on one side of the back of the stage. This was my entry for the well-known scene with the heroine's companion, who was none other than my old friend Sprod. She was there with all her baggage waiting for the departing coach. Feldman, having learned a phrase or two in English, is supposed to remark jovially: "I see you have everything on but the kitchen stove!" In a fit of exuberance on the opening night, I said, "I see you haf nuttin on but the kitchen stof!" The line was a show stopper, and D'Arcy got me to keep it that way for the rest of the run.

After some weeks in the cook-house I thought I would like a change of occupation, and applied to work on the wood-pile, where we sawed up wood for the cook-house boiler. It was reputed to be the hardest work in the camp and I liked the thought of the challenge. We worked long hours, two men to a cross-cut saw, and received a little extra rice "pap" for our pains. I enjoyed another spell in "D" Block with a bedspace next to Hamish Tod again, but I found myself growing progressively weaker from the strain of excessive physical work with inadequate food, so I asked to go back to the cook-house. To my relief I was again accepted by Frank. I did not try any further experiments with location. It became very obvious to me that the cook-house was the place to be.

As we moved into the second half of 1943, the pattern of news which we had been receiving from clandestine sources began to be more exciting. When the atom bomb was dropped over Hiroshima, we knew of it, as by then a radio was regularly assembled at night from parts kept separately by individuals.

I was sick a couple of times during those final months in the gaol. The first time I felt a familiar tingling in my finger tips, a prelude to a shivering fit, which I knew heralded a bout of malaria. I went off to have my finger pricked, and hoped I would be treated quickly, so that I would not be off work long. Having returned to duty in the cook-house I was surprised to be confronted by two medical orderlies from the hospital, who had come to fetch me with a stretcher. I said I was fine, and could walk to wherever I had to go, but they insisted that my blood sample had shown a PT infection which could lead to cerebral malaria, so I complied with their request. Apart from the malaria symptoms I felt in excellent physical shape at this time, and was muscular and quite heavy, so that the two men from the hospital decided that they needed a man at each corner of the stretcher before they carried me off. On the journey there was a good deal of banter from the stretcher bearers about fat, greasy cooks. Fortunately, I responded favourably to treatment, and was soon back on the job.

The second time I was sick in the cook-house was with an abdominal complaint which was diagnosed as a rumbling appendicitis. By this time the world news was so propitious that I thought it a good time to undergo appendectomy, especially as it was known that new medical supplies were being flown into our makeshift hospital. I remember looking joyfully from my bed through the window of the recovery room to watch stores being dropped by parachute nearby. I felt enormously elated, as though parting with an appendix was symbolic of the end to our confinement.

Wonderful things happened in rapid succession around that time. I heard that the gaol had been taken over by the allies in spectacular fashion. A young paratrooper lieutenant with a plum -coloured beret had been parachuted into the gaol with a letter from Mountbatten calling upon the Commandant of the gaol to hand over his command. There were no problems, for the Emperor of Japan, after the bombing of Hiroshima and Nagasaki, had ordered the Japanese general in charge of Singapore to surrender. We knew that Force 136 had been consolidating its strength in Ceylon to mount a counter-attack against the Japanese in Malaya, but we learned afterwards that the Japanese general in charge of Singapore would never have surrendered but for his Emperor's orders, nor would he have allowed any POWs to be recaptured.

Now suddenly the gates of the gaol were opened, and in came people from the outside world. Some were officers of the newly formed British Military Administration (BMA). We tended to be unimpressed by these newcomers. "Banana colonels" we called them. But some unexpected visitors we welcomed with joy. While I was in hospital Geof had been summoned to the front gate to meet with Major General H. H. Fuller, Mountbatten's Deputy Chief of Staff, who gave Geof, a lowly Volunteer corporal, the marvellous news that his wife Louise was safe in Australia. She had become confidential secretary to Major-General Marshall, Deputy Chief of Staff of General MacArthur in his Australian Headquarters, and held the rank of captain in the United Sates WACs.

I was glad to be up and about when Lord and Lady Mountbatten came to see us. They drove into the courtyard inside the gaol gates, and addressed us from the back of a truck. That they were ready to greet us inside the gaol lifted our spirits tremendously. Another welcome visitor was Bishop Wilson from the internees' camp at Sime Road. He had been accused of spying, and had been tortured while he was an internee in Changi Gaol in 1944. Only much later did we learn the reason for this. On 10th October, the double tenth, most of the shipping in Singapore harbour had been mysteriously sunk. As the Bishop was the only internee allowed to leave the gaol to visit the town he was thought to be involved with this event and was made to suffer for it. Actually the sinkings were the result of a daring submarine commando raid organized in Australia.

The Bishop conducted a service in the gaol, and confirmed into the Anglican Church a number of POWs, of whom I was one. A few days later I hitched a ride into town on a jeep, and there witnessed, mingling with a great crowd on the Cricket Club Padang, the official surrender of the Japanese Command.

There was much waiting still to be done before repatriation could be effected, however, and naturally we became impatient, especially as we had no opportunity of getting in touch with our wives and families. We were nevertheless pleased to participate in a number of meetings set up for us to learn what had been happening in the world outside, and particularly in England, while we had been cut off. We were all astonished to learn that Churchill, our hero, had been voted out of office, and we wondered where the policies of the new Attlee Government would take us. Finally, we were told that we would sail for England on the "SS Almanzora", and have facilities for sending cables to England as soon as we arrived in Colombo.

The "Almanzora" sailed from Singapore on 15 September 1945. Some called it "the hell ship", because of the congestion on board and the poor food. But I remember enjoying much of it. We slung hammocks below for sleeping, until most of us learned to sleep on deck, which was cooler and more pleasant. There were morning exercises for those who wanted them. I took part in these, although my appendicitis scar was still red. Above all, I appreciated the privilege we Volunteers had of meeting with the internees, who were better housed on the upper deck. There I met Jean, Tom White's wife, again, and Nella McDonald, a Domestic Science Education Officer who had been a friend of Phyllis's. There was a good deal of bureaucratic red tape on board, but also an undercurrent of rebelliousness, which made the authorities wary. It was rumoured that some unpopular NCOs feared to take a walk on deck at night.

Our arrival in Colombo was something I shall never forget. All the shipping in the harbour gave us a hero's welcome, with their horns blaring as we steamed slowly past. We anchored close to shore, and there on the quay below us were a bevy of Wrens (WRNS), the women's arm of the Royal Navy, waving to us. We were ecstatic. On shore the Wrens were rationed – one per truck on our way to the rehabilitation camp. Starved of women's companionship for nearly four years, we gazed and gaped, and talked in shy bursts of enthusiasm.

The rehabilitation process in Colombo was well organized. We were fitted out with new uniforms, and were allowed to send cables home. I sent two, one to Phyllis and one to my parents. It proved to be the first intimation they had that I was truly alive. During the whole of my period of imprisonment I had been allowed to write just three postcards to my wife, Phyllis, and only to her. We still have them. They are all addressed to Phyllis at her sister's address in Twickenham. The address side has on it a number of Japanese characters and a British government stamp saying "Passed" with an identifying number. But there is no date. All I know is that the last one was written from Blakang Mati before we were sent off to Thailand.

They read as follows;

1st

7869 Pte LUKE K.D.
DARLING PHYLLIS
PRISONER OF WAR
UNWOUNDED, HEALTHY, GOOD SPIRITS.
DEAREST LOVE TO ALL AT HOME.
WITH ALL MY LOVE TO YOU UNCHANGED UNCHANGING

KENNETH

2nd

7896 Pte LUKE K.D.
DEAREST PHYLLIS

FIT CHEERFUL PLENTY
DOING, HAVE BEEN WITH LES. LOVE DEAREST
TRIO. YOU ARE EVER IN MY MIND'S EYE.
ALL MY LOVE
KENNETH

3rd

7869 Pte LUKE K.D.
PHYLLIS DARLING
CHEERFUL WELL
LONGING FOR NEW LIFE TOGETHER.
MAIL RECEIVED TO SIXTEENTH LETTER.
DEAREST LOVE TO TRIO. YOUR OWN
RETURNED A THOUSAND FOLD.

KENNETH

The last postcard records an interesting fact. From the beginning of 1942 until May 1943, when "H Force" went to Thailand, while Phyllis received only three postcards from me, I was receiving airletters from her at fairly regular intervals. But our being sent off to work on the railway marked the end of all mail for everyone. Her aerograms appeared to have been photocopied, reduced in size at some point, then sent to reach me via Tokyo months after they had been written. It was ironic that I knew of Phyllis's teaching in London, her decision to return to the Colonial Service and teach in Tanganyika, and of her experiences as a headmistress in Tabora and Dar-es-Salaam, while she knew virtually nothing of my whereabouts or prospects. There was plenty of time for me to have died between postcards. Indeed, when in the end she had a hunch that the Japanese would capitulate and she headed back for London, there was still no news of me. When she arrived in London news of the capitulation of the Japanese had just come through, but there was still no news of me, so that all but her closest friends began to avoid her for fear of being the first to hear the worst. In those final months the first and only news she had was my cable from Colombo. I have never ceased to marvel at her faith, love and courage.

Our next port of call was Taufik at the southern end of the Suez Canal. Here we were told what medals we were entitled to, although official confirmation of our entitlement was to be given much later in Malaya. I found I had collected four – the 1939–1945 Star, the Pacific Star, the Defence Medal 1939–45 and an Efficiency Medal.

Because wartime conditions still prevailed in Britain, we understood that our families had been told to keep away from the docks at the time of our arrival in Southampton. There were therefore no civilians waiting for us when we docked: only an army band which added a festive touch to our anticipation and excitement. We were to be billeted overnight in Southampton in Nissen huts adjoining the docks, and then we would be allowed to proceed to our individual destinations by train on the following day. I found I was able to explain this to both my parents and Phyllis by telephone. It all seemed like a dream.

And then someone came by with the news that if anyone wanted to get to London quickly, he might do so that very evening without waiting for official departure permission the next day. I therefore grabbed my kit-bag, and set off for the station to see what could be done. Sure enough there was a train just leaving which would get to Waterloo station about 8:30pm. So I got aboard without realizing that there would be no–one to meet me, as I would be expected to arrive the next day. Fortunately a young soldier in a similar situation to mine was getting off at Woking, so I persuaded him to telephone Phyllis at her sister Elsie's house in Twickenham, to say that I was on my way.

Phyllis received the call while Ronald, Elsie's husband, was deep in conversation with a fellow beekeeping enthusiast. My friend in Woking had asked: "Do you know a chap named Luke?" Phyllis, struggling to block out the bee talk, allowed that she did. "Well," said the voice, "he's just passed through here" "Where's here?" said Phyllis, as calmly as she could. "Woking," said my friend. "And where was he going?" said Phyllis. "I don't know," said the voice. But it was enough. The terminal for Woking was Waterloo, and there near the gate when I arrived, although she had been assured no more POWs would arrive that night, was Phyllis. What a reunion! We each have a vision of the other at that time. I saw the girl I loved transformed into a well-dressed woman, wearing a light brown suit with a light blue velour type hat. She saw the man she loved, much larger than she had expected, dressed in khaki and wearing a forage cap. After we had kissed and hugged each other a little, along came a St John's Ambulance worker, who insisted on driving us the ten miles or so across London to my parents' house in Abbey Wood. The warmth shown by everyone we met was heart-warming and touching. This was home.

I had not seen my parents' house in West Heath Road, but I knew they had moved there. My father had reached retirement age, and therefore had had to give up his job as librarian of the Plumstead Public Library, and the flat over it. Fortunately, he was able to take on the librarianship of the public library in the nearby town of Erith, Kent, in the absence of the young incumbent librarian, who had been mobilized. This job was a godsend to him, for he was still energetic and gregarious. It was a wonderful meeting, the first time my mother, father and sister Barbara had been with Phyllis and me together. We sat around the fire, and gazed long at one another, and talked, and drank endless cups of tea. The date must have been early in December 1945 because 16th December was a special date for celebration, it being the anniversary of our wedding as well as of my birthday. On that morning, while Phyllis and I were still in bed, my mother brought me as a gift, among other things, a copy of the Book of Common Prayer, inscribed by her "From Mother – 'I will fasten him as a nail in a sure place'. Isa. XXII V.23."

After we had celebrated Christmas together, and met with Phyllis's sister Elsie and her husband Ronald, their daughter Fenella and their son John, it was clear that Phyllis and I could not stay long with my parents, for their house was very small. Moreover, they had made careful enquiries about accommodation for us to get away by ourselves. We accepted the recommendation of an address in Portreath, Cornwall. I suppose at that time of year it must have been quite difficult to find a place. We were certainly on our own. Our bedroom window looked straight out onto the Atlantic Ocean. There were no curtains to block out the bleakness by day or the blackness by night. We were not enamoured of Portreath, but we revelled in each other's company. Phyllis had brought with her a box of Cuban cigars bequeathed to her by her father, who had been knocked down and killed by a bus in the blackout, shortly after she arrived in Malaya. I smoked one every night while we talked after supper. We enjoyed being alone, but kept in touch with our families by telephone. At that time one could phone anywhere in the British Isles after 8pm for one shilling for the first three minutes.

Our stay in the Lake District was more pleasant and memorable. We were lodgers with a Mr and Mrs Bindlass in Ambleside. Rationing had not affected the Lake District nearly as badly as it had London, and we marvelled at the plentiful supplies of meat and fish in our menu there. We climbed Kirkstone Pass in the snow, saw swans rise in flight from Windermere Lake in the early morning, admired the beauty of Tarn Howes, though when we visited this last beauty spot, my admiration was tempered by my having a kipper bone in my throat. We also looked up my cousin Elsie Johnson, who taught from choice in a one-room village school in an enchanting setting. She drove us around tirelessly in her tiny Austin 7, showing us the beauty spots of Cumberland.

Malayan personnel who had been "in the bag", either as POWs or internees, were encouraged to return to Malaya as soon as possible in 1946, to assist in rehabilitating the country and restoring confidence. We in the Education Service especially were urged to return to rebuild the "English Schools". Phyllis had conceived our daughter Carolyn after our reunion and, because it would be her first child and the war had delayed her starting a family, we requested an extension of leave to enable her to have pre-natal care at Middlesex Hospital. When we were assured that all was going well, we decided that the baby could be born in Malaya, and agreed to the next sailing offered by the Colonial Office.

Return to Malaya

To my surprise I found that I had been posted to be Headmaster of Clifford School, Kuala Kangsar. So it was to be the same small town, but the "other" school. We found Kuala Kangsar still suffering very much from the aftermath of war. Phyllis and I had to live with the District Officer, along with other government officers, up in the house on the hill I knew so well, in a kind of mess, and Phyllis soon found herself in charge of the commissariat of the place. The house compound was surrounded by barbed wire and Japanese POWs still tended the garden. There were few vehicles. The one belonging to the DO had to be reserved for any journeys to Ipoh or Taiping. The Malay College was still being used as a military hospital. The Clifford School headmaster's house had been occupied by Gurkha troops and was not fit for our occupation. The Senior Inspector of Schools, Mr. E.C. Hicks, who was now my immediate boss, came over from Ipoh to see us by motorcycle.

I had wondered at first why the DO's house was surrounded by barbed wire. The reason soon became clear. During the "Reoccupation" as it was called, there was a good deal of lawlessness. Quite soon after our arrival, our bedroom on the ground floor was burgled during the night. Phyllis's handbag and her few pieces of jewellery were taken from the small table between our beds without our being aware of it. The whirring clunk of the ceiling fan, and our mosquito–nets had deadened the sound of the intruders. My rifled despatch case was found near the barbed wire and on the barbed wire itself there was blood. John Cumming, the young bachelor PWD engineer, had a room upstairs. One night he thought he heard a noise, so he looked out over the verandah to check that his car was still under the porch. It seemed all right, so he returned to bed. But in the morning he found the car jacked up – without its wheels.

As Headmaster of the Clifford School I also had responsibility for the Malay hostel in the school compound, which housed about forty Malay boys from the more distant kampong (villages). One day a Malay police officer came to my office to report that one of the hostel boys, Abdul Karim, had been accused of extortion. I called the boy from class and went with him and the officer to the boy's bedspace in the hostel, because the allegation was that Abdul Karim had threatened someone with a gun. Sure enough, under the boy's pillow the officer found a loaded revolver. On the way back to my office Abdul Karim wrenched himself free from the grasp of the officer– why he had not been handcuffed I cannot think– and ran off towards the centre of town. The officer seemed unperturbed, saying he would catch him later. I knew that Karim was a misfit, well over-age for the class he was in, so I was not surprised when he never returned to school.

On the Clifford School staff were a number of excellent teachers, some of whom I had known slightly when I had been at M.C.K.K. Mr Arumugam, my senior assistant, had reopened the school as an English School after the Japanese left. He was a good man and I trusted him implicitly. Phyllis took over the primary school, and the training of its teachers, until she had to go to Penang to await the birth of her baby.

By the time our daughter Caroyln was born, the Clifford School headmaster's house had been cleaned by the PWD after its occupation by Gurkha troops, and made ready for our use. It was a large two-storeyed wooden house, which looked quite well repainted, but certain parts of it, such as the floors and the water closets, had been damaged irreparably. The garden when we moved in had an unmistakably military accent. There were grand paths lined with whitewashed bricks, set at an angle to make a zig-zag border, and where one might have expected flowers, pineapples seemed to be growing, except that on closer inspection these turned out to be pineapple tops buried lightly in the soil – a simple deception for a last–minute inspection perhaps.

Our life in Clifford School was made immeasurably easier by our sudden acquisition of two Chinese servants, who transformed our lives. Ah Lin and Ah Soon had arrived unannounced one after-noon at the DO's house, and offered us their services as a team. We had no hesitation in accepting their offer, because we knew a good deal about them. They had in turn been servants of the Careys, and then of the Woods. Ah Lin was the mother of Ah Soon's wife, who had died during the Occupation, leaving three small children Ah Chee, a girl, and two boys Ah Fook and Ah Wah, aged six, five, and four respectively. Ah Lin was a tiny woman, but one with an iron will, and in her younger days, we were told, a sharp temper. Mrs Carey, who had formerly been the Lady Medical Officer in Kuala Kangsar, told the story of how Ah Lin had so infuriated her Indian cook in a quarrel, that he had cut off the tip of her nose with a kitchen knife. Mrs Carey had rushed her to the hospital and sewn the nose back on. I noticed that the scar was barely visible when Ah Lin came to see us. The offer of her services, together with those of Ah Soon, was made above all because she was a baby-amah, who needed a baby to look after. She had looked after the Careys' daughter, and the Woods' son John. In our situation we were a per-fect match for the Ah Lin/Ah Soon team. Ah Lin accompanied Phyllis to Penang, and Ah Soon became our cook. However, there was never any doubt as to who ruled in the servants' quarters in our establishment. It was Ah Lin.

Shortly after we had settled down in Clifford School I received a letter from Carey, asking me about the Malay College. He had been a POW in Sumatra, where the Japanese had broken his nose while giving him a bashing. He had been taking recovery leave in England, but also in the United States, as his wife Enid, who was American, had been working in an American hospital.

I had to tell him that the College buildings were being used as a military hospital, and that there was no indication that the College would be opened in the near future. Phyllis was still in Penang at that time waiting for her baby, so when Carey arrived in Kuala Kangsar in August 1946, he lived with me in the Clifford School house. He had obtained permission from the Director of Education to buy a certain amount of equipment in London before he sailed, and on arrival had spoken with some of the Sultans and other influential Old Boys about getting the College reopened. His hand was greatly strengthened by the growing unpopularity of the Malayan Union idea, which had been floated by the British government, and the ever increasing strength of UMNO., the United Malay National Organization.

The actual evacuation of the College buildings by the Military was accomplished, according to Carey, by his making a deal with the major-general in charge of North Malaya to get polo going again in Kuala Kangsar, on condition that the hospital buildings were handed over for the re-opening of the school. The College buildings were indeed evacuated by October 1946, and the first boys returned late in January 1947. By that time the tents and huts of the hospital had been removed, and the holes in the games pitches filled in. The Prep School ground, however, remained a military dump until the end of 1947, when the last armoured car and Japanese tank were removed.

By the time Phyllis returned to Kuala Kangsar with baby Carolyn, Carey had moved up to a house on the hill, next to the DO's house, which adjoined the Experimental Agricultural Station and had, before the Occupation, been the Agricultural Officer's house. We saw somewhat less of each other after this. Phyllis, with the help of Ah Lin and Ah Soon, made the Headmaster's house into a home. Meanwhile lawlessness persisted everywhere, fuelled by high prices and the lack of consumable goods, particularly clothes. As burglaries were frequent I used to make a circuit of the house each night with a stout stick, checking the locks and the windows. Our "jaga" (watchman) had his charpoy (bed) set up inside the house across the locked front door. One night I heard a noise in our bedroom, and startled a would-be thief. He jumped from the second floor verandah and fled, leaving his rubber shoes at the bottom of the drain-pipe he had scaled. I ran downstairs, but there was no way of finding the burglar in the dark. I nevertheless bicycled immediately to the police station, and made my report. Looking back I am amazed at behaviour which I would now deem to be foolhardy and reckless, but the incidence of violence against the European in 1946 was remarkably low. I never considered acquiring a gun of any sort, and we treated the danger of being robbed as inevitable, considering the circumstances of the country.

We did lose one major item for a time. The CSKK headmaster's house had a large separate garage in its grounds and as we had no car, at Carey's request the MCKK's truck was kept in it. One morning we found the garage door broken open and the truck gone. But this was really an inside job. A disgruntled sais who had been sacked by Carey had made off with the truck. It was recovered in Penang, and in due course returned to the College.

Carolyn had been born in the General Hospital, Penang, on 8th October. After being brought to KK she could be seen most days in the cool of the early morning being pushed in her white pram, either by Phyllis or Ah Lin, along the short roads which divided the playing fields of CSKK from those the MCKK.

In 1947 both the Kuala Kangsar schools were visited by Malcolm MacDonald, the Commissioner-General for South East Asia. I am not sure now which school he visited first. However, I remember escorting him as he looked in on Clifford School classes in a heavy blue suit, sweating profusely, and crooning "bagus" (good) from time to time after being shown samples of the students' work. It seems that he profited from these early visiting experiences, for later in Singapore it was he who pioneered an open-necked short-sleeved shirt as appropriate dress for the highest councils of

Government, a practice which is continued in Singapore Government circles to this day.

The conditions which caused people around us to steal also had their effect on us. The food we needed, and particularly cold storage items, was ordered by telephone, and reached us by train from Ipoh. It had to be fetched from the station by Ah Soon on the bicycle we had bought for him. The cost of food constituted a larger proportion of our income than ever before, so that there came a time when our salaries scarcely covered our day to day living expenses. We nevertheless had confidence in the Government, and knew that a revision of salaries was under consideration. In retrospect I believe the Malayan Education Service Branch of the Colonial Service, like its other technical branches, was a most beneficent employer. We reckoned to work hard, but we were always treated generously and with consideration. Not surprisingly, most Education Officers, and I believe most officers of the other technical services too, were dedicated servants of the country in their respective areas of expertise.

One of the happiest aspects of this early post-war period was our participation in the Government's teacher training programme, the so-called Normal Classes, which consisted of courses of lectures on Saturday mornings, combined with teaching practice over a two-year period. The Normal Class Certificate was actually awarded some time after the examinations had been successfully completed. The student teacher had to demonstrate his or her capacity to teach in the classroom as well as to pass examinations. Phyllis lectured and demonstrated in Primary Teaching Methods, for which her own training and experience made her eminently qualified. She not only had the usual teaching qualifications of a London College (Furzedown) but had also successfully completed courses in Froebel Training, worked with Rachel MacMillan in her original nursery school in Deptford and been personal demonstrator to Dr Montessori herself in London. I gave classes in English Language and Composition.

Phyllis and I would travel the twenty-two miles to Taiping with a truckload of young teachers, as there were no buses immediately after the Reoccupation. The teachers would sit precariously on benches, and we would have a happy time, for they were keen to improve their skills.

As far as English was concerned, having continued to speak the language secretly during the Occupation, they now pratised it with enthusiasm, and took pleasure in attempting to write creatively in English on a variety of subjects.

One of the teachers who travelled with us to Taiping for Normal Classes was Kim Kee, a young Chinese woman who taught in the Primary Department of Clifford School, Kuala Kangsar, and was one of Phyllis's students. She was married to Chuah Cheong Yong, who had a brilliant career in CSKK., obtaining distinctions in most of the subjects he took for the Cambridge School Certificate Examination. Cheong Yong seemed wasted serving in his father's hardware store in KK, and I had been happy to recommend him for admission to the Medical School of the new University of Malaya, which was opening in Singapore. He also had exceptional ability in the graphic arts and was responsible for a new crest for Clifford School, which was used on the cover of the school magazine for some years. While he was available I enlisted his help as a tutor in Chinese, after I had obtained official permission to study the language. However, as I found I was making poor progress, I gave it up after a few months. Apart from aptitude, of which it seemed I had no particular measure, the successful study of Mandarin demands a dedication and singleness of purpose, which I regret I was unable to devote to it at that time, given my other responsibilities. The Cheong Yongs went on to successful careers in Singapore. Kim Kee became a headmistress there, and Cheong Yong the Secretary of the Singapore Medical Association.

I imagine the demands of home leave, coupled with sickness, made postings quite difficult for the Education Department to organize, until air travel made continuity in a post easier to arrange on account of shorter tours of service and shorter leaves. While the round-trip sea travel from Malaya to England took six weeks, there was a tendency for an officer to be assigned to a new post on his return from home leave, and for these postings in turn to cause transfers within the country of officers who were not due for leave.

I was not specially surprised, therefore, when we learned that I was to be assigned to the post of Examinations Secretary, Federation of Malaya, in Kuala Lumpur, after I had been Headmaster of the Clifford School for less than two years. My duties in the new post began on 19th February 1948, in the head-quarters office of the Federation Education Department, which was housed in temporary single-storey wooden buildings on the Batu Road. The work consisted of monitoring, co -ordinating and pro-cessing applications for all the public examinations of the school system, and some outside it – including examinations in law, accountancy and technical subjects (the City and Guilds examina-tions) and seeing that these examinations were properly administered and conducted. One most interesting facet of my work was responsibility for the co-ordination of the Cambridge School Certificate test in Oral English, which was carried out by teams of native English speakers working in the various States. A core team worked with a sample cohort of the immediate past year's School Certificate graduates and disseminated an agreed-upon standard throughout the country. A pass in Oral English in the School Certificate examination was of vital importance in the pursuit of a job in Malaya, and the Oral examination, though suf-fering from the weaknesses of personal value judgements, did much to establish a reasonably high quality of spoken English in the country.

Phyllis and I were allotted a house in Kuala Lumpur which really belonged to the Victoria Institution, the largest government boys school in the city, and began to enjoy the change of pace which the capital offered us. Our contentment was short–lived, however, because on 15th June, a little less than four months after our arrival in KL, an event took place in Sungei Siput, a small village halfway between KK and Ipoh, which left the country in a state of shock. Three European rubber planters were murdered in cold blood on their estates by Chinese communists, murders which were followed sporadically by others across the country. The so-called "Emergency" had begun.

The story of the Emergency is admirably told by Noel Barber in his book The War of the Running Dogs,' Malaya 1948–1960 (William Collins, 1971). I do not wish to give a detailed analysis of it here, but only to highlight those aspects of it which touch upon my own story. It was a war certainly, though it was never called that. The term "Emergency" was used in order not to undermine confidence in the Administration, but also because the Malayan economy relied on the London insurance market for coverage, and insurance rates covered losses of stocks and equipment through riot and civil commotion, but not through war.

When the Japanese invaded Malaya, there were among the Chinese population communists who took to the jungle and harassed the invaders. The British, as had been done in other theatres of war, assisted these communists when they could, as a matter of expediency, against the common enemy Japan. An example of similar clandestine help is that given by the British to Tito's communist guerrillas fighting against the German Nazis in Yugoslavia. Elements of Force 136, the British guerrilla fighters, were therefore dropped into the jungle, not only to attack the Japanese themselves in commando-type raids, but also to make contact with the communists and help train them. Spencer Chapman in his book The Jungle is Neutral, describes his personal involvement in such action. When the surrender of the Japanese took place in Singapore, the Chinese communist guerrillas were much in evidence. They marched through the streets fully armed as part of the victory parade, trying to give the impression that they were the real heroes of the conflict. There was unfortunately a period of turmoil and uncertainty between the capitulation of the Japanese and the actual taking over of the government by the British Military Administration, during which many old scores were settled. When the BMA re-established law and order, the communist guerrillas were ordered to hand in their arms, but many did not do so. Instead they hid their weapons in caches in the jungle for use later. In June 1948 these Chinese guerrillas, or communist terrorists, CTs as they were called, declared open warfare on the government.

Although on paper the Government army chiefs and civilian leaders seemed to have an obvious advantage over the CTs in the jungle, the advantage was largely illusory, because the actual number of fighting men in the army battalions was quite small, and the political machine of the government, comprising eleven separate administrations linked by the Federal Government in Kuala Lumpur, was most unsuitable to deal with the insurrection. Added to this was a complete misreading of the situation by the British High Commissioner of the time, Sir Edward Gent. He had no sympathy with the planters' complaints, and was indisposed to listen to the old hands, who understood what was going on. Fortunately, Malcolm MacDonald, the Commissioner General for South East Asia, had a more realistic perspective of what was happening and was responsible for Gent being recalled to London on 29th June. Four days later Gent was killed when the aircraft in which he was travelling collided with another over London.

In September the British government appointed Sir Henry Gurney as successor to Sir Edward Gent. Gurney had been Chief Secretary in Palestine during the last two years of the British Mandate. He was immaculate of dress and unflappable in manner. It was typical of him that after finishing his work in Palestine, he took the last plane out of the country. Gurney made important contributions to the conduct of the war. He decided to resettle the 600,000 Chinese squatters living on the fringe of the jungle into what were to be called New Villages.

Gurney also announced two further steps for bringing stability to the country – a system of rewards for information leading to the killing or capture of CTs, with Chin Peng their leader at the top of the list, with $80,000 on his head, and the introduction of a nation-wide registration, whereby every man, woman and child over twelve had to possess an identity card bearing a thumb-print and a photograph.

Gurney was widely admired for his firmness and conviction, but the Malayan Police Force, who were to play a vital role in this war, were unhappy when he sacked the incumbent Police Commissioner, Langworthy, and replaced him with Colonel Nicol Gray, who had worked with Gurney in Palestine as Inspector General of Police. There was already dissension in the ranks of the police force between those who had remained in Malaya and been taken prisoner, and those who "escaped". When Gray brought in several hundred ex-Palestine Police, police morale dropped even lower. Morale in general in Malaya was not helped when, in 1949, Attlee gave official British government recognition to the Mao Tse-tung regime.

However, Whitehall did assist Gurney by appointing a new Director of Operations, Lt General Sir Harold Briggs, who was to make a significant impression on the conduct of the war. Briggs was required to work as a civilian, partly because the struggle was conceived as political rather than military, but also because it was necessary to maintain the proposition that the country was suffering from an emergency, not a civil war, for the reasons already mentioned. The Briggs Plan, as it came to be called, was based on the creation of the New Villages, through which the squatters were to be resettled, and government control of these centres of population. There was, of course, some reluctance on the part of the squatters to go to these New Villages to begin with, but when it was realized that the land on which they were building their houses was to be theirs on long–term leases, they were slowly won over.

In November 1948, Phyllis, Carolyn and I went on home leave, and on our return I found I had been posted to act as headmaster of the Malay College. This lasted until Carey retired on medical grounds in June 1949. I then became the substantive headmaster. It was the first time, and will probably be the last, that a headmaster of the Clifford School, Kuala Kangsar, also served as headmaster of the Malay College. Although we felt reasonably safe in the Malay College setting, as it was not the policy of the CTs to antagonize the Malays, there was always an element of danger when we travelled outside KK, and our planter friends, who lived outside the towns, were never free from the threat of attack. They armoured their vehicles, flood-lit the barbed-wire fences round their bungalows at night, and mounted Bren machine-guns in strategic places. One day my old friend Pete Byrne was driving down a jungle road with his wife, when he was stopped by a tree-trunk laid across the road. The CTs opened fire from ambush positions and shot his wife dead beside him.

Pete got out of his car and returned fire with his carbine. Then in a lull he reversed down the road, and reported the incident to the KK District Officer. Incidents such as this, and intimidation of the work forces on estates through selective assassinations, became commonplace.

All this was naturally disturbing to the work of the College, which had already been excited by the enthusiastic celebration of the establishment of the Federation of Malaya on 1st February 1948, a step which was widely interpreted as representing a penultimate move towards total independence of the country.

One result of the establishment of the new Federation was the reconstitution of the Board of Governors of the College. Under the new order it was to be composed of the Mentri-mentri Besar (prime ministers) of the nine States, representatives of Penang and Malacca, a representative of the University of Malaya, and the Director of Education of the Federation. This new board was a very powerful body, which could make quick decisions, and it was a pleasure to work with its members. The Mentri-mentri Besar, I am sure, also enjoyed the opportunity of meeting together informally before and after Board of Governors meetings to discuss privately things other than College business. The University member for a time was T.H. Silcock, Professor of Economics, a post which Harold Wilson, later to become prime minister of Great Britain, had applied for unsuccessfully. Afterwards it was C.W. Northcote Parkinson, Professor of History, later to become famous for his "Parkinson's Law": "work expands to fill the time available to do it in".

Another result of the new Federation was the setting up of a Post School Certificate Class in the College, which comprised boys from other "English" schools in the Federation, besides those who qualified from the College itself. This group of Malay boys were later to proceed to the University of Malaya and be groomed for the junior branches of the Malayan Civil Service. A third change was the introduction of primary Education into the College. Malay boys who had completed four years in a Malay medium primary school were admitted to the College for the first time in 1950. They were accommodated in the King's Pavilion, a grand mansion which had been the summer residence of the High Commissioner of the Federation. This gracious building, with a magnificent view over the Perak river, was to house sixty boys and a resident master until 1961, when the College reverted to being exclusively a secondary school. The King's Pavilion was actually presented to the College by General Templer before he left the country.

I had been a strong supporter of the primary school intake experiment, although there were complaints about the boys leaving home at too tender an age. I believed the disadvantages complained of were largely offset by the boys being given early encouragement and facilities to study, and their having an opportunity to do so in a disciplined way. The pay-off came, I believe, when those who had been admitted to the King's Pavilion in 1950 took their School Certificate examinations in 1957. All candidates passed, and twenty–nine of the sixty–two candidates obtained

Division One Certificates. I do not believe this standard of achievement has been surpassed by Malay College students in any subsequent year. In my experience, moreover, all Old Boys who lived and studied in the King's Pavilion seemed to have enjoyed it.

My period of headmastership at the college was one of transition. Discussions took place with the Board of Governors as to what its future should be, given the urgent need for the strengthening of Malay Education. It was mooted for a time that a second college, possibly in Ipoh, might be better than an extension of the existing facilities in Kuala Kangsar. But in the end a programme of expansion of the MCKK was decided on, and I was deeply involved in its planning. The extension comprised two dormitory wings, one on either side of the Big School, each providing accommodation for another one hundred and eighty boys, a completely new teaching and administration block with eighteen classrooms, three laboratories, a library, and a new assembly hall to be named Hargreaves Hall after the first headmaster. These buildings were to be ready by late 1954, and officially opened during the Golden Jubilee celebrations of the College in 1955.

The transition, however, was not merely a question of expansion of facilities. The College also pressed forward with the teaching of science, though boys and staff had to manage for a time with makeshift laboratories. Emergent Malay nationalism had required that the College at its reopening should change from being an elite institution, for which admission had been based on birth and privilege, to one which would admit deserving and intelligent Malay boys irrespective of their birth or social status. The College was also influenced by the creation of UMNO. (United Malay National Organization) which awakened the political consciousness of some of the senior students so that they preferred politics to their studies, and became restless and occasionally rebellious. This rebelliousness manifested itself in political speeches in the school debating society, and tentative challenges to school authority.

Hamish Tod had been posted to serve at MCKK. when I returned from leave to become headmaster of Clifford School, and he had made debating a very important College activity. To this day there is an Inter-House Debating Competition for the Tod Cup. The most politically minded boys were from Pahang and the east coast, and during the early 1950s this group wrested the leadership from those of the west coast States, who because of their larger numbers had traditionally been expected to provide leadership. The Pahang boys also, I think, were inspired by the prominence in UMNO. of Abdul Razak bin Datok Hussein, a Pahang student who had been head prefect in 1938. Razak was to become Deputy to Tunku Abdul Rahman, Malaya's first prime minister on Independence, and was later to succeed him.

During my time as headmaster (June 1949– July 1953), there was a certain undercurrent of restlessness in the College, due no doubt to the upsurge of Malayan nationalism, the decline of British prestige and the continuing Emergency, though for the most part school life went on smoothly. Outside the College, on the political front, on 6th October 1951, Sir Henry Gurney was killed in an ambush, when he was on his way for a short vacation to Fraser's Hill, the nearest hill station to Kuala Lumpur. Typically he had travelled with a very small escort, the union jack fluttering from the radiator of his Rolls Royce. When the CTs riddled his car with their bullets he opened the car door, and walked slowly to the side of the road to draw fire from his wife. And there he died. His wife and his ADC escaped unscathed by lying on the floor of the car. Although it transpired that the ambush had not been planned for Gurney– it was intended to waylay a small military unit to obtain their arms– –this murder of the Governor had a devastating effect on the morale of the country. Churchill sent out Oliver Lyttleton, the Colonial Secretary, to appraise the situation, and as a result of Lyttleton's recommendations he appointed General Sir Gerald Templer to be in complete control of all political and military operations in Malaya.

Templer arrived in Malaya in February 1952 and immediately revitalized the fight against the CTs. He was rarely in the capital, making his presence felt in every corner of the country by personal unheralded appearances. One Friday morning, Friday was the Sunday of the Muslim week, when the boys all attended mosque, I noticed from my office window a policeman at each of the school gates. Suddenly a jeep swung into the College drive, followed by an armoured car, out of which jumped the General. I quickly explained to him that Friday was a holiday, but at his request summoned the boys to the school dining hall so that he could speak to them. He gave us all a tense pep-talk and departed as suddenly as he had appeared.

But to return to 1951. In that year the College hockey team made a successful tour of Seremban and Johore Bahru, and played two games in Singapore. In 1953 the Dramatic Society sprang into prominence under the direction of Jimmy Davidson, and its open-air production of "As You Like It" was taken to Kuala Lumpur in the September holidays, where it played to full houses in the Town Hall.

As mentioned above, however, there were in the College occasional outbreaks of what might be called non-co-operation, which challenged school discipline. One of these related to food. Complaints about food had been common enough over the years, and I had organized a representative committee from the student body to make recommendations regarding messing. The committee knew the level of funds available from the Government for food, and the possibility for variety, and its suggestions, where practicable, were accepted. I was not happy with the amount of money allotted for food in the College budget, and had so reported, but these were the funds available. Unfortunately, the fees the boys paid came nowhere near covering the cost of their board and lodging.

One day news of complaints about the College food appeared in the Malay Mail newspaper, apparently based on a letter written by a College boy. The boy declared himself eventually when the paper threatened to reveal his name if he did not. When asked his motive in writing to the newspaper the boy confessed that he was more interested in challenging school authority than in criticizing the catering. In this period of political change some boys felt a need to do this. I sympathized with their mood, but I also shared the view of the Government that the time when independence could be granted had to be postponed until the communist insurrection had been subdued. The Malays would certainly not profit from a communist takeover. The matter of the complaint about the food was resolved with the help of an excellent head prefect, Ungku Omar, who later became head of the Institute of Medical Research in Kuala Lumpur.

The full brunt of student rebelliousness, however, fanned by contemporary political events, hit my successor as headmaster, J.D.R. Howell, when the whole of the sixth form went on strike, and left for their respective homes without permission. This act of indiscipline resulted in the intervention of Malay members of the Government at the highest level, and the students involved were only allowed to return to the College on probation. The turbulence of this period is reflected in Anthony Burgess's novel "Time for a Tiger"; Anthony Burgess being the pen name of none other than Education officer J.B. Wilson, who taught English to Form V at that time.

Jimmy Howell stayed on to see the new buildings filled, and a smoother progress towards independence. Attitudes had changed a good deal by 1955, the Golden Jubilee year, and by 1957 when Jimmy "retired" at the time of "Merdeka" (Independence), he found his labours rewarded by some fine examination results. The College by then was almost four times as large as it was in 1941. Only years later did I realize that Carey's departure on medical grounds was in no small measure due to changes in the running of the College from the traditional English "public school" model, which he believed in, to something for which he had no stomach.

Domestically this was a very happy period. We lived in the house that the Careys had vacated, which was opposite the King's Pavilion across a section of a nine-hole golf course, and Phyllis delighted in retaining and improving the garden that Enid Carey had created. We had an excellent domestic staff headed by Ah Lin and Ah Soon. We took afternoon tea under the bougainvillaea hedge before College games started in the afternoon. Carolyn enjoyed her parties with other children of her age group and had a special boy friend, Stephen Horne, son of Roger Horne the DO, who came through the hedge to play with her.

It was not always smooth sailing, however. Late in the afternoon one Christmas Eve, Donald Keel, our local police officer (OCPD), a lively character, strode into the garden dressed as Father Christmas. His red coat trimmed with white bunny fur, his shiny–top boots and his long white beard excited Judy, our black Labrador, near to frenzy, so that a well-meant surprise for Carolyn became a source of tears and upset. When I think of that house I can still hear Judy's excited barking. She was always there to meet the car with swinging tail, when I came in from school. Later on to greet us was also the squawking of Rosie the goose, who was given to us as a present by Mr Chingar Singh of Clifford School. Though she was a better burglar alarm than Judy, she over did it, and did not last for long.

Because there was an acute shortage of trained teachers in Malaya at this time I obtained permission for Phyllis to be employed as the teacher of the lowest form of the school in the King's Pavilion. Carolyn, aged five, would accompany her and sit at a desk in the front row. This worked beautifully until one day Judy walked in from the back of the class, her tail thumping the desks as she passed. This caused a good-humoured minor disturbance. Some of the little boys, being strict Muslims, jumped on top of their desks, pulling their sarongs tight about their legs to avoid being touched by the unclean dog, and Carolyn had to lead Judy home in mild disgrace.

I have stated earlier that I thought we employees of the Education Service were treated well by the Government. This is true except in one important respect, which actually applied to all departments of the Government Service. If a woman in any department married she was immediately obliged to resign from her job, although she could be re-employed at a reduced salary on a temporary basis. This was the case with Phyllis when she taught at the King's Pavilion. We had friends, medical doctors in the Malayan Medical Service, who lived together but refrained from marrying to avoid a reduction in the salary of the wife. I still smart today at the inequity of this regulation.

During this period we had a close association with the Church of the Resurrection. I had been a member of this little wooden church since my arrival in Kuala Kangsar as an assistant master at the College in 1936, and in October 1947, while headmaster of the College, I had been appointed a lay reader for the church by Bishop Leonard Wilson. Carolyn was christened there by the Rev.John Hayter. I had asked John to perform the christening ceremony because of our Oxford connection and our renewed association in Singapore, but Phyllis and I were sorry afterwards, for by so doing we felt we had hurt the feelings of dear old Canon Gnanasihamani, who came over from Taiping once a month to conduct a communion service for us.

When I returned to KK in 1949 to become Headmaster of MCKK., my lay reader's licence was renewed by Bishop Henry Wolfe Baines, who had succeeded Bishop Wilson as Bishop of Singapore. Our tiny congregation of mostly Indians was then swelled by British Ghurka officers, while we had a Ghurka contingent stationed in KK. Later the Ghurkas were replaced by a contingent of Royal Marines. One regular church-goer among the Marines was Sergeant Fox. He had a magnificent singing voice, and made our services seem specially significant no matter what the size of the congregation. But only on Christmas Eve did the Marines fill the church to overflowing.

A particular joy on the hill in KK was the beauty of the setting, and the flowers of the King's Pavilion. The King's Pavilion reflected its past glory modestly in its numerous pot plants tended by a dear old Tamil gardener named Lechumanan, who prayed for them every evening by his sacred tree – his "pokok keramat". Living just across from the first tee of the golf course, we tended to benefit from his pots, which could be borrowed for tea parties at the house. He had a green thumb par excellence. He burned his soil in a pit to sterilize it and tested it on his tongue. Periodically he would appear at the house, twisting the grey hairs on his scraggy brown chest with his fingers, to cajole us into buying him a buffalo-cart load of manure, "tai lembu". I don't think we ever refused him.

The road curving down to the river and the town, where my little "Standard" car had collided with a Indian officer's truck, was lined with huge rain trees covered with pigeon orchids. On certain days in the year all the orchids on all the trees would burst into flower simultaneously. When that happened we always paused on our way up or down the hill to wonder at them and inhale their fragrance.

Although there was undoubtedly a certain turbulence in the life of the Malay College in the early 1950s, I am sure the College played an important role in the smooth transition of the country to independence. From 1905 to 1955 the College had concentrated on producing the kind of boy who would enter the Malay Administrative Service, the MAS, while relatively few qualified to enter the technical services of government. These students, trained in administration, formed the Malay nucleus of the new independent government for Malaya in 1957, which provided stability and a certain bureaucratic continuity at a crucial time in the country's history. The role of the MCKK in helping to provide this nucleus of an independent government for Malaya is discussed in Robert O. Tilman's book Bureaucratic Transition in Malaya (pp. 76, 111–112, 127). It has been claimed that the College was too "English", and its product modelled too closely upon the typical MCS officer. There is, of course, much truth in this. Nevertheless, the training provided by the college, and particularly that given by its Probationer classes, gave the young MAS cadets a basic understanding of the British bureaucracy, and the beginnings of a familiarity with international diplomacy which served the newly independent nation well.

As I remarked earlier, it was not unusual for Education Officers to be transferred from one posting to another within a short time span. I was nevertheless surprised when, in the summer of 1953, the Director of Education, L.D. Whitfield, informed me that I was to be posted to Kuala Lumpur to become Senior Inspector of Schools, Selangor. Although I was quite pleased by this news, for I felt I had been stationed long enough in Kuala Kangsar in one capacity or another, I was glad to know that the MCKK Board of Governors had agreed to this move "with much reluctance".

This time our house in K. L was in Brockman Road, which led up to the residence of the British Adviser on the top of a hill. Our bungalow was the one nearest to the Residency, and below us were those of the State Treasurer, the State Agricultural Officer, the State Chinese Affairs Officer and the State Chief of Police (the CPO). The State in our case, it should be understood, was the State of Selangor, of which Kuala Lumpur is the capital.

It was a very neighbourly road. Our next door neighbours were the Abdullahs. Che Abdullah was the State Treasurer, and we met him and his wife frequently. The State Agricultural Officer, Joe Berwick, I had known in KK where he had been Agricultural Officer. We played squash once a week at night under flood lights at the Lake Club. The State Chinese Affairs Officer was George Webb, a special friend. His wife Margaret was born in Kuching, Sarawak, and was half Chinese. They had two daughters of their own, Rosemary and Ellie, and a third, an adopted Chinese girl, also named Margaret. She was known as "little Margaret". Margaret, a social worker, had been given the baby by a Chinese woman "to hold for a minute" during the Occupation. The mother never came back, so Margaret adopted it. The State Chief of Police was Micky McNamara. The McNamaras had two charming small daughters, Bridget and Claire. They inherited the good looks of their parents, and the athleticism of their father.

I mention this assortment of little girls because they gave me a lot of fun in KL. The little girls of Brockman Road all went to the Alice Smith School together, and I had the pleasure of ferrying them there every weekday on my way to the Selangor Education Office. On the way we had a wonderful game called "fishcakes". The first little girl to see a policeman would shout "fishcake", and win a point. The one who obtained most points by the time we reached the school won the game. Because of the Emergency there were plenty of policemen between Brockman Road and the school, so I would be deafened by shrieks of "fishcake" most of the way to my office. But I enjoyed the game so much I always arrived in fine fettle after it. And this was not the end of my time with the girls. Often when I arrived home from the office they would be playing in our garden, and I would immediately be recruited to chase them around it. It was my object to chase without catching, but I doubt whether I could often have caught Bridget. She had remarkable acceleration for a small girl. Carolyn I loved to catch gently in the end, when the others were gone, and give a hug to. After the chasing Phyllis would organize other games with great skill. "Here we come gathering nuts in May" was one of our favourites. Claire, the tiniest, was deadly serious as she daintily danced up and down as my partner.

One of the reasons why our house was popular with our neighbours' daughters was the presence of a "fairy house" in our garden. We had commissioned a Malay carpenter to build the house for Carolyn. It was constructed of plaited rattan with an attap roof, just like a Malay house, and fitted into a low tree. It had two windows and a door, and two or three little girls could just get into it with a squash. The Webb and McNamara daughters loved to join Carolyn to play in and around the "fairy house," and the game would often involve the wearing of the "fairy" dress – a pink creation with a frilly gossomer-like skirt inspired by Phyllis.

Judy the Labrador, of course came with us from KK, and we also acquired a delightful little Siamese kitten, whom Phyllis christened Charles. As far as we were concerned Charles was the perfect cat. He grew daily in beauty and charm. He never bared his claws. He did not seem to have any. He sniffed flowers in vases like a connoisseur. He himself smelt as sweet as new-mown hay. In the afternoons Charles was commandeered by Carolyn and the little girls, and he allowed himself to be carried in and out of the "fairy house" with splendid equanimity. Every evening he sat on the table beside me while I worked at my files and when late at night we were done he would lollop along the corridor to Phyllis's bed, creep under the mosquito–net, jump onto the bed and make space for himself, almost as if to say "move over if you please!" He would then stretch himself out with complete abandon. At the first sign of dawn he would leave through an open window, but would later wake up Carolyn with a whisker on her cheek. Then when we were sitting round our little rattan table in the bedroom, and Ah Soon brought in the tea, he would rush down the corridor, and make a flying leap onto Phyllis's lap, for she was his mistress. Finally, his day started after he had had a saucer of tea himself. A little later he would give Ah Soon a gentle nip on his Achilles tendon if he did not open the refrigerator door fast enough to feed him.

Charles loved the bathroom and he enjoyed sitting on the edge of the bath watching Phyllis's ablutions. I always took a shower. Once he fell in while Phyllis was bathing, and she had to scoop him out. He also enjoyed unrolling the toilet roll, standing on his hind legs, his front paws paddling furiously. Alas, we lost Charles after a farewell party at our house, just before we went home on leave early in 1955. There was a film show in the garden, and a satay stall, bright coloured lights decorating the trees, much drink and talk.

Charles did not like crowds or noise. We realized afterwards that we should have confined him somehow, for when the last guest had gone, we could not find him anywhere. We suspect that one of the uninvited film spectators took a liking to Charles. We never saw him again.

As Senior Inspector of Schools (SIS), and later as Chief Education Officer (CEO) of Selangor, I was in administrative charge of some 680 schools – Malay, Chinese, Tamil and "English"– with a total enrollment of about 159,000 children. It was exacting work because two new Education policies had to be implemented during my term of office. A number of extra jobs also came my way ex-officio. These included membership of the Council of State of Selangor, and of the following bodies – the Selangor State Scholarship Fund Board, of which I was Secretary, the Selangor Road Safety Committee, the Kuala Lumpur Municipal Cleanliness Campaign, the Arts Council (Schools), the Air Cadet Corps Advisory Committee and the State Branch Committee of the British Red Cross. I also became a lay reader and member of the St Mary's Parochial Church Council, Chairman of the Extension Appeals Fund for St Mary's Church, a Governor of the Federation Military College, a Director of the Kuala Lumpur Rotary Club and President of the Combined Schools Sports Council. I enjoyed all these activities, and especially visiting the various types of schools. Phyllis was in great demand to give away the prizes and trophies at prize-givings and sports days.

I had not had the opportunity of meeting Sir Henry Gurney, because his stay in Kuala Lumpur had been so short, but General Templer made a point of making his presence felt in KL as else-where. So the senior Education Office staff were assembled to meet him. He told us his age, fifty-four, and gave us a brief history of his career with candour and humour. He was, among other things, "the only general ever to have been wounded by a grand piano" (a grand piano had fallen out of an army truck onto his back). In terse, salty language he made clear that he intended to spare nei-

ther himself nor any other expatriate until the communist presence had been wiped out. He had unusual attributes for a military
man. He had a warm, basic appeal for the people of Malaya coupled with a shrewd political sense. He admired Gurney and backed
up the Briggs Plan to the full, but he was prepared to be quite ruth-
less with the enemy. His aim above all was "to win the hearts and
minds of the people". All military action was subordinate to this. In
line with this objective he set up the Chinese Home Guard, organized three-day tours of government activities for ordinary people –
rubber-tappers, trishawmen and secretaries–which ended with tea
on the lawn of King's House with Lady Templer in attendance. He
also greatly strengthened the police force under Arthur Young,
who had been Commissioner of the London Police.

Two stories about Templer's arrival in KL circulated widely while
I was there. On his first journey to King's House he was told by an
aide that about forty servants would be there to greet him. "What
do I do?" asked Templer, "shake hands?" "Oh, no," said the aide,
"the High Commissioner never shakes hands with them." "This one
does," said Templer, and proceeded to shake hands with every servant and gardener. After taking a quick look at King's House and
the extensive gardens around it, he ordered a perimeter fence to
be erected. The assassination of Sir Henry Gurney was still on
everyone's mind. Three days later he phoned the Director of the
P.W.D "Can you hear me clearly," he asked. "Yes, Sir," said the
Director, "quite clearly." "Well, then," said Templer, after a preg-
nant pause, "Where the hell is my bloody fence?" Workmen moved
in to make a start on the fence the very next day.

When, in March 1952, the water supply to Tanjong Malim, a small
town of about twenty thousand people was cut off by the CTs for
the fifth time, a repair party accompanied by police set out to
restore it. About two miles into the jungle the party were
ambushed. Twelve of the party were shot dead, and the eight police
seriously injured. Only one man escaped injury. Templer immediately ordered a twenty–two–hour–a–day curfew in the town, and

sent a questionnaire form to every head of household demanding information. The forms were collected by troops, and opened, read and destroyed personally by Templer in the presence of local community leaders. A second batch of questionnaire forms brought in important information which led to a series of arrests. When the curfew was lifted many Chinese in the district volunteered for the Home Guard, and for the rest of the Emergency, Tanjong Malim became one of the most peaceful areas of the country. Templer certainly was prepared to try unusual methods to obtain the information he needed.

Templer took an active interest in Educational matters and liked to meet school children whenever he could. One day I was informed that he would be visiting the orphanage school of the Pure Life Society, which was run by a saintly man named Swami Satyananda. Phyllis and I, together with others concerned with the orphanage, drove out to the small village of Puchong, a short distance outside KL to meet him there. Together we went round the buildings and inspected the children's extra-curricular activities. Then we shared their simple midday meal. Templer was not impressed with the food. He turned to me and said: "I don't think anything of this meal, do you? Let's help them do better." He tossed a cheque into his general's hat, heavy with scarlet braid, and passed it round the assembled company. It was the beginning of a fund-raising drive which greatly improved the resources of the orphanage.

I don't know to what extent Templer initiated the idea of the Kirkby Teacher Training scheme, but he certainly supported it enthusiastically. It was clear that the Normal Class training of "English School" teachers, in which Phyllis and I had actively participated, was not adequate. But at the same time there was a desperate lack of full-time teacher trainers, and of buildings suitable for teacher training colleges. This need was now met in an imaginative way. In Kirkby, near Liverpool in England, a teacher training college was about to close its doors on account of a lack of students. The Government of Malaya, through the Colonial Office, decided to take over Kirkby College in toto, faculty and buildings, under the direction of a senior Malayan Education Officer named Peter Gurney, for the exclusive training of Malayan teachers. And so Malay, Chinese, Indian and Eurasian teachers were flown to Kirkby for a year's course in teacher training for the "English" schools. The experiment was a tremendous success. The Blue Funnel shipping line supplied the college with a Chinese cook, and the townspeople took the students to their hearts. Very soon to be "Kirkby trained" carried considerable prestige as well as an increased salary in the teaching hierarchy of Malaya. So successful was the Kirkby scheme that a second similar College named Brinsford was opened near Wolverhampton. These two institutions, under Malayan management, continued for some years, with BOAC charter flights shuttling trainee teachers to England, and the trained teachers back to Malaya, until new teacher training colleges could be built in the country. These Kirkby graduates did much to bring the different races of Malaya into a closer and more harmonious relationship.

I have often thought what satisfaction there must be in being a supremo–not just a titular head, but someone able to control and influence the actions of a whole people, even down to tiny details. Supreme power no doubt corrupts and leads to arrogance, but Templer's performance was relieved by his clear–cut objective within a given time frame, self-government by and for the people. Templer certainly took great pleasure in his role of supremo, as when early one morning from the verandah of King's House he saw a squad of workmen about to cut down a large tree to make room for a housing project across the valley. He immediately sent one of his aides to stop the felling, rejoicing I'm sure in his ability to put into practice his early advocacy of conservation.

It was a measure of his stature, however, that HE knew how to leave the country. He knew that after just over two years of stupendous effort he had to hand over the reins to a civil administration led by his civilian deputy, Sir Donald McGillivray, and he believed that the people of the country could progressively take upon themselves the responsibilities of government. Before he left on 30th May 1954, therefore, he announced that during the following year Malaya would hold its first national elections for the Federal Legislative Council. The Council had been composed almost entirely of members nominated by the British government. After the elections there would be fifty-two elected and only forty-two nominated members. The country would clearly now be preparing for self-rule.

On his departure Templer was pleased to receive the farewells of Kuala Lumpur's school children. I therefore arranged a mammoth children's concert in the huge indoor stadium next to the Victoria Institution. The school children themselves were the audience. We had to eliminate dozens of items which the various schools had to offer, but in the end we had a reasonably balanced programme ready, without too many hurt feelings. A Chinese school did a tumbling act, an Indian school offered Indian dances, and the "English" primary schools produced mime and song. The Malay schoolboys showed their skill at clowning (the Malay clown on stage, professional or amateur, I believe is unsurpassed), and the Malay girls danced their famous candlelight dance, in which they gyrate holding gracefully in each hand a lighted candle centred on a saucer. The General and Lady Templer were so pleased with the warmth of their reception that they cancelled a subsequent engagement in order to see the concert to its end. When they finally left KL the school children lined the route to the airport, cheering and waving Federation flags. Phyllis and I were among the hundreds at the airport who watched their plane fly off.

Sir Donald McGillivray slipped easily and unostentatiously into the place left by Templer. He had had distinguished service in Palestine and the West Indies, and was an excellent choice for establishing a smooth co-operation between the civil government and the military. He was the peace-maker, the co-ordinator, the mediator, who laboured greatly offstage to prepare the way for unity and prosperity. I met Sir Donald a number of times in my capacity as Chief Education Officer. When he wished to visit a school I would be summoned to King's House, where I would leave my own car and join him in his Rolls Royce, the same limousine, now with its bodywork repaired, that had borne Sir Henry Gurney to his death. He was always eager for full information, cogent and succinct in his comments, energetic but gracious in manner, appreciative of work well done, whether the visit was an important occasion, such as the opening of the first government school in the satellite town of Petaling Jaya, or a routine visit to a non-government secondary girls' school in KL.

These were stirring times educationally, as the Government was under great pressure from the public to satisfy increasing demands for Education in English, and to supply more opportunities for vocational training in a variety of ways. Two new institutions that played a prominent part in fulfilling this latter aim were the Government Trade School, with specialization in areas such as bricklaying, motor mechanics, electrician training, metalwork and tin-smithing, and a new "secondary modern" school known as the Maxwell Road School, which, under the direction of a New Zealander named Priestley who had headed the Wellington Polytechnic in New Zealand, specialized in non-academic industrial arts courses such as shorthand and typewriting, bookkeeping and commercial art. In a short time Maxwell Road School won a position of high esteem in the community.

Our home leave came round again in 1955, and after our return to Malaya in October we decided that Phyllis should take Carolyn back to England to school. Phyllis and Carolyn left by sea, and reached Suez just about the time of the 1956 crisis over the canal. For the second time Phyllis's ship was the last passenger ship through the canal before it was closed for a protracted period. Phyllis found a flat in Palewell Park, East Sheen, fairly near her sister Elsie, from where Carolyn could travel to school by bus. The school was the Froebel Demonstration School in Roehampton known as Ibstock Place, which Carolyn found greatly to her liking, as it was co-educational with an emphasis on freedom of expression in language, art, dance and music.

Alone in KL I became something of a workaholic, which was quite easy to do, as the responsibilities of the CEO. were extensive and constantly expanding. Under Rotary Club sponsorship, and with the co-operation of the British Council, I organized a series of lectures on careers, geared to help school-leavers choose their field of work. On a given evening two or sometimes three speakers would describe their job or profession, covering in a presentation of no more than thirty minutes, qualifications required, how and where to get them, prospects for employment in the field chosen, and realistic starting and ending salaries. These talks would be followed by a question and answer period.

Before Phyllis left we had more or less decided to leave Malaya on Independence. Most Government Service expatriates were entitled to a "golden handshake" to compensate them for loss of career, and although many of us in the Education Service were invited to stay on after Independence or "Merdeka", my feeling was that if I had to start a new career, the sooner I set about it the better, for in 1957 I was forty-five. Hamish Tod, who had by 1956 become headmaster of the Penang Free School, the most important Government boys' School in Penang, decided to stay on for some time. He and his wife Eileen kindly invited me to Penang for Christmas in 1956, and we discussed our respective futures. In fact before his eventual retirement from the Service, Hamish went on to occupy a number of high posts in KL, and then become head of the Government Teacher Training College in Jesselton, now Kota Kinabalu, in Sabah.

Other friends with whom we discussed our future were Gerry and Janice Dartford. Gerry had been headmaster of the Victoria Institution, while I was CEO. and was designated to take my place during my absence on leave. He had in fact agreed to look after Charles, our Siamese cat, while were away, and no doubt would have done so but for Charles's strange disappearance during our farewell party. We were very close to the Dartfords, partly because their younger son David was the same age as Carolyn, and the two ten-year-olds had attended the Alice Smith School together. One day while Phyllis and I were on holiday at a bungalow in Port Dickson, we were shocked to be informed by telephone of the death of David, who had been admitted to K L hospital suffering from tonsillitis. It seemed a clear case of negligence, but the Dartfords did not press for restitution, though their lawyer tried to persuade them to do so. They felt their son was dead. Litigation would not bring him back. The case was closed. After our return from leave Gerry moved up to be Deputy Director of Education, but Malaya was spoiled for the Dartfords, and they too chose to leave on "Merdeka".

Gerry had served in the Colonial Education Service in British Guiana before transferring to Malaya, and it was in British Guiana that he had met and married Janice McEntee, an American. During the Occupation Gerry had been a POW in Sumatra, and Janice had taken her elder son Ted to New Zealand and put him to school there. After the war Ted was sent to Kent School, an independent "prep" school in Connecticut, USA. I remember being shown the Kent School Year Book, which seemed astonishingly lavish to Phyllis and me by English standards. Janice often said in Kuala Lumpur: "Some time we'll get you two over to the United States." We thought nothing of it, until in that final year I changed my mind a little and began to think of it as a possibility.

The deciding factor, I believe, was a talk at the Kuala Lumpur Rotary Club given by the Editor of the Malay Mail, who had just returned from a lecture tour in the United States. Fired by his example I wrote to the Foreign Policy Association in New York City, requesting their sponsorship for a lecture tour. Rather to my surprise, the FPA agreed to arrange for me to give a series of talks and lectures, coast to coast, at universities, schools and to other interested groups on the emergent Federation of Malaya. US dollars were hard to come by in those days, for our accounts both in the UK and in Malaya were under "currency control". It seemed therefore that some sort of income in the United States would be essential. I need not have worried that much, for I discovered that all the currencies of the world were freely exchangeable in Hong Kong, which would be a port of call on my way to the United States.

Gerry and Janice, I discovered, would also be travelling to the United States about the same time as I would. They too were going via the Pacific, but they had planned to go by sea through the Panama Canal. Gerry, a historian, would use his travelling time to complete one of the text-books he had been writing for use in Malayan schools. We agreed that we should meet in New York City.

There were various farewell functions, official and otherwise, arranged for me in the federal capital, but at last I boarded the night mail to Singapore. As I waved farewell to the small group on KL platform I thought of the schoolboy crowd waving farewell at the station in Kuala Kangsar nearly sixteen years earlier. If I added in the POW years, I reflected, I had spent nearly twenty-one years of my life in lovely Malaya. I felt sadness at leaving the country and the people I had come to love, but was nevertheless ready for new adventures.

In Singapore I spent the night in the home of Michael Campbell, another Education Officer, who had been Headmaster, Clifford School, Kuala Kangsar, after I left KK. On the following day I caught a PANAM flight for Los Angeles via Hong Kong, Tokyo, Pago-Pago and Honolulu. The plane was a DC8, one of the last propeller-powered aircraft before jet propulsion took over, and we were slow moving by today's standards. But I was in no hurry, and had even arranged for stop-overs not only in Hong Kong, but also for a couple of days in both Tokyo and Honolulu.

In Hong Kong arrangements had been made for me to meet relatives of some Malayan friends. At the airport to meet me was the sister of Miss Khoo, the Headmistress of Petaling Jaya School. She met me in her own small car, clad in a white sports outfit as though for tennis. Was I interested in badminton, she asked, because if I were she would call for me at my hotel and take me along to a tournament that night. I readily agreed, and later found myself watching Miss Khoo herself on her way to winning the women's singles badminton championship of the Colony. I was also met and entertained by Dr C.C. Chin, the son of the chief clerk of the Examination Secretary's office in Kuala Lumpur. Dr Chin and his wife drove me out to the New Territories, and regaled me with some of the finest Chinese food I have ever tasted. There seemed to be quite a number of Chinese in Hong Kong who had family connections with Malayan Chinese, and I felt very privileged to have benefited from this relationship.

My most vivid impression of Tokyo was one of pressure of people. The number of people in public places, and in particular railway stations, was so great that I had a feeling of claustrophobia, and realized acutely why the Japanese I had known in Changi as guards were so zealous about fire precautions. Those guards had always insisted that smokers carry around with them a tincan or some other receptacle in which to put their cigarette ash. I went to a theatre one evening, and it took twenty minutes to get out of the building after the show. We were jammed tight, a seething mass of humanity, inching forward in the theatre corridors towards the exits. Had a fire broken out in the theatre there would inevitably have been many deaths. It was a scary experience.

USA

The gateway to the United States from the west is Hawaii, and it is there that an examination of passports and visas takes place. Landing in Hawaii is in a way a salutary experience because one gets an experience of things American ahead of time. As for Hawaii itself several things stand out in my memory – the provision by the hotel I was in of special elevators for bathers, so that the floors of the regular elevators would not be covered in sand; the fact that people walked about in public places in their swimsuits or a minimum of colourful attire, regardless of their shape or size; the wide expanse of stainless steel behind the counter of the coffee-shop in which I took my breakfast – I thought if steel is so plentiful in Hawaii what immense wealth there must be in the United States – and the limited area of Waikiki Beach. The rollers for surfing were the genuine article, but the stretch of sand was much less than I had imagined.

At Los Angeles we were driven by bus from the airport to the Los Angeles Hilton in downtown Los Angeles. This was no place for me, and I immediately picked up my suitcase and started to look around for somewhere to stay within my capacity to pay. I did not have to go far.

Almost overlooked by the Hilton in a side street was The Wellington. It was a small apartment hotel, and for a reasonable sum I was allotted an "apartment", a one-room studio with kitchen fittings, and a bed which came down from the wall on springs – the kind I had seen in Max Sennett comedies, but never in reality – and a very small bathroom with a shower. Right across the road from my apartment was a dry cleaner with a same-day service. I felt I had really fallen on my feet.

My first call in Los Angeles was to the British Embassy, just to register my presence so to speak, and I found a most helpful friend in the Cultural Affairs Officer. He explained to me that I could get anywhere at all in LA by public transportation, provided I was prepared to spend plenty of time on it; and he gave me an introduction to a professor of history at the University of California at Berkeley, who was English. He was also kind enough to entertain me to dinner at his home in the hills in the direction of Hollywood. We were able to look down onto the smog of the city. But, at dusk, he told me, a fox would creep onto his lawn.

My first speaking engagement in the USA. was to the Los Angeles Rotary Club. There was a very large luncheon meeting of the club in the huge hotel I had avoided on arrival.

I soon found that my talk was regarded as a minor side-show, for the club was celebrating the beginning of the baseball season. Members were in high spirits. Many of them were wearing baseball caps and some were tossing baseballs across the room. The protocol officer was handing out fines for infringement of club rules in a most arbitrary way. One member was fined $200. It was difficult to see how the culprit had transgressed any more than anyone else, for a good deal of buffoonery was going on, but my neighbour explained to me that that was not the point. The justification was that the person fined was the president of an oil company and could easily afford it. Then someone who must have been a famous baseball player stood up and was acclaimed. He explained how his side was going to beat all opposition. Finally I was asked to speak, "and make it brief". I did just that: I offered greetings from the Kuala Lumpur club, of which I was a director, and gave the meeting a quick description of Malaya, its people and its politics. The president of the club was clearly pleased with my brevity, and I was warmly applauded. It was a most good-natured meeting.

On my return to the Wellington I examined my little apartment more carefully. It seemed very well appointed. It even had a smell of newness. I looked the carpeting over more closely. It was that which was giving out a slight odour. And then I realized that the carpet was brand new. It was not the carpet which had been in the apartment when I first arrived. The original carpeting had been taken up and replaced with new while I had been giving my talk at the Hilton. I was tremendously impressed. The United States, as far as I was concerned, could not have put on a better welcoming performance of speed and efficiency.

Through my British Consulate friend I visited a selection of LA schools, and through the Berkeley history professor, I met the President of the University, Dr Clark Kerr. My first Foreign Policy Association appointment, however, was a talk to an economics group at the University of Southern California.

My over-riding impression during these first few days was the enormous size of the Berkeley campus of the University of California, both in area and numbers of students, the lavishness of the equipment in the public schools, and astonishment at an item of news – that someone I met was writing his PhD thesis on the subject of "room-mate compatibility".

There was also a sightseeing element to my visit to Los Angeles. I went to Hollywood, called at the CBS studios, and once, with a journalist, went to several bars in search of what he called "personalities", who I assumed would be film-stars. However, I left Hollywood without seeing any.

The itinerary arranged for me by the Foreign Policy Association took me next to San Francisco. Although I had no speaking engagements there, the organizer of my programme, Frances Pratt, wrote that I should see San Francisco because it was a city of character. So I became an enthusiastic tourist, and enjoyed to the full the thrill of looking over the bay from the "top of the Mark", and travelling on the trolley car to Fisherman's Wharf. The stiff breezes encountered in the higher parts of the city were a pleasant relief after the smog of downtown LA. I also enjoyed the artistic luxury of the large stores of the city, and the first-class quality of the Chinese cuisine in Chinatown.

I travelled next to Tacoma by air, where a talk to a civics group had been arranged by the FPA. After a long drive in from the airport, which is halfway between Tacoma and Seattle, serving both cities, I was met by the secretary of the group, who turned out to be a lawyer and a Rhodes Scholar. My talk on Malaya, illustrated with a couple of films produced by the Malayan Film Unit which I had brought with me, was followed by a buffet dinner. The next day after being shown something of the logging industry nearby, I moved on to Vancouver.

In Vancouver I had a speaking engagement on the beautiful campus of the University of British Columbia, and took the opportunity of paying a courtesy call on Professor Scarfe of the Geography Department, at whose feet I had sat at the University of London Institute of Education in 1936. I was much struck by the difference between Canada and the USA. Canada seemed to me to be much less affluent than the United States, and more English, a kind of halfway house between England and America. I felt very much at home with the English-type post offices and red pillar boxes. In Victoria on Vancouver Island the overtones of Englishness were in concentrated form. In a glass-covered orangery in a hotel there, where they served afternoon tea, I was not surprised to see an elderly lady who looked just like Margaret Rutherford playing Miss Marple in an Agatha Christie play.

I called on the Superintendent of Education in Vancouver to see what opportunities there might be in British Columbia in the field of teaching. There were some openings to be sure, but as it would mean "out-back" living to begin with, I decided against pursuing them.

In Chicago, my next stop, I stayed in International House, and gave my talk to a group organized by the English Speaking Union. The lady in charge, who afterwards handed me a cheque for $50, was obviously of British descent. She was fiercely pro-British and fascinated by English royalty. I was also helped by the Chicago British Consulate. One morning, by appointment, I had breakfast with Freyn Utley, who was the director of the Chicago Branch of the Institute of International Education. She asked me whether I would like to be interviewed on local television and I readily agreed. She was very professional when the time came, and under her expert questioning I found I was able to give a reasonably comprehensive picture of the Malaya I had so recently left. Mrs Utley's deceased husband, I understood, had in his time been a very well-known TV newscaster. Her son, Garrick Utley, is well-known nationally as a TV broadcaster today.

Before leaving Los Angeles I had written to my friend of Oxford days, Josephine Saner, who had been with us to Germany visiting Marburg University. She lived in Springfield, Illinois, and was married to a bank president in that city. She invited me to spend a couple of days with her and her family in Springfield.

It was a great pleasure to see Jo again, talk over Oxford days with her, and review our trip to Germany. In Springfield, where Abraham Lincoln spent an important period of his working life, Jo was an enthusiastic guide to Lincoln memorabilia, while I on the other hand was pleased to speak to a local group assembled by her on the political and economic situation in Malaya. I watched baseball on TV in the basement gamesroom of the Saner bungalow, and went with the Saner family to church. It was a wonderful introduction to American family life and I enjoyed it all thoroughly. Yes, we English and Americans were cousins all right. But there were sharp differences as well as similarities. I marvelled at how full the church was, and at the strange "r" sound in "Our Father" in the Lord's Prayer. Church-going in England was certainly not as enthusiastic as it appeared to be in Illinois.

As I have digressed a little to my Oxford days in order to re-introduce Jo Saner, I should like to mention the three undergraduates with whom I "digged" in my last year in Wellington Street, as two of them came with us to Marburg. George Thompson, a Scot from Edinburgh University, lectured at Liverpool University after graduation from Oxford, and then after the war worked in Singapore as its Public Relations Officer. When the MCKK hockey side played in Singapore in 1951, George was most helpful in making the team's stay there useful as well as pleasurable. After Independence George became one of the best-known expatriates in Singapore. He was a personal friend of Lee Kuan Yew, and ran the training programme for government servants at the Government Training School there. Finally, he became a full professor of Government at Singapore's Nanyang University. George died in 1980, in Singapore, as I think he would have been pleased to do, from a heart attack at the airport, after returning from a lecture abroad.

Bill Nield also came with us to Marburg. He stayed an extra year at Oxford, took a first in PPE, became Secretary of the Oxford Union, and joined the Home Civil Service. He retired with a knighthood as Secretary to the Cabinet after a brilliant Home Civil Service career.

Michael Kennan, the fourth member of our Wellington Street household, was non-political. His field was anthropology. But like George and me he ended up in South East Asia. He was the youngest major in the Royal Army Service Corps when he died in Singapore from diphtheria during the Japanese Occupation.

After Springfield, I moved up into Canada again to address a group of university women in Toronto. The group in fact turned out to be a gathering of university faculty wives. It was a pleasant informal occasion, and I was made to feel very much at home. There were also short stops in Ottawa and Montreal, and then I found myself heading south to New York City by train. I checked in at the Winston Hotel on 55th and Madison in the evening, and on the following morning reported to Miss Pratt in her office just opposite the United Nations Secretariat Building. She was most charming and helpful. She introduced me to her bank to change travellers cheques, and explained the procedure of income tax clearance, which I would have to undergo before leaving the United States. She also advised me how I could get the best out of New York City as a tourist in a few short days and at the same time presented me with my final string of talks, which were to be to two independent girls' schools, well outside New York City, then Bryn Mawr College in Pennsylvania, and a junior college for young women in Manhattan itself.

At St Mary's-in-the-Mountains in northern New Hampshire I was an overnight guest of the school, and lectured with my films in a hall which was also open to the local townspeople. As the name of the school implies, it was in mountainous country near well-known ski-slopes, and although it was the wrong time of year for skiing, skis were very much in evidence in various corners of the school. My other assignment was with Foxcroft in Virginia, one of the most exclusive private girls' schools in the country. It was redolent of southern graciousness and charm, affluent and horsey. The seniors were abuzz with news of acceptance or non-acceptance in colleges, and there were special end-of-term celebrations afoot, so my talk was regarded as light relief. I responded to their mood, touching on the humorous aspects of life in Malaya, and at the end of my talk the girls gave me a special sort of cheer, which I was told was only vented on someone they particularly liked. It was most gratifying.

I was invited by the headmaster (that in itself was astonishing to me; in England there would never have been a headmaster of an independent girls' school) to stay the night in the school guest house, and observe certain festivities which would take place the following day. These were truly surprising, for under "Miss Charlotte", the recently retired head of the school, the girls had established a cadet corps of their own, complete with uniforms, band and wooden rifles, which they called their "pieces". Miss Charlotte, to whom I was introduced, was the dominating figure at

Foxcroft, although she had ostensibly retired. Indeed many of the private secondary or "prep" schools of America seem to have grown round a single founding figure. In the case of Foxcroft it was Miss Charlotte. She was clearly still the king-pin, respected and even revered. When there had been a call for officers' cadet corps to be set up in the boys' schools of America, Miss Charlotte was not to be outdone. She would have a cadet corps at Foxcroft too. And so on the morning after my talk I watched a march-past of the Foxcroft cadets. They were inspected by a full general of the Marines no less. One of the girls asked me shyly afterwards whether I thought it was all rather silly. I said I thought it was uniquely impressive, and that I would not have missed the march-past for anything. And then, in the afternoon, they had a fashion parade in the gardens, with the girls modelling creations for the exclusive Julius Garfinckel store in Washington, DC. A nice contrast, I thought. Maybe it was this unusual mix of activity which sharpened the girls' good sense of humour.

My visits to the two women's colleges I do not now recall very well, except that Bryn Mawr seemed to me to be rather stiff and conservative, while the junior college in Manhatten was extrovert and sophisticated.

Back in New York I paid my respects to Miss Pratt, and took her a pot of violets for her office window sill, and she, dear lady, took me to lunch at her club. Then, while waiting for my meeting with the Dartfords, I took in some of the standard tourist attractions of the city: the Metropolitan Museum of Art, the Cloisters, the Staten Island Ferry, the Empire State Building, Central Park and the Museum of Natural History. I also applied for a job at the United Nations, but soon discovered that I was ill-prepared in that I had not sought a letter of introduction from my home government. After a few days I received a communication to the effect that my application was noted, and that I would be informed should a vacancy suitable to my qualifications occur. I later realized that had I sought a letter of introduction from the Colonial Office before I approached the UN I might have been successful even at that time. That would have changed the whole course of my life.

Choate School

I met Gerry and Janice Dartford for lunch in a restaurant off Fifth Avenue a few days before I was due to depart for England. He had taken a job as a history master in Salisbury School in the north-west corner of Connecticut, and he suggested that if I wanted to consider teaching in the United States, I might like to check in with his agency, which was nearby on Fifth Avenue. It seemed to me a good idea. It was not a propitious time of year to offer one's services for recruitment to a good school, but the lady at the agency said: "There is a school in Connecticut named Choate, which has unforeseen vacancies and might be interested in your qualifications. Would you be interested in going there for an interview?" I said I would. The lady telephoned the school immediately, and that weekend I travelled by train to Wallingford in Connecticut to visit Choate. I was met at the station by Charles Rice, the Director of Admissions, who introduced me to the Headmaster, Seymour St John, and showed me round the school. I was greatly impressed by what I saw, and even more attracted by the kindness and consideration of Charles Rice and his wife Tib. The Headmaster offered me a job in the English Department to teach English language and literature, mostly to a sixth form class, and to cover all public speaking classes. In Choate public speaking was a compulsory subject in the upper classes at that time. Stanley Pratt, who had been in charge of this subject, was moving into the position of Dean and I would be taking his place.

I telephoned Phyllis across the Atlantic to see what she thought of the idea. She said "Yes" and I said "Yes" so I sailed with the Mauritania as planned, and as soon as possible after arriving in England got busy applying for permanent residence visas for

Phyllis, Carolyn and myself. Obtaining these visas in 1957 took several months, even though the quota for the UK was not fully taken up. We were relieved when we finally obtained them and sailed on the Parthia to arrive in New York on 7th September 1957.

Charles Rice was there again to meet us at the Wallingford railroad station. He was a welcome sight, for we were all tired, and Carolyn, then eleven, was almost asleep on her feet with exhaustion. We stayed the night as guests of the Rices in their house, the Homestead, before moving over to temporary school quarters. Our ultimate home was to be Wheeler House, a house on Curtis Avenue recently acquired by the school. When we finally moved there we found ourselves in charge of seven seventeen-year-old boys who were to live with us. It was a fascinating new experience. As far as bedrooms were concerned there were two boys to a room with the most senior, the odd man out, in a single. Showers had been installed in the top floor. All meals were taken in the dining hall. Under the Choate house system Phyllis and I became the surrogate parents of our seven teenagers. I woke the boys each morning, and at night before they retired they came downstairs in their dressing gowns and shook hands with each of us. This happened whether we were alone or not. If we had guests they shook hands with them as well, individually announcing their names as they did so. After a couple of nights of this Phyllis and I shook hands in our bedroom before we climbed into bed ourselves. I do not mean to mock this system. It worked well. It is difficult to wake boys in the morning and shake hands with them at night, in addition to advising them, organizing parties for them, and occasionally disciplining them, without coming to know what makes them tick. We grew to know and respect one another. When Phyllis and I remember these boys today we think very warmly of almost all of them.

Our introduction to American social life could hardly have been better. The links between staff, or faculty as the staff of the school were called, were close, and they and their families were encouraged to take part in all school social activities. Coffee for the faculty and their wives was elegantly served in the beautiful lounge of the school library each evening, a faculty wife dispensing it from a silver urn.

As far as our daughter Carolyn was concerned, she went off to school daily to New Haven with the Headmaster's daughter Meg. Both were enrolled in the Day School, which was a private school about half an hour's car ride from Choate. We naturally took our share of the car-pooling, which usually involved my fetching Carolyn and Meg from New Haven at the end of the day. Although the Day School was considered by most people we knew to be a good school, New Haven being the location of Yale University, Carolyn was never particularly happy there, and after a time she asked diffidently whether she might be allowed to return to Ibstock Place in Roehampton. At first we discouraged the idea, saying she would have to go as a boarder, and we doubted whether there would be a place for her. But she persisted, so Phyllis wrote to Miss Priestman, the headmistress. Rather to our surprise there was a place, and Carolyn could be admitted. So at eleven and a half Carolyn started to commute to her London school across the Atlantic. She lived at boarding school, going on alternative weekends to either her grandparents' house in Abbey Wood on one side of London, or to her Aunt Elsie's house in Teddington, Middlesex on the other. On long holidays she flew home to the United States, so she did not feel terribly cut off. This situation continued until we moved to Washington, DC, as I shall describe later. By that time she had to leave Ibstock Place in any case, and choose between going to an English public girls' boarding school (we had her name down for Cheltenham College), or joining us in Washington, and attending "high" school there. We were delighted when she decided on the latter.

On the academic front at Choate I was amazed to find a faculty of seventy–five for about three hundred and fifty boys, and timetables tailored individually to each boy. There were rarely more than fifteen boys to a class, and often less. In sports I quickly learned that "football" was American football, which when played against another school assumed the proportions of all-out battle. Soccer played a minor role in the Choate games hierarchy. Baseball was as important as "football" but played at a different season, while hockey, which is always ice-hockey in the United States, was close in popularity. Hockey, as understood outside the continent of North America, is designated as "field hockey" in the United States. Other options in sport were "crew" (rowing), lacrosse, track or cross country (running), basketball, wrestling, tennis, squash and golf.

One aspect of our new life at Choate I found very striking and admirable. It was held essential that all members of the faculty and the boys should greet one another when they met on the school campus. (The word "campus" encompassing all the school grounds and buildings was a new word for us.) To make this possible, during the first few weeks of a new school year all boys and all faculty, and their spouses, were expected to wear name-tags prominently displayed, so that the name could be easily read at passing distance. In this way everyone on campus could greet and be greeted by name. In England as a schoolboy I was accustomed to being addressed by my surname both by my teachers and boy friends, but in the United States I quickly found that a boy was normally addressed by his Christian name in and out of the classroom, while a master was addressed as Mr So-and-So as frequently as "Sir". The understanding that one greeted everyone met on campus seemed to me to be an excellent rule for the development of a good community spirit and social consciousness.

It was soon clear to me that being a house master in a boarding school in the United States was just as "full-time" a job as it is anywhere else. Apart from classes in the morning, there was sports coaching in the afternoons (I became a soccer coach almost immediately), compulsory attendance in chapel, study-hall supervision duties in the early evening, and special evening activities several times a week. Virtually every master had responsibility for some extra-curricular activity in addition to a sport coaching job. This was inevitable as the school sponsored some twenty-seven clubs, four musical societies and three publications; The Choate News, The Brief, and The Choate Literary News. I shared responsibility for the debating society coaching for example, which entailed travelling to other schools with the debating team; and helped with elocution and handwriting competitions. In short, being a house-master at Choate was a twenty-four–hour–a–day job, except for a blessed arrangement which provided a day off once a week for every faculty member. Other faculty members covered his respon-sibilities for the twenty-four hours, and it was understood that a house master's free day should be virtually inviolable. Tuesday was my free day, and I still remember revelling in the free days I spent with Phyllis, often picnicking in the Connecticut countryside.

One of the main differences between Choate and the schools I had known previously was, of course, the great resources of Choate, an American private school, compared to the extremely limited resources of the publicly assisted schools I had known in England and Malaya. The Choate campus covered some eight hundred acres, and its high tuition fees ($3300 in 1967, plus $1000 for trav-el, clothes, books and sundries), ensured that with few exceptions only the sons of the wealthy enrolled. Its plant and equipment were excellent, its buildings and landscaping gracious. It was well endowed, and from time to time special benefactors, such as Paul Mellon, would provide impressive new buildings. It numbered among its alumni such eminent figures as members of the Kennedy family, Adlai Stevenson and Allen Dulles, and seemed to have no difficulty in calling upon famous living citizens to visit the school and address appropriate societies within it. Eleanor Roosevelt was a regular visitor and a great favourite. She would be introduced to the whole school by the student president of the Current History Club as "the first lady of the world", and would relate her most recent experiences from her travels. Once she entertained a select-ed group of seniors and faculty, in which I was happy to be included, in the small house she occupied as Franklin's widow on the Hyde Park estate. Coffee was dispensed from a large urn such as one might find in a restaurant. It was clear that Mrs Roosevelt enjoyed entertaining groups of this size. Averill Harriman was another such visitor. I remember his soft-spoken fielding of questions from history seniors in the drawing room of the headmaster's house. He maintained a serious and dignified manner throughout, although the meeting was kept informal.

John F. Kennedy was invited back as "Alumnus of the Year". He was already "the Democratic Senator from Massachusetts" when he spoke to the school in the chapel. I happened to be in the balcony immediately above the pulpit from which he was delivering his address. As a teacher of public speaking I was impressed. He had a clear measured delivery. His remarks were spiced with humour, and what he said was to the point. I noted that his speech was printed in large type-written letters in a ring-backed folder. Yet his eyes barely seemed to look down, even when he turned the pages. It seemed to me he was so well rehearsed he scarcely needed his script, or could it have been a masterly display of how to read a speech without seeming to do so?

Choate aimed at producing "well-rounded" American citizens. It had its problems later with regard to student unrest, its reluctance to enrol blacks, and the war in Vietnam, but in general I think it succeeded in its aims. Virtually all the sixth formers went on to good colleges, and many of its alumni have become prominent citizens in many walks of life.

Choate was without doubt a far cry from the Malay College, Kuala Kangsar, though both were elite institutions. One evening at the end of a full faculty meeting in Choate's comfortable, spacious faculty room I was invited by the headmaster to say something about the College. The faculty were very interested, particularly when I described how we dealt with discipline. Choate had strict rules about smoking and drinking on campus. Violation of these rules could mean expulsion. I explained that at the Malay College the punishment for smoking was "six of the best" (drinking did not enter into the picture, as the consumption of alcohol is prohibited by the Muslim religion, and the boys accepted this prohibition in absolute terms). Corporal punishment was banned almost universally in American schools, and certainly so at Choate, but I detected among the Choate faculty at that time a feeling that sometimes in certain very special cases such punishment would not be inappropriate. The senior College boys with whom I had discussed corporal punishment had no great quarrel with it. They found it quick and conclusive, and appreciated that after such punishment the slate was immediately clean. During my headmastership I caned a boy only once. It was for flagrant and very conspicuous smoking. It was the first time I had ever caned anyone, and the last. The victim was a popular fellow. When it was over he gave me a wry grin, and said "Would you like one of my kittens, Sir?" For the rest of his school life we were the best of friends.

  I had no reason in that faculty meeting to describe the college student rebelliousness of the 1950s. Discipline was strict at Choate, but broadly speaking the rapport between faculty and boys was good. It was later, in the 1960's that the authority of the school was challenged, as it was in schools and colleges across the whole nation, partly by the unrest generated by the Vietnam War, but specifically in the case of Choate because Yale University at that time was accepting fewer graduates from Choate than in the past, and a boy had written an article about this in the school newspaper The Choate News, suggesting that the reason might be that Choate graduates were judged to be too insulated from the real world. This story is recounted by Peter S. Prescott in his book "A World Of Our Own", published in 1970 but concerning Choate's academic year 1967–1968.

  Educational institutions everywhere, of course, have their ups and downs. In their different ways Choate and the Malay College in the 1980s reached a new equilibrium and relative stability. Choate is balanced and tempered by its amalgamation with a girls' school, Rosemary Hall. The Malay College, buttressed by a politically powerful Old Boys Association, remains a boarding school for Malay boys only in an independent Malaysia, conscious of its prestige, and anxious to maintain its standards. Both schools have been through their periods of Sturm und Drang.

Adviser to Colonial Students in North America

In December 1958 when we had been at Choate just over a year, I received an interesting proposition from London from the Colonial Office Adviser on Education. A letter arrived from the Colonial Attaché of the British Embassy in Washington, DC, enquiring whether I would be interested in the job of Adviser to Colonial Students in North America under the auspices of the Embassy. There were at that time some 3900 students in North America from territories administered by Britain, who, by virtue of their presence in the United States and Canada,needed help and advice, and also some liaison assistance vis-a-vis their home governments and their American and Canadian institutions. These students were located in colleges and universities spread widely over the continent. The twenty-six countries from which they might come were the Bahamas, Bermuda, British Honduras, British Somaliland, Brunei, Cyprus, Fiji, The Gambia, Gibralter, Hong Kong, Kenya, British Virgin Islands, Malta, Federation of Malaya, Mauritius, North Borneo, Northern Rhodesia, Nyasaland, St. Helena, Sarawak, Seychelles, Singapore, Tanganyika, Tonga, Uganda and Zanzibar.

The original appointee to the job had been Bernard Mellor, on secondment from his post as Registrar of the University of Hong Kong. He had been in office for two years, and was now anxious to return to his post as registrar. The job I was being offered was clearly one which could not last long, as Britain was committed to granting independence to most of its colonial territories. However, it seemed an exciting opportunity, and I immediately agreed in principle to accept it. The official offer of appointment, which arrived from the Colonial Office in February, suggested that I take up the offer with immediate effect. However, although I had no written contract with Choate School, I felt obliged to complete the school year first, so as not to leave my students in mid-stream. I therefore requested the Colonial Office to allow me to complete the summer term at Choate. I would then assume duty in Washington just as soon as term ended in June, and I had completed my reports. The Headmaster, Seymour St John, wrote a carefully worded letter in support of this action, and the Colonial Office understandingly agreed. Phyllis and I set off for Washington the day after I completed my last student report.

I do now know whether our long service in Malaya had sparked a small degree of wanderlust in Chuck and Tib Rice's minds, or whether it was just coincidence, but just as we were leaving Wallingford for Washington in mid-June, Tib and Chuck were doing the same thing. Chuck had accepted the post of President of Athens College, Greece, a prestigious secondary school for Greek boys, supported by American funds, and Chuck had to be briefed at the Greek Embassy before proceeding to Athens. We had been lent a house by the British Embassy, one left by an officer on leave, until we found one of our own, so Chuck and Tib stayed with us for a while.

Although I was under the aegis of the British Embassy on Massachusetts Avenue, my office was a couple of rooms in the Windsor Park Hotel on Connecticut Avenue. The office had been valiantly kept on hold by my predecessor's secretary, Mary Arden, who showed me the files. My first task was to let the governments and students concerned know of my presence. However, as my budget was extremely limited, to begin with I concentrated on helping students who had problems. I would, when necessary, make appeals to home governments for increases in grants, advise students on transfers and special courses, and help them when I could with their personal problems. One of the most important matters I had to deal with was accreditation, or the assessment of the value of academic qualifications. Students from the colonial territories needed to know what value would be accorded to the qualifications they brought with them, usually a Cambridge School Certificate or a Cambridge Higher School Certificate, and what value would be attributed in their home countries to the degrees they would be taking back with them.

In May 1960 Bernard Mellor had written a small book entitled The American Degree, in which he recommended that colonial students seeking to pursue advanced degrees in their home countries should enroll in universities with excellence in the field chosen, rather than in liberal arts colleges, which offered a less specialized four-year liberal arts training to a first degree. This insistence had brought him under heavy fire from the representatives of the Institute of International Education (IIE) located in New York and the African American Institute (AAI) in Washington, who felt that the better four-year liberal arts colleges were being wrongly down-graded. The difference in the purpose of the United States and British institutions certainly caused some misunderstandings. However, these misunderstandings could usually be avoided if students from overseas could be advised ahead of time what their options were. In April 1961 I attempted to help solve this problem by contributing an article to a British government publication, Overseas Education, entitled "The Interpretation of Qualifications submitted by students of British Dependent Territories for Entry into Institutions for Higher Education in North America". This article was afterwards made available for distribution as a pamphlet.

It was useful having a house lent to us in Washington, as it allowed us to look for more permanent accommodation at leisure. After patient searching we found a pleasant house in Hawthorne Street, NW. Phyllis had visited the house with the estate agent to check out what was available. She had been told it was for sale but not for rent. But Phyllis charmed the owner, who happened to be on the premises doing a painting job. This was Rear-Admiral De Witt Hamburger, who replied to her query as to whether the house was for rent "No, it is not: but I'd be willing to rent it to you!" And so we moved in.

Under the terms of our contract Carolyn was entitled to assistance with her Education, and we enrolled her as a day student in the National Cathedral School partly because of this. We were also attracted by the fact that the school was within walking distance from the house. Our house itself was most conveniently located, being about halfway between the school and the Embassy.

My most ambitious activity as Adviser to Colonial Students was to attempt to visit as many students as possible on their campuses across the length and breadth of the United States and Canada. Accordingly I planned to drive in a wide circle to the deep south, across to Texas, up to Colorado and into California; then into Canada, Vancouver, Edmonton, Calgary; down to Wisconsin and Chicago, back to Toronto, Montreal and Quebec; and finally south – through New York State back to Washington, DC. The whole journey would log over 12,000 miles, and would take three months. Phyllis decided that during this period she would make a trip to England, and take Carolyn to Paris during her school holidays. After our respective excursions Carolyn would return to school in England and Phyllis and I would meet in Montreal and drive back to Washington together.

I learned a good deal about the United States as well as the students as I made my journey. Some of the Africans in the deep south suffered from the general race prejudices of white America there. I also found that my contacts in some of the Negro colleges–they were not at that time known as "Black", although the word "Negro" was often capitalized by blacks and by those who respected them-- were being equally discriminated against because they were black. I found, for example, that the black Foreign Student Adviser at Dillard University was unable to accept my invitation to dine at a restaurant with me, because all suitable restaurants were restricted to whites. In the following thirty years all this was to change drastically. At the State University in Baton Rouge I was surprised to find a small group of white French-speaking students from the British administered French-speaking island of Mauritius. They were studying sugar engineering to enable them to improve the sugar industry in their own country.

On these visits my main contact was always the Foreign Student Adviser of the college, and on assuming my job I had quickly become a member of NAFSA, the National Association of Foreign Student Advisers (now the National Association of Foreign Student Affairs, to reflect student participation in the organization). NAFSA was and is a fine organization, providing in the United States, but on a much larger scale, many of the services I knew the British Council provided in the United Kingdom. Each Foreign Student Adviser made a point of helping the foreign student to become accepted in his or her college, and in assisting him or her to satisfy the United States Government's regulations with regard to immigration, part-time employment and income tax. My role was to provide an extra link between the students and their home countries, and support them in every possible way. Usually there was more than one student from a given territory on a single campus, and this was good because they could help one another in all kinds of ways.

On one of my visits to a college in California which had a sizeable foreign student population I was pleased to find a large gathering of Hong Kong students waiting to see me. Usually there would only be a sprinkling of colonial students in a fairly small college, but in this case there were ten or more, all from Hong Kong. I found this surprising as Hong Kong students formed a special category. As a rule they needed little help. They were normally good students, often studying science or mathematics, who had no financial problems. Moreover, I knew that in very many cases they were not anxious to see a Colonial Student Adviser, because they had absolutely no intention of returning to Hong Kong, where jobs were scarce and poorly paid. The reason why they had turned up in such strength in this instance was because of my name –Luke. They thought it must have been meant to be Loke, a common Chinese name, Luke being a misspelling. A Chinese adviser might have had something very special to tell them. They were very charming on realizing their misapprehension. We exchanged information on a number of subjects and parted on the best of terms. This encounter confirmed my belief that the Chinese students were the most self-sufficient of all those who were my responsibility. Most of them intended to remain in the country and eventually to become permanent residents of the United States if they could.

Adviser for East African Students in North America

While I was in Winnipeg I received a call from Douglas Williams, the Colonial Attache at the embassy in Washington. My current assignment, he reminded me, was fast becoming an anachronism, as so many colonial territories were in the process of gaining their independence. Nevertheless, there was a special need for assistance to be given to East African students, who were now beginning to come to the United States in fairly large numbers. Would I be interested in fulfilling that need by working in the future exclusively with East African students? I said I certainly would.

At this time Kenya, Uganda, Tanganyika and Zanzibar benefited from a number of common services – postal, railway, customs and armed forces – which had been established under British rule on a regional basis. It would therefore make sense for the African students from the region to be given extra support as a group, especially as many of them were accepting Educational opportunities in the United States for the first time. Because of their association with Britain, students from the region had traditionally gone to British universities or other institutions of further Education, if they did not attend their home country institutions. Uganda had the highest standard of Education in the area, and was justly proud of its Makerere College in Kampala, which, in association with the University of London, offered University of London degrees. Kenya had a similar arrangement with its Royal College in Nairobi. Tanganyika was less advanced in Education than Uganda or Kenya. Zanzibar, a small island mainly noted for its cloves, lacked an institution at the college level, though it claimed to have a higher proportion of students sitting for the Cambridge School Certificate from its 300,000 population than either Kenya or Tanganyika. Individual students from Zanzibar had attended United Kingdom colleges and universities for many years. I was therefore not unduly surprised when I visited Zanzibar to find that the first Zanzibar Education officer to whom I was introduced, Mr Mohamed Salim Burwani, was a graduate of St Edmund Hall, my own college at Oxford.

I was delighted with the proposition put to me, and agreed to accept the appointment of Adviser for East African Students in North America for as long as required. My employer was to be the East African Common Services Organization, EACSO, which controlled the common services of the region, and my appointment was to become effective on 19th June 1961.

In order to prepare myself for my new assignment I was sent to the various East African territories to meet with representatives of their governments, my itinerary being first to Kenya, then to Tanganyika and Zanzibar, and finally to Uganda. I was delighted to be visiting Nairobi for private as well as official reasons, because Bill Jackman, who as I mentioned earlier had been on the staff of the Malay College in Malaya, had transferred to Kenya on account of his wife Peggy's health, and had now become Chief Inspector of Schools for the territory, stationed in the capital city. I was able to visit him and his family in the house he and Peggy had bought. I also met other officials of the Education Department, in particular John Gregg, Permanent Secretary to the Ministry of Education, Anne Brotherton, who was in charge of Kenya students overseas, and Kenneth Matiba, her assistant, who after Independence became a prominent figure in the shaping of Kenya's Education policies.

I arrived in Nairobi on 20th June 1961, just in time to attend the opening ceremony of the Kenya Institute of Social Services. The opening address was delivered by Lord Dulverton, representing the

Dulverton Fund, which had contributed 40,000 pounds towards the construction of the Institute. Among the distinguished guests was Sir Donald McGillivray, who had been the last expatriate governor of Malaya, and had retired to a farm in Kenya. He remembered me from his time in Kuala Lumpur, and invited me to stay a weekend at his home in the highlands, a beautiful mixed farm in Gilgil. I spent a whole day with him as he made his rounds inspecting crops and cattle. He had played a leading part in improving Kenyan livestock, and had written a pamphlet for the Kabete Veterinary College on artificial insemination.

At this time the British Government was interested in the idea of creating a University of East Africa by integrating and upgrading the existing colleges of the component territories. It was envisaged that specialization would be undertaken by selected students being sent to the strongest faculties in the region according to their needs. Thus, medical students would be sent to Makerere College in Kampala, engineering students to the Royal College, Nairobi, while a new school of law would be established in Dar-es-Salaam. Students would be encouraged to remain in their own countries for general arts degrees. Sir Donald McGillivray had been appointed pro vice-chancellor of this new university.

It was while in Kenya that I first met Tom Mboya, who in 1961 was Minister of Labour in the Kenyan government. He had studied in Britain at Ruskin College, Oxford, which had been established to assist in the Education of leaders of the working–class movement in England, and had already made a name for himself as a charismatic personality and a dynamic speaker when addressing either African or English–speaking audiences. However, he was far from being universally popular in Kenya, largely because he was not a member of the dominant tribe, the Kikuyu, but a Luo, one of the smaller tribes. He was particularly interested in Kenya students in the United States, and had recently been on a speaking tour to United States universities and colleges. This tour had been sponsored by a young American industrialist named William

Scheinman, who, with a former member of the US Delegation to the United Nations and the New York City Commission on Human Rights, had founded the African American Student Foundation AASF, the main objective of which was to bring Kenyan students to American colleges. During his visits to colleges Mboya had been able to obtain promises of scholarship help on a number of campuses. The main purpose of the Foundation was to provide transportation from Kenya to the United States for Kenyan Africans who had already obtained places in United States institutions of higher education.

One of my first moves on assuming office as Adviser for East African Students in North America was to seek an interview with the AASF in New York City. I met with William Scheinman and Frank Montero in the lounge of the Statler Hotel, opposite the old Pennsylvania railroad station (both now long since demolished), in order to express my concern about AASF students arriving in the United States without adequate arrangements being made for them. The experience of our office had been that many of these students from Kenya had been haphazardly chosen, often unsuitably placed in colleges in the deep south, and frequently inadequately financed. The problems that were caused by these inadequacies often ended up in my office. The reply I received from the AASF was, in effect, a polite brush-off. I was told by their representatives that they had complete confidence in their African associates. In fact the AASF seemed to me to be only interested in getting Kenyan students across the Atlantic and into institutions of higher Education of any kind. The Foundation was not greatly concerned about supporting these students, believing, quite rightly in many cases, that the institutions which admitted them would find financial assistance for them from some source or another rather than refuse to continue to support them. The Foundation went out of business in the fall of 1961.

I was to meet Tom Mboya again on two occasions, once in New York when he was meeting with the United Negro College Fund, and for the last time in Washington, for he kept a keen interest in Kenya students. I noted in Washington in 1964 that as a close friend of the President, Jomo Kenyatta, he was becoming increasingly under pressure from his rivals.

In March 1969 the aging President announced plans to call a general election late in the year, and Mboya, as Minister of Economic Planning and Development, and Secretary General of the President's party, the Kenya African National Union (KANU), inevitably found himself obliged to play a leading role in the campaign. Throughout 1969 he had confided to his friends Scheinman and Montero that he feared for his life, and on 5th July he was in fact shot in the head on a Nairobi sidewalk. He was thirty-eight. The government blamed "an international conspiracy" for the assassination, but Montero and Scheinman were convinced that factionalism within his own party led to his death.

As I had no more than a week in Kenya I had a busy schedule trying to see as much as possible, and make contacts with all of those who might be able to assist Kenya students in America. These included not only representatives of government departments and institutions, but also newspaper men such as Mr John Collier of the Associated Press Time and Life magazines, and Mr Curtis, proprietor of the Nation newspaper. My hope was that free newspapers could be made available to African students in the United States and Canada. However, although free newspapers were offered, the stumbling block proved to be the cost of their transportation across the Atlantic, and for that reason none was ever shipped.

As technical training, as well as the creation of the new university, was very much a current issue, I visited the new Kenya Polytechnic which would provide "on-site-training" in a variety of crafts to full technical status. It had five departments: Engineering (Mechanical and Electrical), Building, Science, Commerce and Domestic Science (Home Economics). My visit was a joint one with Mr Biwanuka, Minister of Education, Uganda. A special feature of the Polytechnic was that each student had to be sponsored by a commercial firm or a Government department, so that the student's employment could be guaranteed on his or her graduation. Later in the 1960s, the Kenya Polytechnic became one of the most successful projects of the United Nations Special Fund, which I joined as a staff member in 1964.

At the Royal College I met the Principal, Dr Hyslop, and learned that the Vice-Chancellor of the new university would be Dr Bernard de Bunsen, the then principal of Makerere College. Dr Hyslop was concerned with the problems of the university's Academic Committee, which among other things had to deal with the meshing of academic terms. The Royal College was especially proud of its new engineering laboratory created with American funds. Mr P. Bhagwant, in charge of Electrical Engineering, told us that African students showed little aptitude for engineering, and that even when they started the course they tended to drop out after a year or two. It appeared to me that the superiority of Asian students in the engineering and science fields over African students in Kenya paralleled the superiority of Asian students (mostly Chinese) over Malay students in these fields that I had observed in Malaya. As in Malaya, it was a problem that would need to have a partly political solution.

It was, however, from Mr Lyons of the USIS office in Nairobi, that I fully realized the generally positive attitude of the United States Government towards the admission of Kenya African students to the United States. The Assistant Secretary of State for African Affairs, Mr Mennen Williams, was anxious to help Kenya students as much as possible, particularly at this time in history when African countries were gaining their independence in rapid succession.

In his office Mr Lyons showed me a map of the United States with coloured pins stuck in it representing East African students across the country. He also let me have his latest lists of Kenya students in

US institutions. There was, he told me, a likelihood of at least three planes in a 1961 airlift, with about half the students going to Canada. Lyons seemed completely dedicated to the cause of Mboya, even though he was aware that some colleges had become disillusioned about the quality of the students going to the United States under African American Student Foundation auspices. I felt at the time that the United States as a whole wanted to show its goodwill to the newly independent African countries in a practical way. Almost every college in the United States appeared to want to have at least one African student on campus to show this goodwill openly. At the same time the officials of the Immigration and Naturalization Service in the field were very reluctant to disallow a student's entry into the United States, as that might be construed as thwarting the legitimate aspirations of young Africans seeking higher Education. However, a more professional effort to select suitable students in a new programme was initiated after a time by the Dean of Admissions of Harvard University, David Henry. This programme was called the African Scholarship Program of American Universities, or ASPAU. At first it operated through only a few of the Ivy League colleges, but later it was extended to include most institutions which welcomed the careful screening of applicants undertaken by the Program before scholarships were awarded and placements made.

During my stay in Nairobi I met Dr Kiano, who had been a Minister in the government, and at the home of the Mosers of the United States Agency for International Development (USAID), I met his remarkable wife. Dr Kiano had set an example to the youth of Kenya by gaining admission to an American college, and by hard work and encouragement from an American professor at the University of California at Los Angeles (UCLA), Dr Scalopino, obtaining his doctorate at UCLA. He thus became an inspiration to all Kenyan students. If Dr Kiano could do it so could they. Mrs Kiano is an American black. She had been helping her husband with a venture he had always been intent on undertaking called the "Competent Commercial College". Mrs Kiano was its business manager. Yet most of her work appeared at that time to be concerned with the guidance of students who wished to go to the United States. It appeared that the procedure was for the student to write to a college in the United States, mentioning Mrs Kiano, so that the college could write back to her for an assessment of the student's capabilities. Mrs Kiano obviously believed that there would be another airlift of students in 1961 as there had been in 1959 and 1960, and that the students she had advised upon favourably would be able to participate in such an airlift.

I mentioned to her the troubles we had had with some of the airlift students in the past, who had been inadequately financed and badly placed, but Mrs Kiano was obviously of the opinion that they would get something out of the experience, and would be better off than if they had remained at home. I pointed out that all the students at Philander Smith College, a small liberal arts institution in the deep south (and I had met all nineteen of them), wished to transfer to other institutions. She said she was aware of this, and that indeed she had advised these students to go there with the intention of transferring as soon as possible. When I asked whether this was fair to Philander Smith, she replied: "Well, they agreed to take them." I then added that I hoped we could agree upon the premise that all students from Africa who went to the United States would leave the country with a warm feeling for it. I said I was beginning to doubt whether this would be the case with some of the airlift students. It was generally agreed round that dinner table that more secondary schools and institutions of higher Education were desirable in Kenya, but Mrs Kiano was emphatic that something had to be done immediately for the students who required higher Education.

Mrs Kiano was obviously a remarkable and very energetic woman. She had taken over all the Education aspects of her husband's work, and no doubt she was under considerable political pressure to do this. Parents would come to her with their sons and daughters and say in effect: "We voted for Dr Kiano. Now get my child to an American university!" Not only was Mrs Kiano business manager of the Competent Commercial College, which she was hoping to rename the Ralph Bunche Academy if she could obtain Dr Bunche's permission to do so, she was also business manager of her husband's Kikuyu newspaper. All this she did in addition to looking after her husband and four children ranging in age from ten to a few months.

The question of the airlifts, which I realized from the start would be one of my main concerns as Adviser for East African Students in North America, had been thrown into relief by my meeting with Mrs Kiano. By far the largest group of East African students in the United States were from Kenya, and the example of Dr Kiano and the personal promotion of Educational opportunities in America by Tom Mboya with the help of the AASF had fired all Kenyan school-leavers with the ambition to pursue "higher studies" in the United States. Admissions officers of institutions of higher Education of all kinds across the continent had been beset by a flood of blue air-letters from Kenya school-leavers asking for admission and financial help to enable them to enroll. Admissions officers would write back indicating the academic and financial requirements needed for admission, but from time to time a Kenya student would appear in an admissions office unannounced without having received any notification of acceptance. The student had accurately gauged the prevailing sentiment in the country, namely that every effort would be made by college authorities to support any young African who had shown enterprise enough to travel to America in search of higher Education. In practice this could mean that the student would receive gifts of clothes and financial support from interested individuals as well as a waiver of tuition fees.

As mentioned earlier, the first airlift, which took place in 1959, and the second, which took place in 1960, were sponsored by the African American Students Foundation. After 1960, however, the AASF drastically curtailed its activities, and handed over all its files to the Institute of International Education (IIE). The 1959 airlift, the original airlift of 81 students, had been a cause celebre in Educational circles concerned with foreign students. The eighty-one were officially received in convention facilities in the Commodore Hotel on 42nd Street, New York City (now the Regency Hyatt), where they had been welcomed by the AASF's representative Cora Weiss, and addressed by Bayard Rustin, a well-known black activist, who urged them not to distance themselves from American blacks, but to identify themselves with them, since American blacks were Americans of African descent. I also was given an opportunity to speak to the group, and explain the services my office was able to offer. Since these students were not sponsored by the Kenya Government, and therefore critical of the Government in many cases, I was grateful to the AASF for allowing me to do this. The AASF, however, was careful to give me limited exposure.

The students were accommodated for at least one night in the Great Northern Hotel on West 57th Street, four students to a room, and were then transported by Greyhound bus to their respective campuses. In this operation valuable help was given by the Committee for Friendly Relations Among Foreign Students, which some years later changed its name to the International Student Service. The Committee had a few paid workers, but its workers mainly comprised young American volunteer students, who simply wore arm-bands at Kennedy Airport, and met and helped the foreign students as they arrived.

Over the next two years I visited on their campuses as many of these eighty-one Kenyans as I could. It was true that their selection had in a number of ways been arbitrary and haphazard, but in the end I came to respect their determination and dedication. Though many of them had difficulty in maintaining an adequate standard in the institution to which they had been admitted, they persevered. If they were rejected in one college they would seek and usually gain admission to another in which the standards were less exacting. They would rather have died than return to Kenya without some significant academic qualifications. The reason for this was in part because of the high hopes pinned on them by family and tribe, for the first step in each individual's pilgrimage to America had often been a collection of money in the student's home village.

There were four charter flights for students in the fall of 1961, the three of the Council on Educational Cooperation with Africa (CECAF), which included some students for Canadian universities under African Students Foundation of Canada sponsorship, and that of 27th September, sponsored by the Kenya Education Fund Directors. The African Scholarship Program of American Universities (ASPAU) students travelled by sea. The East African Governments paid for the passages of students under the ASPAU and CECAF programmes. The Kenya Education Fund paid for most of the students flight of 27th September from local contributions and a loan. Some students on this flight paid for their own passages.

Under the ASPAU programme the greatest care had been taken with regard to selection, placement, reception, orientation and financial support of the students concerned. The CECAF programme was one of semi-sponsorship through the IIE, with the help of State Department funds. The African students of CECAF were met and looked after by the representatives of the State Department and the IIE. The airlift of 27th September, however, was an arrangement to meet a local demand of Kenya students travelling to the United States, which provided no continuing support. My secretary, Eileen Fox, and I had to deal with this airlift alone, except for three volunteers from the Committee for Friendly Relations Among Foreign Students, whose help proved to be invaluable.

Meeting the 27th September airlift was a remarkable experience, exhilarating but disturbing. Our office had no information about the students who had arrived, and our first business was to accommodate them in the Great Northern Hotel, as had been done with the AASF students. In a room there Eileen, who had brought along her portable typewriter from Washington, made a list of names and campuses, and we checked our lists by telephone with college admission offices. Some students bound for Californian institutions thought they could travel straight on without wasting money on an overnight stay in New York. One student had been accepted for admission to a high school in Alaska. Another had boarded the flight in haste with almost no luggage. The Committee for Friendly Relations Among Foreign Students in a number of cases kindly put up funds to cover the travelling costs of some students to their places of study. Most students decided to travel by the cheapest possible way, so we arranged for a Greyhound representative to come to the hotel to ticket those who elected to travel by bus to their various destinations. While the students were waiting for these arrangements to be finalized, I took the opportunity of explaining to them some of the things they needed to know quickly in the United States, such as the value of the dollar, and the items they most likely would first need to spend their money on.

I think it was generally realized that this last kind of student movement to the United States was chaotic and unsatisfactory, and from that date onwards the interest of Kenya students in higher Education in the United States was directed towards the officially approved programmes by most authorities concerned, both in Africa and in the United States. The ad hoc placement of East African students thereafter diminished almost to vanishing point.

***

But to return to East Africa .No–one passes through Nairobi without seeing something of the marvellous wildlife which is to be found in the nearby national park. The Jackmans called on me at my hotel when I had a little free time, and drove me out there. Soon we were watching a pride of lions at very close range. The huge beasts, having just fed, were sleepy and quite unperturbed by the closeness of our car. Later, we had a number of jabbering monkeys surrounding us, with some of the more venturesome sitting on the hood of the car. I also enjoyed a more ambitious excursion to "Treetops", the famous hotel from which one can watch a herd of wild elephants assembled below one's eyes at a saltlick. To undertake this excursion one travels to the highlands by car, and stays first at the Outspan Hotel, which is built in a solid Dutch style. Then, for an extra fee, one can set out to overnight at Treetops, which, as its name implies, is actually constructed in the tops of trees. One is advised to travel to Treetops in warm safari clothes, to wear rubber shoes or sneakers, and to be prepared to wait long hours in absolute silence. Treetops provides mattresses and an artificial moon so that the elephants can be viewed at night. If one's luck is in, as many as twenty or thirty elephants can be seen together at one time at the salt lick.

As I write this chapter in the closing weeks of 1983 I read in the press of cheering crowds greeting Queen Elizabeth II in the streets of Nairobi. The colonial yoke and the unhappy days of MauMau seem to have been forgotten. Jomo Kenyatta, at one time denounced as the "symbol of darkness and death", later surprisingly became the toast of his former implacable enemies, the settlers. Now the country, still headed by Kenyatta's successor, Daniel Arap Moi, besides being the recipient of substantial British government aid, receives a greater investment in Kenyan industry and commerce from British industry (some £1 billion) than from anywhere else in the world, and the Queen, on her way to preside at the Commonwealth Conference in India, has paid a sentimental visit to "Treetops", because that is where she was staying thirty years before, when she received the news that her father King George VI had died, and that she was from that moment queen.

I was due to leave Kenya for Tanganyika on June 30th. However, the flight was postponed until the following day, so I took the opportunity to visit Carola Jackman, my god-daughter, at her

211

school in Limuru. Limuru is considerably higher than Nairobi, and has a cool pleasant climate. The buildings of Limuru School were attractive, but the facilities, especially those for science, were very limited. On the way back I noted the beautiful Limuru highlands farmed by the white settlers, and an overcrowded Kikuyu settlement on their outskirts. One could understand the land hunger of the Kikuyu.

Eventually I left Nairobi at 6pm and arrived at Dar-es-Salaam at 9pm, thus unfortunately missing a reception given by Jefferson (Pat) Murphy, Director of the African American Institute in the region, in honour of Harold K. Hochschild, chairman of its Board of Trustees. I was met by Miss Maud Watt, who was in charge of Tanganyikan students in training overseas. She kindly drove me to the New Africa Hotel, and afterwards gave me supper at her house. Her car, I, noticed, was a Peugeot. This surprised me as I assumed she would be driving a British car. When I commented on her choice she merely remarked, "The French make good cars." I smile now when I think of this. Phyllis and I have driven Peugeot cars a lot since that time, having owned a 404, a 504 and a 505.

I was very interested in the New Africa Hotel because Phyllis had spent some time there when she was in charge of the African Girls School in Dar-es-Salaam in 1944-1945. An unusual feature of the place was that tea was delivered to one's room at 6:30 every morning regardless of whether one ordered it or not. There would be a heavy hammering on the door, and in would come an African in a long white robe, bearing a tray on which would be set a teapot, a cup and saucer, a small jug of milk and a bowl of sugar, all in heavy white crockery. I appreciate a cup of tea in my room in the morning, but my efforts to get it served a little later without the onslaught on the door proved to be of no avail. The ritual of morning tea is still today observed in many modern African hotels in countries which were formerly under British rule.

On my first morning in Dar-es-Salaam I met with officials of the

Education Ministry, and then the rest of the day I spent with Miss Watt learning about the various scholarship programmes with which she was associated. Fourteen Tanganyikan students were going to the United States under United Negro College Fund auspices. For these students the Tanganyika Government was paying fares, at about, £200 a time. It was understood that the Government would repatriate any of these students if necessary, and would also be prepared to finance any Tanganyikan airlift students who needed help, provided they were making satisfactory grades. As far as the 1961–1962 airlift students were concerned, all money in the regular votes was committed, and the figure I had submitted from Washington had been accepted. With regard to the 1962–1963 year, a decision on the amounts of Government bursaries had been arrived at. Those selected under ASPAU were expected to go on a chartered plane leaving about 21st July. The itinerary would start in Rhodesia, continue through Tanganyika, Kenya and Uganda, and thence to Naples and Paris. The journey to the United States would be by sea. No loans were given to Tanganyikan students other than to students to Makerere. The list of ASPAU selected students for the year 1961–1962 included two Europeans, who claimed to be Tanganyikan, and one Indian.

In Dar-es-Salaam I was greatly impressed with the thoroughness of ASPAU's selection process. The marking of candidates at the interview was for a hundred-point total – twenty-five for the United States Preliminary Scholastic Aptitude Test (PSAT), twenty-five for the Cambridge School Certificate results, ten for any Cambridge Higher School Certificate results, twenty for school reports given by heads of schools and twenty for the interview itself. It was Murphy's opinion that the PSAT did have a rough correlation with the total worth of the student. He thought that the PSAT scores often identified those students who would be successful in the United States, but not necessarily so successful in institutions based on British practice. If this were so, he thought it would mean that the African Scholarship Program of American Universities was, in a sense, complementary to what was being done both in East Africa and the United Kingdom. Three hundred students had applied for ASPAU scholarships. Fifteen had been selected for full scholarships.

On 4th July I had an interview with the Principal Assistant Secretary, Celebrations, Mr J.P.Jones, whose office was in charge of all Independence celebrations. Mr Jones had already received letters from England and elsewhere asking for money in order to allow Tanganyikan students to celebrate their country's independence in the country in which they were studying. He had not received such a request from America, but expected to receive one at any time. Would I be responsible for the distribution of Independence celebration material? A request for £1000 had been received from New Delhi, and a similar one from Addis Ababa. I said I would speak to the Tanganyikan Students' Association to see how they would like the materials sent, and that our office would be glad to help in any way possible. Included in materials which were being distributed was a souvenir booklet in English and Swahili, a gramophone record of the new National Anthem, a copy in miniature of the national flag, a photograph of the Prime Minister, and possibly some cash in an amount to be determined.

As soon as possible I visited Jefferson (Pat) Murphy, Director of the African American Institute Program in Dar-es-Salaam. Pat Murphy had been in this post since January 1961, and had set up an attractive air-conditioned office. The office notice boards showed the procedure for the selection of students for the ASPAU associated programmes, with photographs of the selection board comprising admissions officers from various colleges, copies of the forms used, maps showing the areas in Africa from which the students had been chosen, and the colleges in the United States to which they would go. Murphy had prepared a statement describing the Program, which had been approved by David Henry and the Governments and sent to every secondary school in East and Central Africa, all members of selection committees, all Ministries of Education, and all Provincial Education Officers.

I asked Pat Murphy what Tom Mboya's reaction was to the statement that had been issued with regard to ASPAU. He said it was generally favourable. Mboya thought that it met a need, but not the whole need. His case was that there were hundreds of Kenya Africans over twenty years old who were bright, but had not had the opportunity to pursue higher studies. This was a talent lying fallow for which something should be done. There was no doubt also an unspoken aim- that there should be a sizeable cadre of trained Africans who would not be "beholden to the Government or the settlers". He did not need or want trained professional people at this time, but rather a cadre of leaders who could be sent out to be district commissioners. This, Murphy thought, was the African concept of Education for Power, which did not necessarily coincide with the British or Western concept of what should be done to train talent in Africa. When Ghana and Nigeria became independent, West African leaders, Murphy believed, had been quite willing to push people who had no special ability academically, but who later nevertheless could be put in positions of power. Such people were not normally associated with formal Education. This philosophy was probably a major part of the motivation embodied in the airlifts, although it had not been fully vocalized.

In a sense what was happening now in East Africa was a reflection of what had already happened in West Africa. Ghana had led the way, when it became independent in 1957 under Dr Kwame Nkrumah. In his early years before he became obsessed with the trappings of power, Nkrumah had been a philosophical leader in Africa, and his cynical twist of the Christian ethic "seek ye first the political kingdom, and all these things shall be added unto you" had been widely believed and accepted. The main plank in Mboya's platform had a similar thrust. It was that throughout the programme the African initiative should have been retained. His criticism of ASPAU was that it had not been endorsed by African leaders, and that therefore in the minds of the people it would fall into the category of being Government sponsored.

While in Dar-es-Salaam I was glad to meet again Mr H.S.H. Stanley, who had been First Secretary, Commonwealth Relations, at the British Embassy in Washington. He was now in charge of the United Kingdom High Commissioner's Office in Dar-es-Salaam. At a party given by Mr George Baker, Controller for Tanganyika Information Services, I also came into contact for the first time with EPTA, the United Nations Expanded Programme of Technical Assistance, and UNTAB, the United Nations Technical Assistance Board. Mr John Symonds of the UN office in Geneva was setting up an EPTA office in Tanganyika. Mr Symonds' assistant, Jane Weidlund, sparked my interest in the work of the UN, and I was glad to meet her again in the UN Secretariat building in 1964, when I joined the UN Special Fund.

On the following day I met Mr Oscar Kambona, Tanganyika's Minister of Education, who had returned from London by comet the day before, Saturday,8th July 1961. Mr Kambona felt that the financial difficulties which had been the lot of airlift students generally would not occur in the case of Tanganyikan students, except in rare instances, since in practice virtually every Tanganyikan student who went to the United States was supported either by TANU, the ruling political party, or by the Tanganyikan Government.

This was my last appointment in Tanganyika, and on 19th July I left Dar-es-Salaam for Zanzibar in a tiny plane capable of carrying only four passengers. It was a very short ride, less than half an hour, and the pilot, who was quite visible to the one other passenger and myself, seemed so confident of his bearings that he had the morning newspaper spread comfortably over the controls for the greater part of the flight. I was met by Mr A.A. McGreig, Assistant Director of Education, and accommodated in the English Club in an air-conditioned room.

Zanzibar is an island from the Arabian Nights. The narrow streets, so narrow that there is barely room for two loaded donkeys to pass each other, and the twelve-foot-high brass-studded doors give the place an air of mystery and intrigue. In 1961 the island was troubled though peaceful on the surface. The Sultan toured the city each day in his red Rolls Royce. He was a popular figure. But underneath the surface the place was in a ferment. The party in power was the Zanzibar Nationalist Party, which had thirteen seats, and was predominantly Arab, though supported by some Africans and Indians. The largest party numerically, however, 36,500 out of a poll of 90,000, was the Afro-Shirzai Party, which was almost entirely African. The Zanzibari Pemba Party was also mostly African. There was much envy of the Zanzibari aristocracy who held positions of privilege in the government and society. Zanzibar had been a marshalling ground for the slave trade, and some of the imperious attitudes of those days were still prevalent. Within a few years the country was to be joined with the mainland of Tanganyika to form the independent Republic of Tanzania.

On 12th July I flew to Entebbe in Uganda and went by car to the Imperial Hotel in Kampala, which is about twenty miles north of the airport. The next day I was collected by Dean Bright of Makerere College and Dr Field who was in charge of liaison between the American teachers in the African American Teachers Programme and the respective East African Education Departments. The American teachers were being given courses at Makerere before being posted to East African schools. These courses would cover background information on East Africa, African Education, including the organization of the Education Department and schools, and an East African language. The Director of Education, Uganda, Mr C.R.V. Bell, with whom I had a long discussion, was at pains to point out that there were more facilities for higher Education in East Africa than was generally supposed. He suggested that to offset the tremendous pull of overseas Education there should be a period of such training written into employment training schemes. Thus it might be possible for a student to have two terms at Makerere and one term in Europe or the United States.

To allow me to see as many Ugandan schools as possible, and at the same time something of the country, a tour had been arranged for me, with the Assistant Director of Education (Girls), Miss Buckerfield, as my guide. On our way to Mbarara, some one hundred and twenty miles from Kampala, we passed mile after mile of parched countryside which appeared also to have been deliberately burned in many places. This burning was done by the local people, we were told, in spite of Government regulations forbidding it, in order to catch animals, and in the belief that the burning encouraged new grass for the next season.

After a night at the Ankole Hotel, we visited Ntare School which had an enrolment of three-hundred and fifteen boys, all boarders except five Asians. There was one Asian boarder, the rest were Africans. There were sixty-three in the School Certificate class, thirty-two in the first year of Higher School Certificate and twenty-eight in the second year; seventeen doing Science and two Arts. The swing to science subjects I found interesting, as most of the students from East Africa already in the United States were for the most part Arts students. The staff at Ntare were all graduates with the exception of two Africans. Twelve were expatriates, eleven straight from the UK, and one Fulbright teacher. Two Ntare boys were at that time exchangees under the American Field Service programme.

We now had a weekend ahead of us which we could use to see some of the beauties of the country. We were approaching Queen Elizabeth National Park, and on our way there saw two small herds of elephant, buck and a great variety of wild birds. Mweya Lodge, where we stayed the night, is a hunting and game-watching lodge situated on a promontary which runs into Lake Edward. On Sunday morning we took a boat trip around the lake which was most rewarding. The lake teems with hippo, and its banks abound with the most remarkable bird life. On the edge of the lake birds flocked together in scores and hundreds. One felt surrounded by great beauty. But the water was tainted with bilharzia, and in the evening at the Lodge, myriads of lake flies caused guests and staff alike to turn out all the lights and retire behind mosquito nets.

The next day we proceeded to Fort Portal to stay in a small hotel at the foot of the Ruenzori Mountains. On the way I enjoyed two unforgettable experiences. We passed a lake which was surrounded by a thick skirting of flamingo. The birds were so numerous that the lake appeared to be surrounded by a broad dazzling fringe of pink. The second memorable experience on that day was that we crossed the equator where the equator was marked, so that one could stand with a foot in each hemisphere. I have a photograph somewhere of myself doing just that.

During the next few days I visited a number of Government and Mission institutions. Nyakasura School is a Government boys, senior secondary school dating back to 1926. It had a proud tradition, and was distinctive in that the boys wore a kind of kilt made with khaki material, and scarlet stockings without bottoms, so that they could have bare feet with warm leg coverings. They also wore scarlet sweaters which gave them a very striking appearance. We were taken on a thorough inspection of the school premises, including dormitories, kitchens and workshops for metalwork, carpentry and tailoring.

After lunch we visited Saint Scholastica's Primary Teachers' Training College for women, which had one hundred and fifty students. The students followed a four-year course after "Junior Secondary II". Mother Mary Dominic had been in charge only six months, but impressive progress had been made during that time.

St Leo's College, Virika, which is just outside Fort Portal, had an enrollment of two hundred and thirteen, and a Cambridge School Certificate class of thirty–five. Its principal, Brother David, was an American, and I was therefore very interested to hear his views on School Certificate courses and the suitability of American degrees for teachers teaching in Uganda. He thought the nearest approximation to the Cambridge School Certificate in the United States was the New York Regents Examination, where a student could take six subjects and get the Regents Certificate. In his view the senior secondary schools in Uganda were similar to "preparatory schools" in the United States. In mathematics, which was his subject, he thought that the standard reached in the School Certificate in Uganda was inferior to an average Senior High School standard in the United States. Because of the differences in approach and material both the history teacher and the biology teacher from the US were having difficulty in their first years. African boys tended to do very well in biology, partly because their parents had a knowledge of animals and insects, and partly because there is no necessity for abstraction in biology as there is in physics or mathematics. Father David deplored the fact that many African students suffered because they did not do well enough in their English Language papers. For example in an essay subject a boy might write on "A Fire" when the subject was "Fire", and so be a failure. Perhaps, he thought, a "credit" in English Language should not be a requisite for Higher School Certificate classes or for admission to various other courses of higher Education.

After returning to Kampala I visited Trinity College, a senior secondary girls' school at Nabingo. The Canonesses of St Augustine had just taken over from the White Sisters, and the school was planning to expand from two hundred and thirty-five to four hundred and become a three-stream secondary school. I had the opportunity to address the Senior IV class. They were all enthusiastic about the possibility of going to the United States for higher Education.

Next I visited King's College, Budo, which is perhaps the most famous boys' secondary school in Uganda. There I was handed over by Mr Robinson to two senior boys, Aweri and Amukum. Aweri had a short time before done the one hundred yards dash in 9.4 seconds, and had just been awarded a scholarship to Harvard University. Amukum held the school records for two hundred and four hundred yards, and had represented Uganda at the Olympic

Games in these events. He had been awarded a scholarship to Fisk University in the United States. After lunch with Mr and Mrs Robinson I was given the opportunity to address the whole class of Senior IV, between sixty and seventy students. There were many keen questions regarding the possibilities of higher Education in the United States.

At St Mary's College, Kisubi, I had only a short visit. Brother Marcel, its director, was a Canadian trained in English at the University of Montreal. He was worried about his best students going overseas. He had over a hundred students applying for such Education in various ways, and was inundated with forms of application he was being asked to help fill in. With regard to the PSAT, the Scholastic Aptitude Test which was being administered by the AAI and associated programmes, he said he thought that the African students were very definitely at a disadvantage with regard to these tests, since from his own experience he knew that they did not understand the English in the instructions, and were not accustomed to the rapid filling in of squares in the pages of an answer book.

After a session with Mr Tom Gleave, Acting Director of Education, who was concerned about the political aspects of the numbers of students going overseas and the expectations of his Minister, I paid a visit to the Kampala Technical Institute. The KTI offers a variety of courses in Architectural Draughtsmanship, Building Technology, Carpentry and Joinery, General Clerical Training, Dressmaking, Electrical Installation, Foundry and Pattern Making, Laboratory Technology, Mechanical Technology, Machine-shop Engineering, Motor Vehicle Mechanics, Pottery and Sign-Writing.

At KTI all students, five hundred men and forty women, were boarders. The principal, Mr L.H.S. Eitelberg, told me he had had a good deal of help from UNESCO, and had planned requirements for 1962-1967 based on a manpower survey of the requirements of commerce. Some of the deficiencies were glaring. For example, there was a great need for laboratory technicians, and the Institute could take from two to three hundred of them, but the planned output was only twenty as from 1962.

On my return to Washington I moved from the Windsor Park Hotel into new quarters in the British Embassy on Massachusetts Avenue. The Embassy's new building had recently been completed so that I was allotted a rather handsome office in the Old Chancery, where security was less tight. Ironically the office I was given, I understood, was the one once occupied by Ian McClean, the notorious spy.

As mentioned earlier, in an effort to encourage a community feeling among East African students our office produced a regular newsletter, "The East African Students Bulletin", which was published four times a year, and with the help of the African Governments I set up an emergency fund to assist students with their financial problems when necessary. However, when the office finally closed there were quite a number of debts outstanding, which I had to pass back to the Governments concerned. In a few cases when certain students were very hard pressed for funds I had made personal loans, which when the office closed I had to write off. Two young ladies who were often in my office seeking help were the Kagwa sisters from Uganda. Juanita and Emily were charming, and had the distinction of being the first Ugandan women to qualify and practise in the fields of medicine and dentistry respectively. As the time for independence drew near some students tended to become highly politically motivated, and suggestions were made by a few of them that the purpose of my office was to spy on students rather than to help them. However, most students appreciated our genuine efforts to help them in every possible way.

Soon after my return to the United States I found myself deep in preparations for the celebration of Tanganyika's independence, which was to take place on 9th December 1961. At the same time I began to realize very clearly that my job was a self-liquidating one, which would end as soon as the last East African country under British rule became independent.

Two important events stand out in my memory of this time. The first is the elaborate preparations made by one American college for the celebration of Uganda's independence on 9th October 1962. Glassboro State College in Glassboro, New Jersey, decided to make the celebration of Uganda's independence a project in which the whole college would participate. Students from Uganda, and anyone intimately concerned with its future were invited to a whole --day celebration on the Glassboro College campus, and many of those invited were given hospitality including overnight accommodation. The gathering was addressed by the Ambassador Elect of Uganda, Mr Kironde, who was in the process of opening new offices in New York City, and on the platform was a representative of the Department of State. A highlight of the day was the announcement that John F. Kennedy, President of the United States, had invited the President of the Student Council of the college to travel to Kampala with the State Department delegation, flying in Air Force one. These activities reflected the generally warm feelings across the United States towards the newly born African states.

As my responsibilities regarding East African students were drawing to a close I became particularly concerned with the question of their return to East Africa after their graduation, and the availability of jobs for them there. Tanganyikan and Ugandan students were usually government sponsored, or under some official programme which ensured their return passages home, so it was with the Kenyan students that the greatest problems were foreseen. They were the most numerous, and because many Kenyan students had reached the United States by the airlifts, they had not the means to buy themselves air tickets back to Kenya. There was also the challenge, which a number of students felt, to continue their Education and take a Master's degree or even a PhD rather than go back to an uncertain future.

As, in the Government's view, it was important that Kenya graduates with a first degree should return to Kenya as soon as possible to take the places of expatriates departing on Independence, the Kenya Government decided, with USAID assistance, to send a recruiting team to the United States to meet with Kenyan graduates and those about to graduate, and offer them jobs combined with a free passage home to Kenya. This team comprised three high officials from the Ministry of State for Constitutional Affairs and Administration, the Secretary of the Civil Service Commission, the President of the Nairobi African Chamber of Commerce, the Chief Engineer of the Ministry of Works, the Assistant Secretary, Ministry of Education, and the Assistant Localization Officer of EACSO (East African Common Services Organization). My responsibility was to organize the reception of this team in Washington, DC, and to schedule its interviews with Kenya students in selected centres around the continent. We were able to make known to students what the employment opportunities in Government Service and elsewhere were through the East African Students Bulletin, which, as I mentioned earlier, was published by our office approximately four times a year.

In my meetings with Kenya students I was also able to point out the advantages to them of accepting these offers of employment, as the exodus of the white expatriates from Kenya had left vacancies which had to be filled immediately. If the trained Kenyans in the United States did not return home to fill these vacancies, they would undoubtedly be filled permanently by less qualified Kenyans already in the country.

The successful operation of this recruitment effort was one of the most gratifying aspects of my job. The team travelled widely throughout the United States and Canada during the period 20th May to 20th June, and interviewed one hundred and eighty–two students who wished to be considered for employment in the Kenya Government Service. A second Kenya Guidance Study Team, under USAID sponsorship visited the United States and Canada during the period 12th April to 14th May 1963, and a guidance team jointly for Tanganyika and Uganda, administered by the Institute for International Education under a Ford Foundation grant, made a similar visit during the period 14th May to 22nd,June 1963 to offer employment opportunities to Tanganyikan and Ugandan graduates ready to return to their home countries.

In the summer of 1963 I visited East Africa again and attended a meeting of East African Governments' representatives, held on 20th August 1963 in Nairobi, under the chairmanship of Mr A.T. Adu, Secretary General of EACSO, to discuss the future of the Students' Office in Washington. The meeting hoped that the office could remain as an East African unit, but the representative for Uganda, speaking on behalf of the Uganda Government, informed the meeting that his government had decided to set up a separate students' unit in the new Uganda Mission to the United Nations in New York.

In accordance with this decision, the Uganda student work was transferred to the Uganda Mission to the United Nations on 24th October 1963. From 14th October 1963 until 16th March 1964, I continued to be responsible for the affairs of Kenya, Tanganyika and Zanzibar students, operating from the Washington office, with my title changed from Adviser for East African Students in North America to Adviser for Kenya, Tanganyika and Zanzibar Students in North America.

The signs that my job as a students' adviser was ending were becoming more frequent and obvious towards the end of 1963, and I had been looking for alternative employment. I note from my files that I was in touch with the Department of Technical Cooperation in Britain in January 1964, and that that Department was considering supporting me for an appointment either with UNESCO, or somewhere overseas under their own auspices. I had also applied for a post in Washington in the international student field, but it soon became apparent that my not being a US citizen could possibly be an insuperable obstacle to my being appointed to such a post.

In addition, I applied for the position of president of a private junior college for young women in Washington, the Mount Vernon Seminary, where I had given a talk on Malaya to the students and faculty. After Phyllis and I had met Dr Lloyd, the president, and his wife, Dr Lloyd informed me that he would recommend me to his Board of Trustees as his successor.

At the same time I thought I might make another attempt to seek employment with the United Nations as a second string to my bow. This time I wrote to the office of the Adviser on Education in the Department of Technical Cooperation in London, and in due course I received a letter of introduction to David Owen, Head of the United Nations Technical Assistance Board and Administrator of the Expanded Programme of Technical Assistance (EPTA), who worked in close co-operation with Paul Hoffman, the Administrator of the Special Fund. It was with the Special Fund, I was told, I might be considered for employment.

The United Nation's involvement with technical assistance to the developing world began in 1949 when it established EPTA under a Technical Assistance Board, TAB. EPTA projects were small in size and of short duration. In 1958 the Special Fund was established under the leadership of Paul Hoffman, who already had had a distinguished career as President of the Studebaker Corporation, Administrator of Marshall Aid under President Truman and President of the Ford Foundation. The Special Fund was created to finance technical assistance projects on a larger scale and for a longer duration than those of EPTA, and had an initial budget of 26 million dollars raised by voluntary contributions from Governments. A typical project might have an input from UNDP of about 1 million dollars over a five-year period, with a counterpart contribution of at least as much from the recipient Government.

In due course I received a letter from the chairman of the Board of Trustees of Mount Vernon Seminary informing me that the Board, after careful consideration, had decided not to pursue my candidacy for the post of president of the college. The chairman apparently knew of my application to the UN, for he wished me success in it. Understandably, I felt, the Board would prefer an American citizen for the job. I was in fact amazed from the start that Dr Lloyd had entertained an application from someone who was not a US citizen, though at the time I think I was prepared to become one if the job depended on it.

After my meeting with David Owen I was interviewed by Mr Horst Quednau, chief of the Research and Training Division of the Special Fund, and after various other meetings was accepted in principle as a "Project Officer". There remained the formality of a medical examination. I explained to the UN Director of Medical Services that I had recently had a complete physical examination in Washington carried out by my private doctor. Would the organization, I wondered, accept my doctor's report instead of my undergoing a second complete check-up? The UN agreed. A copy of my doctor's report was duly sent to New York. And therein was my undoing.

The exceptionally thorough physical examination of my Washington doctor had revealed a very small kidney stone, so small that his advice was to leave it alone as it was causing no trouble. A few blood cells in the urine had sparked the further investigation which led to the stone being discovered. However, when this fact was revealed to the UN Director of Medical Services he regretfully informed me that the UN medical standards for admission were extremely high, and that the existence of that kidney stone disallowed me from being recruited. I asked whether I could be accepted if the kidney stone were removed, and was told that I could be as far as medical requirements for acceptance were concerned.

So I asked Mr Quednau whether he would still accept me if I took time out to have the kidney stone removed. He agreed that I could start as soon as possible after the necessary operation. Accordingly I made arrangements to enter the Washington General Hospital. The surgeon, after noting the size of the stone from the X-rays, was quite reluctant to operate, but nevertheless agreed to do so when he knew the job I was seeking depended upon it. The operation took place on 26th March, and on 1st May 1964, rather pale, I reported for duty on the twenty-sixth floor of the UN Secretariat Building in New York City.

United Nations – Special Fund

When I moved to the British Embassy from Choate I had the option of changing my permanent resident visa to a diplomatic one. But bearing in mind the uncertain duration of my employment in Washington, Phyllis and I decided to retain our permanent resident visas. In those days the possibility of someone in my situation becoming an American citizen was regarded simply as an option, as immigration to the United States was on a quota basis and the quota for British subjects tended to be under-utilised.

However, when I became a UN staff member, I found I had to relinquish my permanent resident visa, revert to my British citizenship status and take out a G4 visa, although Phyllis was allowed to retain her permanent resident visa. This proved to be fortunate, because when finally we wished to retire to the United States, the law had changed, and I would not have been able to regain permanent resident visa status without a prohibitive waiting period, but for the fact that my wife was already in possession of that little plastic card. I found I could regain my permanent resident visa by reason of being her husband. By that time being a British subject was far from enough.

My work as a project officer in the Research and Training Division of the Special Fund was very satisfying. Each project officer had been selected for his or her expertise and experience in a certain field. My projects were Education projects in the developing countries worldwide. Typically a request for assistance would be received from the government of a developing country asking for help with Educational planning, teacher training at the primary or secondary level, or vocational training. A summary of the request would be made which would be circulated to all agencies concerned asking for their comments. In the case of Education projects the comments of UNESCO would particularly be sought. There might follow a mission to the country concerned comprising a UNESCO member and a UNSF staff member, which, in consultation with the government, would prepare a proposal. This proposal would be finalized in the form of a "project document", committing the Special Fund to an input of international funds, typically of about $1 million over a five-year period, and a government counterpart contribution of an equal amount or more in cash or kind. UNESCO would undertake to execute the project by recruiting experts, training national counterparts to the experts through fellowships, supplying equipment and supervising the project's implementation.

In 1965 the Special Fund and EPTA merged to form the United Nations Development Programme, UNDP. In 1968 a "Capacity Study" was undertaken with a view to making the organization more suited to its larger scope, and by 1972 the merging was complete. As a result of this study the focus moved from headquarters to the field. "Country Programmes" of five years duration were set up, basically through consultation between the Governments and the Resident Representatives of the UNDP in the field assisted by the specialized agencies, and an "Indicative Planning Figure" or IPF for each developing country was determined. The IPF was the amount a developing country could expect to be allocated over a five-year period for planning purposes and was based in large part on the figure of earlier assistance, per capita income, and population. At the same time project officers at UNDP headquarters became "Area Officers," backstopping the programmes of one or more countries in a region, or in certain cases "Technical Advisers" to the four new bureaux for Africa, Europe and the Middle East, Asia and the Pacific, and Latin America.

During the four years 1964–1968 that I was a project officer in the Training Division of the Special Fund I went on missions to Rwanda and Burundi in 1965, Cameroon and Sierra Leone in 1966, Nigeria in 1967, and Ivory Coast in 1968, in each case with at least one UNESCO staff member, to help governments prepare requests for projects in the field of Education.

In 1968, I was appointed Chief of the Human Resources Programme in the Programme Division of the Bureau of Operations and Programming and, in 1971, when the Capacity Study began to take its full effect, I became a Senior Technical Adviser for Education and Training in the Bureau for Programme Policy and Coordination. In this capacity I went to Mali in 1969 and 1972, Jordan in 1970, Papua/New Guinea in 1971, and to Morocco, Lesotho, Botswana and Swaziland, Tanzania, Zambia and Guinea in 1972.

Phyllis and I lived for eight years in Manhattan in an apartment on East 62nd Street overlooking the East River. I walked the fourteen short blocks to the UN every day, and sometimes home again. But a bus ran north on 1st Avenue, so I would sometimes take a bus home. I think we adapted quite well to the change from Washington. We learned how to enjoy New York City. We loved visiting the Metropolitan Museum of Art, walking down 5th Avenue and through Central Park, and on Sundays taking early morning communion at St Thomas's on 5th Avenue followed by breakfast at Clark's coffee shop. We also enjoyed a French meal on West 65th Street occasionally, or a wander through Bloomingdale's. Phyllis became a very active member of the U.N. Women's Guild, and was for a time in charge of the preparation and sales of the UN Calendar Towel, the proceeds from which went to help needy children around the world. (We were happy to propose and have accepted a recommendation for a grant to Swami Satyananda's Pure Life Society home for orphaned children in Petaling Jaya which we had visited with General Templer). Carolyn had graduated from Earlham College in Richmond, Indiana, in 1969, so we did not see much of her in New York. She married her College sweetheart, Philip Lynes, on 15th March in that year, and we were

231

delighted to attend the wedding ceremony in the College Meeting House in Earlham.

Phil taught mathematics to start with, and Carolyn took a Master's degree in Education at Boston University. For a time she was secretary to the President of Swarthmore College, and then worked in the Dean's Office of Harvard University. They rented apartments in various localities, first in Pennsylvania, but afterwards in Massachusetts – Reading, Natick, Newton, Watertown. Eventually frustrated by his students' lack of interest in mathematics Phil moved over to work in computers, first with Hendricks in Manchester, New Hampshire, then with Key Data in Watertown, Massachusetts, and finally with Prime Computer in Natick, Massachusetts. After hesitating about a family – they had considered adopting a child, being concerned with over-population around the world and the orphans from Vietnam – they started one of their own with Megan Lara, born in March 1977. We were delighted.

The day to day work of the Special Fund/UNDP during my time, until the Capacity Study took its full effect, was controlled by Myer Cohen and Paul Marc Henry. Paul Hoffman, the Administrator, was a father figure, immensely respected, but because of his age he no longer concerned himself with the day to day work of the Programme. Myer Cohen, Assistant Administrator and Director of the Bureau of Operations and Programming, was the policy planner and business manager of the organization, while the details of the Programme and individual projects were in general left to Paul Marc Henry, who had a truly remarkable grasp of the details of each project. Together these two ran a most efficient and effective operation in a happy, family-like atmosphere. Each letter from a project officer would be cleared by his division chief and submitted to Myer Cohen for his signature, so that a huge pile of files would accumulate on his desk to be signed by the end of each day. The signed letters would duly catch one or other of the various pouches going out to the field or the Agencies.

Being a Senior Technical Adviser whose advice might or might not be sought by the Bureaux was a far less satisfying job than being Chief of the Human Resources Programme, so in 1972 I was actively seeking a posting to the field. After a number of possibilities had been discussed it was decided that I should be posted to Laos as UNDP Resident Representative. This was a small country, one of the least developed, and politically unstable, but we were very happy to be going there.

Laos

We first arrived in Vientiane on 4th August 1972, having travelled up from Bangkok in a small Thai Airways plane. A delegation of rather nervous faces met us as we stepped down from the aircraft. Formal introductions to Laos government officials and UN personnel were made. Phyllis received a bouquet of red roses from the fiancee of the Deputy Resident Representative, and we moved off to the VIP lounge where thirty or so people were waiting. More introductions took place, and I made a little speech in French thanking everyone for their welcome. The Resident Representative's black Mercedes was ready with its blue UN flag flying. The two back doors were opened by white-clad chauffeurs, and we were in and on our way. Fifteen minutes later we arrived at the Lang Xang Hotel – a modest establishment of tropical character, different from those of our early days only in that all the rooms were air-conditioned (each with its own air-conditioner). The lobbies, corridors and entrance hall, however, were not.

We did not find the hotel food much to our liking, and soon learned that most of the experts, through the UN office, ordered a broad cross-section of foodstuffs and liquor from Oesterman's, a firm in Denmark. Even sugar was brought from afar, because the Government permitted only one kind and quality to be produced, a coarse grey kind which clinked in the bottom of the cup and took a long time to dissolve. It was, however, really sweet. We liked neither the local tea nor the coffee. The tea was an Eastern variety with a cardboardy, scenty flavour. The coffee had a reasonable taste but we found its smell unpleasant.

As soon as possible after our arrival, in accordance with protocol, we made a series of courtesy calls to various ministries and embassies. I had to go alone to call on the ambassadors wives. Only in two cases did we go together to call on an ambassador and his wife. We did this with respect to the UK and Thailand. Ambassador Lloyd and his wife (UK) were most charming and popular. They had a cocktail party on the 10th at the embassy, just for the "Brits", prior to their departure on home leave for two months. There were about fifty people at their drinks party. It seemed to us rather a lot of "Brits" for such a small place as Vientiane. Everyone was very friendly, and among the guests were some ex-Malayans – one, named Whitbread, had even been a master at MCKK.

We also had a very pleasant session with Mr and Mrs Nimad (Thailand). The Thai Embassy was almost next door to the UNDP office, so we solemnly drove out of our drive into theirs to arrive on the second of the appointed time. They were charming, delighted that we spoke English because their French was not strong, and expressed a love for London which included a warm acquaintance with Harrods and Marks and Spencer's. Mrs Nimad liked Soho best, however, for there she had found a restaurant which offered "Peking Duck". She had wanted to take a sample of this delicacy back with her to Brussels when they were living there, but her husband had dissuaded her.

Phyllis's star turn I think was a visit to Mrs Leum Rajasombat, wife of the Secretary General of the Ministry of Foreign Affairs, who had spent six years in Paris as Laos's Ambassador to France. She, poor woman, had been too busy having children to learn French (she had ten), so Phyllis and she enjoyed a conversation in pantomime. Mrs Rajasombat was completely uninhibited, and the "conversation" had been so free that Phyllis had come home looking like the cat that had swallowed the canary.

I imagine that a repeat performance of this kind took place when Phyllis called on the wife of the Ambassador of South Vietnam, Hoang Co Thuy, whose language abilities were similar to those of

Mrs Rajasombat. I found him a charmer. He said to me in excellent French: "We in the Diplomatic Corps are on very friendly terms, you know. You must call me Thuy. What's your first name, and the name of your wife?" He invited us to a dinner party to meet the Foreign Minister of South Vietnam, and I said we would be delighted to come provided I could find my tuxedo trousers in the luggage that had so far arrived. We agreed that we had got down to "affairs of state" very quickly.

The week culminated with my calling on the Prime Minister, Prince Souvanna Phouma, at 10am on Saturday, 12th August, at his residence. My driver, Vi Van Ngau, a Thai Dam, had very little French and less English, but fortunately an excellent sense of timing. We liked each other. He was duly at the hotel with the Mercedes at 9:45am in his best clothes. We looked each other over, and he pointed out with a solicitous finger that I had cut my chin while I was shaving and had better wipe off that little spot of blood. Then he unfurled the UN flag on the mudguard above the right headlight, put on his driver's cap, and we were off. I was to learn afterwards that Ngau's punctuality was superb. As I mentioned earlier he reckoned to swing into a driveway as the second hand of his watch swept over the appointed hour. His Highness, ("Altesse" in French) was just a trifle aloof, which was not surprising when one considered the problems he was facing. He was seventy-one, although he looked younger. He conceded that he would like to retire. But he was now a father figure, like Kenyatta of Kenya, and his continued presence in public affairs helped the country maintain an uneasy political stalemate. After three not very successful attempts to form coalition governments with rival Laotian factions Prince Souvanna Phouma died on 10th January, 1984, at the age of eighty-two, in his villa on the Mekong River. He had been bedridden for some years.

In September 1972 we were happy to accept an invitation to participate in the inaugural flight of Royal Air Lao from Vientiane to Chengmai as guests of the Government of Laos. Chengmai is the second largest city in Thailand, up in the north, and is a most fascinating place. Even though it is the second largest city, it is tiny compared with Bangkok, having only 120,000 inhabitants. But what we found especially fascinating was that it is a centre for traditional Thai handicrafts: Thai silk and cotton weaving, wood carving, silverware, lacquerware and pottery. There was even a village, just outside Chengmai itself, devoted entirely to the making of umbrellas, the kind made with waterproofed paper and bamboo – the "payong" we knew so well in Malaya. But in the Chengmai village the umbrellas were all beautifully painted and decorated. Each family seemed to produce its own particular kind. Under one house made of wood,men and women were working together making large umbrellas five to six feet across for use in a garden or perhaps for a produce stall. We bought one beautifully painted with a dragon-headed long rowing boat, and had quite a time getting it back to the aircraft along with three more ordinary small ones bought as presents. The plane left Vientiane on a Thursday afternoon, and returned on the following Saturday afternoon. Before landing we had to circle a little to allow an Aeroflot plane to come in from Hanoi. It was supposed to be bringing in US prisoners of war, but in fact did not, and no prisoners ever came.

Our plane was an Electra turbo-prop, one of three bought second-hand by the Lao government with the assistance of American entrepreneurs. The hope was that the new run to Chengmai might prove to be a financial success. But this was a forlorn hope, because not many Thais were likely to wish to visit Vientiane, while those who could afford to make the trip from Laos were few indeed. Chengmai was prosperous compared with Vientiane. In some of the shops there one could buy all the provisions one could need. Phyllis in fact found some face powder of the kind and shade she liked.

By and large we found Chengmai a carefree place compared with Vientiane. We felt surrounded by bustle and smiles. We visited a Buddhist temple three thousand feet up a mountain, climbing hundreds of steps, and afterwards, on the summit, admired the summer palace of the King, who had entertained Queen Elizabeth II there in the February of that year. Chengmai also has a famous university, whose campus we drove around. At this point we lost Mr and Mrs Nimad, because they peeled off from the party to visit their son who was an undergraduate there.

Royal Air Lao had a rather checkered history. During the time we were in Laos the three Electras were reduced to one by a process of cannibalization. However, the Electra was a solid, reliable plane, and the American pilots and maintenance personnel were excellent, so we never felt unsafe when flying in one. This was not always the case when we were flying up-country over mountainous terrain to Luang Prabang in one or another of the company's ancient DC3s. Nevertheless we felt grateful to Royal Air Lao for its promotional generosity. We took advantage of a five–day excursion to Hong Kong from 13th to 17th December, as well as the free trip to Chengmai, and came back with two beautiful rugs, a Bokhara twelve feet by nine feet, and a Sarouk six feet by four and a half feet, which looked extremely well on our polished teak floors.

October 24th is United Nations Day. This does not mean much in the United States, but in Third World countries it is considered important. In Laos the Government's Department of Information, with the assistance of our office, provided materials about the UN and its activities. On the day itself, as the chief representative of the UN family in Laos, I was escorted by a posse of police on motorcycles to the banquet hall of the Lang Xang Hotel, where I inspected a guard of honour, and then read the UN Secretary General's message in French to a gathering of high government officials and the Diplomatic Corps. In the afternoon there was a tennis tournament for which the UNDP office had provided a number of silver trophies, and in the evening Phyllis and I put on a party in our house and garden for three hundred people.

All this went off smoothly on Tuesday, 24th October 1972, but beneath a calm exterior we were greatly perturbed. On the morning of Saturday, 21st October one of our experts had been found naked and dead on the floor of his bathroom together with the nude body of his girlfriend. The weekend and a public holiday on the Monday made any postponement of UN Day difficult, so we decided to proceed with the arrangements we had made. I am glad that we did this, because although foul play was at first thought to be a possibility, the autopsy I insisted on indicated that the probable cause of death was carbon-monoxide poisoning from the gas water-heater. The verdict accordingly was accidental death.

On Monday, 12th February 1973 we of the Diplomatic Corps and our wives received an invitation to visit the royal palace at Vat Phou for Friday and Saturday, 16th and 17th February, to witness the Fete of Vat Phou. The invitation was from Boun Oum, Prince of Champassak. In the 1700s the Prince of Champassak was one of three kings, the other two being the King of Vientiane and the King of Luang Prabang. In 1973 the King of the ancient capital of Luang Prabang, Srisavong Vathana, was the King of the whole of Laos, but in the south Boun Oum, half-brother to King Srisavong Vathana, ruled like a feudal baron. Two other brothers of the same family were Prince Souvanna Phouma, the Prime Minister, and Prince Souphanouvong, a leader of the Pathet Lao, known as the Red Prince.

We were taken to Champasak by military plane and we sat on benches in the aircraft without seatbelts. The planes were not pressurized or air-conditioned, so we were very cold during the two-hour flight. Then we landed in hundred-degree Fahrenheit heat, and had to stand under the wing of the aircraft to shelter from the sun until an assortment of cars came out to meet us. We were accommodated in barrack-like buildings, and we made up our own beds with bedding we had been asked to bring with us. These rather primitive travelling conditions, however, were thoroughly compensated for by the lavish hospitality of our host. We fed buffet – style from long tables laden with light soup, the Lao glutinous rice in baskets, fish, poultry, meats and fruits. Then we visited a market of locally made goods, silk and cotton weaving, and coarse pottery. There was boat racing on a lake, and acrobats performing on its banks. Elephants carried the guests to and from the wat, which was almost half a mile from the upper end of the lake at the foot of a range of mountains. Though smaller than Angkor Wat this wat was similar in shape and design, and possibly of equal antiquity. Rumour had it that there had been human sacrifices there in the distant past. I mounted the elephant I was to ride on from a special platform raised to the height of its back. I had to remove my shoes, then step onto a seat in the howdah. It was not exactly a comfortable ride. But the elephant moved so slowly that one could accommodate easily to the lurchings of the howdah. There were also tug-of-war matches between elephants, and one between an elephant and a large number of men. Some of the elephants appeared to enjoy their turn at this, but one, when losing against the men, got angry and chased his opponents so that they scattered at top speed.

In March 1973 there was a regional meeting of UNDP Resident Representatives in Bangkok, and Phyllis and I spent a week there at the Erewan Hotel. During that time Phyllis had an opportunity to top up her wardrobe. There was a dressmaker named Sunee Vichitrananda, manager of the Liat Export Company, right near the hotel, and Phyllis found that the careful fitting that she obtained there was quite the best she had had anywhere ever.

My day usually began with a quick dip in the hotel pool at about 6:45am. Air-conditioned buses took us to the conference hall in the ECAFE building each morning, and back again for lunch, the operation being repeated in the afternoon. The traffic in Bangkok is appalling, so that each journey took about half an hour. We had a long agenda and covered much ground, but the most useful part of the conference in my view was meeting the more than twenty Resident Representatives of the region, and the regional representatives of the Specialized Agencies, and getting to know their views.

Back in Vientiane, Phyllis had been active trying to help the wives of the local UN staff control the size of their families. It all began with Pha, who heard that Carolyn had not started a family after four years of marriage, and asked how she could avoid having a fifth child. Phyllis took Pha to the Family Welfare Office, and as a result Pha's family was thereafter limited. Pha, a highly intelligent and courageous woman, did not hesitate to spread the word among the local UN staff wives who came to seek her advice.

This was a bad time of year for water. No water at all came through our pipes during the month of March, and if we had not paid a year's rent in advance, we would have been looking for another house. Even when water was running through the pipes it was often stopped by the electric pump failing, so we used a system which activated a different electric pump outside the house every time a tap was turned on. Because of this uncertainty of supply, water was delivered daily by truck to tanks at the back of the house. Unfortunately the truck often failed to appear at weekends and we were sorely tried.

One morning before 8 o'clock I was driving the Peugeot to the office as usual when I was hit by a motor-cyclist turning into the office driveway. Vehicular traffic in Vientiane was extremely heavy and chaotic in the early morning, and the movements of motor-cyclists were especially unpredictable. The driver leapt clear, but his pillion rider struck his head on the side of the car and was knocked unconscious. As we were so near the office I was able to get help immediately, and I took the unconscious soldier to the hospital in my car. Unhappily the young man never regained consciousness. I was badly shaken and upset by this incident, and stopped driving myself for a time. I realized that technically I was in the wrong, because I was turning into the driveway against the flow of traffic, but I was blocking a long line of cars behind me, and at that moment there seemed a reasonable space for me to turn in. Although the motorcycle had defective brakes, and the young man wore only a beret, it was assumed from the start that my insurance company would pay compensation to the family of the deceased, as Lao drivers rarely if ever carry any insurance. The claim was accepted by my UN insurance company without hesitation.

In a letter to Carolyn and Phil at this time Phyllis wrote: "This accident to a Lao national in a country where Dooze is the UN representative is especially horrifying." I felt the truth of this. Yet I was amazed at the calm acceptance of the fact of the accident by the family of the victim, and by the Lao community in general. This was a Buddhist society in which acceptance of death seemed as easy as acceptance of life. Instead of flowers for a funeral, Lao mourners present large intricate paper decorations which are placed on the funeral pyre. I bought mine at a shop in Vientiane which specialized in them, and took it to the house of the soldier's parents. They in turn showed their sadness, but I saw no hint of animosity or bitterness in their faces. I felt humbled by their passivity. Later there was the material reckoning. Representatives of the family were paid the insurance money in cash in the presence of a high government official. The money, in Kip notes of medium denomination, filled a large box-type briefcase.

We had planned only one night in Bangkok, and then to fly to Penang. Our journey to Penang, however, was not quite direct. After about two hours of flight we came down at the small airport of Hai Yai, a popular Thai seaside resort, where we waited for a couple of hours before resuming our flight on another small Thai Airways plane. In a very short time we dropped into Penang airport. At the customs counter I had some slight trouble opening my suitcase. Suddenly the Malay customs officer said "Aren't you Mr Luke, my old headmaster"? I agreed I might be, and was quickly ushered through the remaining formalities. Speaking Malay we soon made friends with our Malay taxi–driver, and before long we even tried a bar or two together of the well-known Malayan love song, "Rasa Sayang ee, rasa sayang sayang ee ...", which all Malay school children know. It was, we thought, an auspicious beginning to our return to Malaya.

When we had first made our plans, we thought we would stay a short time in Penang, then drive down to Taiping and Kuala Kangsar in Perak, and afterwards spend some time up in the Cameron Highlands. But when we sought out the Lone Pines Hotel which we remembered from our Malayan days more than thirty years earlier, we decided we would return to it after visiting our haunts in Perak. On someone's recommendation we had checked in first at the Palm Beach Hotel which is two plots nearer Penang than the Lone Pine. One night there was enough, however, for we rediscovered the stretch of grass and sand between the chalets and the sea punctuated by casuarinas, which, unique to the Lone Pine, captivated us when we first learned to love Penang. We decided we would savour this place to the full rather than spend time travelling to the highlands.

The Lone Pine hotel is at Batu Ferringi, some fifteen miles along the coast from the capital Georgetown so we rented a car to see the shops. We found Boon Hak's store, our old favourite for objets d'art of quality, closed. It stood on the same site as before opposite the shell of Whiteaway Laidlaw's, also closed. This was a little sad. But we called through to the towkay, and he opened up for us. Poor old Heng Hang Kwang had retired after a heart attack, and no longer conducted any business. The Government had made life too difficult, he said. All Chinese objets d'art had to be purchased through the Government. So with all his children well-educated and well-placed (one of his grandchildren was secretary to a Member of Parliament in London), he had given up. He remembered us, though, and the Tods, and a dozen or so other old customers.

We then went to the E&O Hotel and arranged to stay a night there for old times' sake. The lawn by the sea with its low wall and ancient cannon was just as I remembered it when I arrived back from England on the "Ulysses" in August 1941, and Phyllis was there to meet me – the only non-official on the quay. We changed some money at the Chartered Bank, bought some langsats just outside (a kati for forty cents), and drove back to the Lone Pine. After watching some Indian fishermen drag their catch of tiny fish up onto the beach, where their net was immediately surrounded by a group of small Indian boys squatting on their haunches, we stayed to see a reddening sun drop into the sea. Later we dined under the casuarinas by candlelight, fanned by a gentle sea breeze, savouring the "Captain's Curry" with a bottle of wine between us.

On Tuesday morning, 17th July, we rented a small car – a Toyota – and set out on our own sentimental journey. The ferry from Penang to Butterworth was well-organized and efficient, and soon we were on the mainland and driving south. For some time we saw many changes – factories and houses where before the country and hills were covered with jungle. But by the time we entered the State of Perak the changes were less obvious. The plantations of rubber and oil palm were still there, and the bright green padi fields with the jungle-covered hills in the background. Bordering the road were the waterways filled with lotus lilies and water hyacinths. Malays were using the same kind of nets that we remembered for fishing in that water – nets spread out on a framework and strung up on a long pole; plank bridges were still the only way to reach the stilted houses set back from the road.

Soon we became aware that this was a season of ripe fruit. There were durians in large piles along the road, and rambutans, jackfruit and langsat in profusion. We could not remember seeing so much fruit for sale by the roadside in all our years in Malaya. After about two hours of leisurely driving we arrived in Taiping. The new rest house (rumah rehat), in which Phyllis had booked us a room, was in a beautiful position in the Lake Gardens on the site of the former Residency. Some of the pillars of the old building had been retained in the garden, which gave it an air of special distinction. The Lake Gardens were as lovely as ever, and at night, as a backdrop, there were the lights of the cottages on the top of Maxwell's Hill, some three thousand feet up.

We had not told anyone that we were coming to Taiping, and we therefore expected to renew old memories just by ourselves. We looked in at the New Club, now the Taiping Club. There were the portraits of its presidents hanging on the wall, most of them known to us, but most of them no more. I had a pleasant chat with the old Malay barman behind the counter, and Phyllis spoke with two young Indian women playing badminton in a part of the ballroom, the ballroom where I had first met her, surrounded by young Dogra officers, when we saw the New Year in in 1939. The Indian young women were teachers working in one of the schools. We then went to the Shanghai Furniture Store to enquire after our old friend Towkay Num Seng, who used to make furniture for both the College and Clifford School. We did so with some diffidence for we had already discovered that our old friend Towkay Taik Ho, owner of the best-known general store in town, was dead. When we were last in Taiping, Towkay Num Seng was sixty-two. He had told us he had cancer of the liver, and that since Western doctors had given him no hope he had turned to acupuncture. To our delight he appeared smiling and energetic, and absolutely delighted to see us. He asked after Carolyn by name, and we spent a happy evening eating Chinese food with him and his son in a nearby restaurant. His son of course had been educated in Phyllis's school – the King Edward VII School, Taiping. This was a happy reunion.

We returned to the rest house to find a very large Sikh gentleman awaiting us. We soon recognized him as a former King Edward VII School master, Chancell Singh. It appeared that one of the girls we had spoken with at the club had gone home and said she had met two Americans, and they had said this and that. Her father, Chancell Singh, immediately replied, "They were no Americans. They are Phyllis Sharpington and Kenneth Luke," and he chased around until he found us. That was only the beginning. Soon the telephone began to ring, and several of Phyllis's students – now in their fifties – spoke to her. Five or six of them came to see her before we set off for Kuala Kangsar early the next morning.

Kuala Kangsar was even better – beautiful and rewarding. We stayed in a new rest house on the site of the old ADO's house, where Tom Hart and his wife used to live, just by the little cemetery on the hill. The view from our balcony over the Perak river was just as we remembered it–magnificent. And the price of our room, $6 Malayan or US $3, was in striking contrast with that of the E&O room they first offered us in Penang, which was $54 Malayan. We had settled for the cheapest in the end, which was still a large room in the annex overlooking the sea, at $35 Malayan a night.

KK had changed very little, and we were soon on a network of old friends – the Partridges being the connecting link. Joe Partridge was the only retired member of the MCKK staff living in the immediate neighbourhood, partly because Mrs Partridge, a Chinese, had become headmistress of the Methodist Girls, School, which now occupied the King's Pavilion. I had written to the Headmaster MCKK, who was at the time Che Nordin, but otherwise we had made no overtures. From the point of view of personnel the College had changed entirely. We did not know any member of the current teaching staff, and because the College has always been a Federal institution there were no old boys living locally. However, the Tamil gardeners of our time came out to greet us and we were very glad to see them. Singgaram, Phyllis's gardener, we learned, had died in 1963. No-one seemed to know what had happened to dear old Letchumanan at the King's Pavilion.

Phyllis and I dined at high table with the Headmaster. and his wife, and I had the fun of addressing the boys, telling them about the past in a way which seemed to amuse them. They were astonished to know that the huge rain-tree by the corner of the main building had been one on which Mr Bazell had hung his coat when he first arrived in Kuala Kangsar in 1922. I also noted with some pride that the row of tembusu trees which I had planted to provide shade for spectators alongside the playing field were now thirty to forty feet high.

As far as personal contacts were concerned our visit to Clifford School was much more successful. Although only one member of the staff of our time (1946-1948), Mr Soh Kai Jan, was still there, by chance the school prize-giving and speech-day was the day following our arrival, so we stayed on at the invitation of the headmaster, Mr Goh Kee Meng. Two prominent old boys were on the platform – Datok Haji Hamdan bin Sheik Tahir, then in his eighth year as Director of Education (Che Hamdan and his wife had visited us in Washington when we lived there – he is now (1994) Vice-Chancellor of the Universiti Sains in Penang), and Tun Jamil Rais, who had just returned to Malaysia after being Ambassador in London. He had been State Secretary of Selangor when I was Chief Education Officer there. They all said friendly things about us in their speeches, and then in a surprise presentation I was given a picture by a local artist in appreciation of past services. It was all rather touching, and more so when we met many friends in the audience afterwards. I was particularly happy to meet some old soccer player colleagues among the locals. We used to play together for the KK Sporting Union. Big stuff!

Karam Singh, who had been headmaster until a short time before our visit, was not there. We understood he was sick. We had a phone call, from Ipoh, from Bhagwan Singh, who had taught in the primary department, and a visit at the rest house from Isa the driver. A session at the KK.Hospital was extremely pleasant. All sorts of old boys (MC and CS), hospital attendants and paramedics, seemed to appear from nowhere. One of the doctors there was the son of Fateh Singh, at whose house we met all his family, and had "breakfast" – curry and chapatis – at his insistence. Unfortunately, we had to leave early for Penang the following day because we had a dinner appointment with a friend who was teaching at the Universiti Sains there.

Dear Fateh Singh, he had a struggle qualifying as a teacher, but the quality of his character was never in doubt. I remember particularly an end-of-year concert at CSKK.which was attended by Major

Scott, a rather bristly former headmaster of the school, and his wife. A young Eurasian boy was belting out the song "Don't fence me in", accompanying himself on his guitar when the lights went out. The electricity did not return at all that night, but Fateh Singh went down to the town, and returned in due course with a clutch of hurricane lamps which saved the evening from disaster. Now in 1973 he had four sons who were doctors, and a fifth who was a dentist. When Phyllis told Pha about Fateh Singh and his family on our return to Vientiane, she said: "What good parents they must have been. They started with only themselves!"

While we were in Laos Phyllis and I wrote three "round - robin" letters for our friends in different parts of the world which covered in brief the non-professional aspects of our stay there. They seem to capture the flavour of the country, so I include them here.

Started by Phyllis

We arrived in Vientiane early in August 1972 during the wet season and went to live in the Lane Zang Hotel, a less than mediocre establishment by world standards, but the best the town has to offer. The wide Mekong River flows in front of it, and at the time of our arrival was high and wide. Flooding was anticipated. However, the water receded steadily until now the river is half as wide as it was then.

After two months in the hotel we were fortunate to obtain a suitable, if rather large house in Sisangvone, which is ten minutes by car from the town centre. It is a little more than one year old, of rectangular concrete construction, with inside rooms of good size and shape and with excellent fittings, all the woodwork being of local teak. Two young people appeared on our first day seeking work, and as they were recommended by the previous Resident Representative we took them on. One was Ehah pronounced Fah, an intelligent twenty-six-year-old Tahi Dam woman. All of her childhood was spent nomadically, moving from place to place with her family, so she had no opportunity for schooling until she was nearly through her teens when her group became permanent residents of Vientiane. Here she obtained some English lessons in the Lao American School and began working as a servant in English-speaking homes. For us she cleans the house and does the laundry, but her great value is that she has a little English, much Thai and Lao and some Vietnamese. Her English is only basic. How could it be otherwise? But at least it enables us to get some things done, for as you will appreciate the house is now a veritable Tower of Babel. The young gardener who came on the same day is also Thai Dam and his family arrived in Vientiane with Fah's. Heung is eighteen, and he was full of joy and energy until last Sunday when his only possession, an old bicycle, was stolen! He does the outside work, cutting grass, watering in the dry season and caring for plants and trees. To my surprise we have roses of good quality enough for keeping the dining table decorated, but the plant life is mainly tropical; palms, rubber trees, franzipanni, bougainvillea, alamanda, hibiscus and gardenia. Heung looks after them all, and keeps the roads and the outside grass verges and surface-water drains tidy. The house is on a corner, so we have roads on two sides; earth roads, mud in the wet season, dust in the dry. To keep the dust down Heung waters them at least once a day, sometimes twice.

On the third side and close, in fact with only our banana and papaya trees between us, is the house of an Air America pilot and his family. They have a swimming pool and all modern electric appliances, also full-time military guards equipped with walkie-talkies. On the fourth side and just as close, is a Lao village of ten wooden and plaited-leaf, stilt houses. In it there are many small brown-skinned children, some naked, some wearing one garment, a shirt or pants, seldom both.

At night there are twenty or so neat, brown cows in the village (they are out during the day) and at all times dogs, chickens, ducks, geese, turkeys and cats. For these people day begins shortly before dawn, when the cocks are crowing vociferously and ends with the setting of the sun. Sometimes at night the light of a candle or of a minute oil lamp can be seen. Occasionally melancholy bamboo pipe-music can be heard over the barking of a dog, but for the most part there is silence and darkness. They sleep on plaited rush mats on the wooden floors, and in the cool season use cotton quilts as coverings. For meals the family sits in a circle on the floor with the glutinous rice and vegetable in the centre; each member has a piece of banana leaf for a plate, and fingers are used in place of cutlery. After eating, fingers are washed and water drunk. The cooking is done on an open wood fire and at most two pots are used.

Across the road is Sisangvone Pagoda, a tall thin building surrounded by a bare earth compound and enclosed by clumps of bamboos. Here live a number of Buddhist priests all clad in orange robes and with shaven heads. I can see them through the bamboo tree trunks performing their rites and doing chores. A deep gong is struck to call them to prayer and sometimes we are awakened by it during the night. The fires seem to be kept alight at all times and when it is dark they glow prettily among the trees. The passing pageantry of our roads is of interest to us. Hawkers of bread, sections of papaya, sugarcane and pineapple go by frequently as do communal taxis, the only kind of public transport there is in the town. Children riding bareback gallop by on ponies, and most mornings around 7 o'clock an enormous horned grey water buffalo trots purposefully towards our flowering potato-creeper hedge hoping to demolish it for his breakfast. If Heung is already here he goes outside and tells the buffalo he cannot do so. If not I rush across the garden and make a big noise inside the fence, and so far he has retreated peacefully. I would not get near those horns.

I believe I am not exaggerating when I say that life is a little more dangerous here than in some places. Lights are kept on all night on the gates and in the porches. Moreover we have a guard on duty from 7pm-6am. He is an Indian, by the name of Abu Bakar and he comes from a small village near Madras. There is no work for him there, and he comes all this way and leads a solitary existence in order to be able to send back to India enough money to keep his mother, his wife and three children alive. He goes to visit them every few years when he has saved enough to buy the cheapest possible passage.

After a time the house and garden were being well-cared for, but we had no cook and I had realized that it was important to have one. I cannot work in the kitchen in this temperature, and much entertaining is expected of us. We had already been wined and dined lavishly by the French, US, British and Vietnamese ambassadors and others and some of the meals had been of high quality. How did they do it? The food served in the hotel we had not found to our liking: the fresh food I had seen in the market had been of poor quality. There is no fresh milk here, all drinking water has to be boiled and filtered, sugar is coarse and grey, coffee is distasteful and tea often unobtainable. We had begun negotiations to import from Denmark and then good fortune came our way again. A French-speaking Vietnamese, having, I am sure, carefully made enquiries as to K's and my temperaments, called by appointment and proposed with dignity and assurance that he should cook for us. He told us he could make all French dishes, some English, Vietnamese and Chinese, that meals for large numbers were within his capacity, and that by large numbers he meant a hundred or two. We accepted and he has been with us now since mid-October, during which time we have had luncheon and dinner parties and a buffet dinner for thirty. The food is very good. Mr Lak's eyes glow with pride as he produces soups, roasts, pies, cakes, crepes, charcoal grill, quenelles, quiche lorraine, anything I can think of and much that he suggests. Even when we are alone he writes a French menu for lunch and dinner! His story is that as a young man he worked in the residence of the Governor of Laos in the days when this country was a part of French Indo-China. One of the French officials took him and his wife and children back to Paris. There he worked with that family for fifteen years obtaining a Cordon Bleu along the way. Then World War II began and Mr Lak returned to Vientiane. You must be thinking that he must be old and he is, looking like a tiny frail bird, so we are just hoping that his health and strength will continue indefinitely.

Continued by Kenneth

Laos itself I think is a fascinating country – exciting in many ways. Certainly frustrating and unpredictable, often incomprehensible and almost incredible. Like Vietnam and Cambodia it has now lived with war for many years, but the easy-going people of Vientiane seem largely unperturbed by the fact that their country is bankrupt and that the so-called tripartite government under Prince Souvanna Phouma rules no more than an eighth of the country in area, and about one third in population. The Pathet Lao forces control vast areas of the countryside, and journeys to anywhere outside Vientiane beyond ten to twenty kilometres have to be made by plane. To travel by air is in fact the only way to reach the ancient capital of Luang Prabang, where King Savang Vatthana usually lives, and the other two main towns of Savannakhet and Pakse. Any journey on the ground outside the environs of Vientiane can only be made after a careful security check.

In Vientiane itself there is a Pathet Lao headquarters occupied by a delegation and a few soldiers in uniform. Their presence is justified by the fact that the Pathet Lao in principle have a share in the government, although they have not taken up the ministerial posts allotted to them.

There are some thirteen embassies in Vientiane, whose protocol order of precedence is Vietnam, France, USA, UK, USSR, India, Thailand, Australia, Indonesia, Cambodia, China, Malaysia and Czechoslovakia. Then comes the United Nations, represented by the UN Resident Representative and the International Control Commission (ICC), with the heads of its Indian, Canadian and Polish delegations. From time to time we of the Diplomatic Corps are called, usually at rather short notice, to attend official functions at a precise time, clad in white suit or evening dress (black tie, white dinner jacket). Any absence is noted. Tucked away in a corner close to the Embassy of the People's Republic of China is not quite an embassy but a North Vietnamese presence. One invites their representatives to a comprehensive cocktail party anyway.

Laos is very "protocolaire" as the French say. During our first month a good deal of my time was taken up with making formal calls on the Prime Minister, the heads of his Ministries and other dignitaries, and on the various ambassadors. To fulfil this duty I would be driven in the official UN car, a black Mercedes 220, the UN flag streaming from the front mudguard, to arrive at the ministry or embassy concerned exactly on time.

Round Robin No. 2

Christmas 1973

I suppose today, Friday,30th November, is as good a day as any to begin a round-robin letter. There was some trouble with the water this morning. The electric pump which normally is activated when you turn a tap on, did not turn on at 6:30am today. It had to be thumped by Bone, our house servant, and then it worked. So Phyllis had her shallow bath and I had my low pressure shower, and in due course we assembled for toast and coffee: the toast small, board-like squares to be covered with butter and marmalade or marmite, and the coffee, Colombian, packed by Oesterman, and sent to us from Copenhagen. Life seemed good after the coffee.

Mang drove me to the Office today as our usual driver Ngau is on leave, preparing for his daughter's wedding, an elaborate affair in which we shall participate on Sunday at noon.

Friday is pouch day and so there was a special flutter of last minute letters and cables for most urgent decisions or avoidance of them. And then a visit from Fritz Lhérisson, the new Representative of UNICEF, to introduce Mr Louis Gandron, his Director of Administration from UNICEF Headquarters in New York. We tend to think of ourselves as disadvantaged in Vientiane, but the director assured us we were rather better off than, for example, our colleagues in Saigon, Phnom Penh or Hanoi.

We were in better shape for the pouch today than usual, that is to say all letters for New York and Bangkok were ready for sealing in the cotton sacks for dispatch to the airport by 12:45 or so.

This afternoon was of special interest. I called on the Prime Minister alone to ask him what assurance could be given that the new government, still to be established, would endorse projects and priorities we of the United Nations were setting up in cooperation with the Royal Lao Government Planning Commission. I wondered whether he would have any objection to our meeting with the Pathet Lao (Neo Lao Hak Xat) representatives to clarify the matter. The Prime Minister's reaction was that any commitment made by the existing government would be honoured by the new government, and that was that. But at a cocktail the same evening, I discussed the point with Mr Soth Pethrasy, representative of the Neo Lao Hak Xat in Vientiane. His view was somewhat different. The new government would wish to give a new look to the Administration and would scrutinize all programmes carefully. Where does one go from there? We have a second Country Programme to prepare for the period January 1975 to December 1979 for presentation to the January 1975 session of the UNDP Governing Council. The various preparation deadlines do not allow for prevarication. We must prepare therefore and be flexible.

We have just got back from a trip to Bangkok, where we had four days happily undisturbed by strikes or student unrest. The purpose of the visit was to study the report of an ECAFE Planning Team which had visited Laos in October. The Planning Commissioner from Laos was also there with two of his colleagues, and our meetings were held in ECAFE Headquarters in Bangkok because the

255

Government team were en route to conferences in Wellington (Colombo Plan), Manila and Tokyo. The team from le Plan arrived from Vientiane on Saturday morning and we worked over the weekend. I hope some strengthening of the planning machinery and programming will result from these joint labours.

I also touched base for discussions with Mr van der Oord, the Executive Agent of the Mekong Committee at 7:00am on the Monday (we are old friends from New York), and with representatives of UNDP Bangkok, UNFPA, UNICEF and the Regional Office of ILO at other times, but Phyllis and I slipped away on the Friday before the weekend to visit Kanchanaburi and the Bridge over the River Kwai.

There was nothing there which really evoked the past for me. That particular bridge I had never seen, and where the long bamboo and attap huts of the POW hospital had been I could not guess, but the cemetery was peaceful and well-kept, and we found on that glorious afternoon, for the weather was just perfect, the bronze plaques of the graves of some of my dead friends – George Tacchi, Prigge, Pike and Timm.

We are now in the cool season, and social life is beginning to blossom. The Lao International Women's Association (AFALI) ran an International Gastronomic Gala for charity by the swimming pool of the Lane Xang Hotel. It was a great success and very exotic in the choice of dishes, decor and dress of the nine hundred guests. Each embassy offered samples of its international dishes, and the UN stall, which Phyllis organized, served the desserts provided by fourteen ladies of different nationalities. Behind our counter were Jenny and Joëlle from our office staff, Jenny (Lao) and Joëlle (Vietnamese) in their national dress, Cynthia Baer (American married to a German) in a dirndhal, and Pilar Le Xuan (Spanish with a Vietnamese husband) in a mantilla. They are all beautiful, and they looked their best in the soft coloured lights of the garden. The organizers made 2,500,000 Kips (over $4,000) for charity.

Some days have passed since this letter was started, and now we have less than two weeks to go to Christmas. The wise have packed in their entertaining early before the final rush, which culminates on 31st December with the Prime Minister's Ball. We went to a "mechoui" last Friday, given by the head of our Telecommunications Training Project, a Frenchman. A mechoui is a kind of barbecue in which whole carcasses are roasted over an open fire. In this case there were two whole sheep grilled in this way. You are expected to help yourself from the spit. The mutton was washed down by a Corsican red wine and topped off with French cheese and fruit salad served in half a long melon. Mechouis come from North Africa, and Frenchmen of a certain age group favour them through their Algerian military experience.

Continued by Phyllis

And now it is January 1974 and we have moved on to the very middle of the good season. The sun shines, and sky is blue, the temperature around seventy degrees, and the garden lovely. The house is large and we have expanses of polished teak floors; rattan lounge furniture with upholstered pads; even rattan beds; but the dining room is three sides of teak and has a Swedish-Danish air. There are wide windows of tinted glass on three sides of the reception room and outside a veranda and four steps down to lawns, flowering shrubs and rose beds. Hibiscus, plumeria, oleander and bougainvillea are constantly with us; morning glory, gardenia, marigolds, roses and phlox drummondi visiting companions. The lawn is of good quality for the tropics, and we shall be attempting to keep it green until the end of May when rain comes again. We have a well now so I think we shall succeed.

It is the trees that give the garden its tropical air. There are three traveller's palms, the kind that stand up like giant fans. Six other palm trees of varying sorts, a tamarind, a mango, three Norfolk pines that we used, lighted as Christmas trees and a clump of banana plants that have produced more than four hundred bananas during the year.

Carolyn and Phil have been here visiting and are even now on their return journey to Boston. They arrived, to our delight, on Christmas Eve; saw what there is to see in Vientiane and a little of the surrounding country; were entertained a great deal and then left with us for Penang to revisit Carolyn's birth place and the country in which she had lived for the first ten years of her life. We had two pleasant days at the Lone Pine by the sea. From Penang, Kenneth and I returned to Bangkok and Vientiane whilst they drove on to Taiping, Kuala Kangsar and Kuala Lumpur. Climatically their visit was unusual. As they arrived a cold spell, said to be from Mongolia, came down upon us and the temperature dropped lower than we had ever experienced. After one and a half years of almost continuous heat and sometimes of great heat we were using all the blankets, top coats and undies that we had with us. Even in Penang it was cool, much cooler than it had been in the many years we had lived in Malaysia. So Phil and Carolyn have been in the tropics and returned to the cold of a New England winter without having felt the heat. Most extraordinary. I have since heard that they were hot in Kuala Lumpur but cold again in Hong Kong.

Copying from 1973 diary:

Feb. 15

There has been a shortage of water. Often we cannot take a bath or wash clothes. The roads around the house are of deep dust which the traffic sends up in clouds to descend on the garden and the porches. The leaves of the trees are encrusted with dirt.

Feb. 25

The sun is a glowing orange-ball in a slate grey sky. The light is misty luminous. Figures emerge from a sunset-coloured dust: the chair covers, usually white, are tawny, my hair stands up like wire, the sun burns through my clothes and I sneeze frequently. In the garden nothing stirs with the exception of a long angular lizard who scuttles from one shadow to another.

And so this drought continued for six months and water was delivered daily by truck. It was somewhere during this period that I decided that a two-year stay in Laos would be as much as I wanted. Kenneth's decision was, I think, based on other factors. In any case when he was offered a year's contract from January 1973 he accepted only six months and we plan to leave here at the end of June 1974.

Continuing from the diary: (Phyllis)
May 22

And now the rain has come, and as if by magic all around is green. The lawn is perfect and without weed; the izoras are flowering and we have roses for the table. There are many kinds of butterflies and of all colours, ranging in size from one to eight inches wing span. Some are so large they look like birds.

The rainy season lasted until mid-October often with the paths and flower beds well under water and with real flooding in some parts. It is surprising that after such trying conditions any plants should survive, but the truth is that the majority do.

The year here has been politically calm, at least apparently so. There are more Pathet Lao in evidence, and they have officially taken over some of the buildings, one indeed that was WHO Headquarters. Probably you read of the coup in August and how it fizzled out. But that was the only violent disturbance that we heard about during the year.

The servants, with the exception of Mr Lak, our old cook, have stayed with us. Mr Lak we were forced to replace in October owing to his ill health. With the passing of time we have become more attached to Pha, Boune and Heung. Pha is an intelligent young woman of twenty-seven who works in the house and laundry for six and a half hours every day excepting Sunday which is a holiday. She comes from a Thai Dam village twenty minutes by motorcycle, goes back at midday to cook for her husband, four children and her husband's mother, and returns in the afternoon. During the year this family, with the help of neighbours (for such is the custom) have built a home. It is of teak on stilts, has four rooms and a corrugated-iron roof. The garden is planted with coconut palms, papaya and banana trees. The children look bonny, well fed and clothed. Vivat and Vijan, aged six and five are attending school, and we hope they and the two smaller ones will be able to obtain good Education. Boune, whose real name is Am Noi Chantavong, is nineteen nearing twenty. His parents live in Pakse a town in the south of Laos. He came to us without experience and without having even visited a European type of home. Here he enjoys having his own room and keeps it in good order. During the year he has learned to look after the downstairs part of the house, to serve at table and drinks for cocktail parties, to cook simple food and to take responsibility when we are away. He is slim and tall for a Lao and looks well in a white uniform. Every afternoon he goes to the Lao American School for an English lesson, so that I hope when we leave he will have at least a smattering of English to offer together with the fair French he learned in the Lycée at Pakse.

Heung who works in the garden is about the same age, but he is shorter and more sturdy than Boune. His whole name is Thao Heung Louvanh. He has a perfect set of teeth and likes hats. In the cool weather he has been wearing a Mexican wide-straw hat and when it was really hot he had a thick woollen balaclava. For a period he wore a shiny peaked hat with a French squareness of crown. He came to us recommended by the previous Resident Representative, energetic and with a desire to cut down or burn everything that grew. Working with me he quickly showed a feeling for plants, learned to care for a lawn, both weeding and feeding, to plant seeds and transplant seedlings, to make marcots on roses, on night-scented jasmine and other woody-stemmed plants and to prune trees. I have used the Latin names here and he has learned them all and can write them too. He speaks some English and goes to school after work. He has the makings of a good gardener. When the time comes for us to leave Laos I shall be sorry to say goodbye to these pleasant people.

Round Robin No.3   (Kenneth)
Christmas 1974

In our last Christmas letter Phyllis said we planned to leave Laos at the end of June 1974 and indeed we did expect to do so. But there were interesting possibilities of continuing with UNDP somewhere else which seemed so promising, especially if there were extra time for decisions to be made, that we decided to take home leave, go to New York for briefing and return to Vientiane for the extra six months necessary to pay for it.

So we took the home leave and will now depart from Vientiane in February 1975. My successor will be Mr Reifenrath, a Frenchman, who has been acting Resident Representative in Somalia.

Home leave was a great success. We had exactly two months door to door, leaving Vientiane on 11th June and returning on 11th August. We very much enjoyed the flight from Bangkok to Copenhagen by SAS with just one short stop in Tashkent, overnighting in Copenhagen at the airline's expense, and revelling in the elegance of the Royal Hotel. Shopping in Copenhagen's traffic-free pedestrian-only arcades on a summer's morning was also a delight.

There followed happy family reunions in England with Phyllis's sister Elsie and her husband Ronald and my sister Barbara, both families in the London area. We did not make our favourite sweep in the West Country this time, only a trip to see old friends in Cambridge, as I had to have a hernia repair. We left for Boston on 1ST July.

Carolyn and her husband Phil were there to meet us at Logan Airport, and we were carried off to their charming apartment in Watertown. Both were happily employed, Carolyn with a counselling job, and Phil finishing off courses in computer science for his Master's degree. Later we had a most memorable holiday in lovely weather in New Hampshire, Vermont and Connecticut, partly with "the children" but mostly as guests of very close old friends.

There followed a week of briefing in New York, two days with dear friends in Washington, a twenty-four-hour family reunion in London, and on to Singapore to participate in a meeting of the World Confederation of Organizations of the Teaching Profession (WCOTP).

We were pleased to have another look at Singapore after seventeen years. We stayed in the Phoenix Hotel which overlooked Singapore Cold Storage on Orchard Road. The slight rise of the road is the same as before, but virtually everything else has changed. The Phoenix Hotel block now houses a complex of shops and restaurants and includes the relocated Robinson's after Robinson's was burnt out in Raffles Square last year.

Still part of the Singapore scene is George Thompson who was a dig-mate of mine at Oxford. After more than twenty years in Singapore he is now a professor of Government and Public Administration at Nanyang University. We had curry tiffin together at the Cricket Club watching a cricket match on the padang the while, and reminiscing on the Japanese capitulation, which we both had witnessed in strange circumstances in 1945, on the steps of the State Building nearby.

Going back to Kuala Lumpur together was a very special experience. Phyllis left there in 1956 to put Carolyn to school in England, and I on Independence in 1957, though I have passed through since then. There have, of course, been many changes. We stayed in the Merlin Hotel which did not exist when we left, but is now one of the older hotels, and we found our old bungalow on Brockman Road derelict. In fact Brockman Road had half disappeared to make way for a fly-over, and what was left of it had been renamed Jalan Dato Onn. St Mary's church and the Selangor Club still grace the padang, but we fear their days may be numbered.

Our visit to Kuala Lumpur was memorable on two counts. First we were invited by Tun Razak, the Prime Minister, and his wife to a buffet dinner. It was very much en famille, the only other guests being Dato Hamzah, Minister of Defence, and General Ungku Nasaruddin, Commander-in-Chief of the Army, all of the Malay College, Kuala Kangsar of course – old students and old friends.

The second real pleasure was meeting Aw Ah Wah again, the son of Ah Soon our Chinese cook. We have corresponded with him over the years and Phyllis tried to phone him at Sime Darby and Co. He had moved on from there and is now a sales supervisor for Carlsberg beer. We duly met in the Merlin coffee-shop. Ah Wah is a fine young man of thirty-four, married with a family. He came to us with Ah Soon at the age of five. Ah Soon,who was our cook for more than ten years and who on our departure became cook to the first US Ambassador to Malaya, alas died three years ago.

Continued by Phyllis

Rather to our surprise we have spent almost the whole of 1974 in Laos. As Kenneth wrote, we were away in England, the United States and Malaysia for two months, those of June and July, and the rest of the year we were here. Changes have occurred politically in the country, Prince Souvanna Phouma has been sick, Prince Souphanouvong, sometimes called the Red Prince, has returned. He works in Luang Prabang and the Pathet Lao share the power of the government. But the feeling of waiting or indecision is with us still. A unanimous agreement to proceed with any project is rarely arrived at because the two sides of the government do not agree among themselves. They have experience of French methods, US methods, UN methods. Now what they want is the money and a free hand. And this is understandable when you see the results of the many well-intentioned efforts that have been made. But it is also impossible from the UN point of view for many reasons which I cannot go into here.

The Lao are a people who live in equanimity with poverty. They are not yet mainly materialistic in attitude though we have successively tried to indoctrinate them. Within three yards of our side windows is a Lao village. Two of the dozen houses or so have electric light, the rest none. Water is carried by hand from a well or caught in buckets from the roof during the rainy season. Sanitation is a toilet sunk level with the ground, or none. A few months ago a baby was born in the nearest stilt house. For the event a neighbour fixed a wire from his house so that there was some light, and the experienced women of the village came to help. Cooking is done outside or under the house, and not more than two pots will be owned by a family. There is no furniture as we know it, just a few woven grass mats and some cotton covers woven on looms in the house for the cool season. A well-equipped house may have a round wicker stand 9" high and 24" in diameter on which the prepared food is placed when ready for a meal. Glutinous rice steamed and served in a woven wicker basket will be the main body of the meal and will be eaten with the tips of fingers. There will be fresh green salad, a cooked vegetable, chilli and spices, and on rare occasions, meat, fish or eggs. Water is the only beverage. They sit down together around the stand and eat in an orderly almost dignified fashion, age taking precedence. Guests are customarily invited to share the meal. Often there are dogs, ducks, chickens and geese around. Neat little brown cows too are not far away, and water–buffaloes are in the adjoining fields, coriander and chilli grow around the houses in a somewhat disorganized manner and are used with the food. Probably some few miles from Vientiane each family has a piece of ground that it cultivates for rice. It is unlikely that they can produce more than enough for one month's supply, but the fresh new grain is something that they look forward to and enjoy. There are two crops a year. Sadly there is almost no communication between our neighbours and us because we have no common language. It is as if they do not see the big "elegant" building right on their doorstep, and as the windows are of tinted glass they cannot see inside. Perhaps too they think how hot and uncomfortable a concrete construction must be, and so it is whenever the electric power is not working, which is often.

There has been little change domestically in our home except that Boune, one of our household servants, has chosen to leave us. His full name is Am Noi Chantavong. He came to us as an under-nourished, stocky, tousled-haired seventeen year old. Mr Lak, our first old Cordon Bleu cook brought him along with him to do the rough work of the kitchen. It wasn't many months before he suggested that he learn to work in the house. I was dubious. He did not look the part, but servants were hard to come by and I agreed. My reserve was ill-founded. In six months he had learned to do everything well. Never was silver so well polished, meals more gently served. He had grown tall and slim and in his white uniform he looked almost handsome. He spoke a certain amount of French and wanted to learn English, so we arranged that every afternoon he went to the Lao American School for a lesson. He bought a bicycle, a good bed, a few clothes. But from early days I knew that there was no content in him. A fierce anger not particularly against us, but against the injustice of a world that gave others so much more than it gave him. So in October (after he had been with us more than two years) he told us he did not want to work any more, and he left to live in a nearby pagoda on a share of the rice that is prepared in the wat for the orange-clad resident monks, itinerants and the very old and the young males. He visits us occasionally but he has no inclination to return to work. Boune is struggling to enter the clerical world. He may succeed. He is intelligent and determined but it seems unlikely that he will find contentment.

In his place Pha's younger sister, Phian, came. She is eighteen, jolly and plump, and she and the cook get on well. These sisters, of whom there are five, all have names beginning with Ph, "Pha", "Phoon", "Phin" and "Phian", the fifth I do not remember. Phian has high cheekbones and long shiny black hair. Bishop Chiu Ban

It, who was here last weekend, thought she looked like an American Indian! Mr Chi, the Vietnamese cook whose whole name is Truang Van Chi, deplores her inexperience and does himself some of the things he thinks she should do, such as taking Kenneth his slippers, putting his coat on a hanger, carrying his despatch case. He is minute, weighing somewhere around 80lbs, and he is all of sixty-eight years of age. We are thoroughly spoiled by his excellent cooking, but he finds the work for the many big parties we give rather too much. We have become increasingly fond of him and I think he is happy as things are. There is a special affinity between him and Kenneth and I wish you could see them together, a Saint Bernard with a miniature poodle! Pha is the same balanced intelligent woman. Her children; Vinai eight, Vichi six, Vivat four and Vihan two are doing well, the two who go to school leading their classes. As Ah Lin was in our Malayan household Pha is in Laos, the majordomo to whom the others defer. They too recognize her superior intelligence. And as for Heung, Thao Heung Louvanh the gardener, he is now twenty years old and a pleasant person. His early-morning smile when we meet among the flowers is as of one who thinks he has inherited all God's Kingdom. Perhaps he has in spite of his worldly possessions being so very few. There is a quality of life here that is invaluable and Heung has it. During 1973 he attended a course on radio engineering, as well as two regular English classes, and having acquired some skill he offered to mend any broken radio in the village. No, he asks no fee, occasionally someone would give him something, but as a general principle it is a service – a service from a young man without material possessions and with no "prospects in life".

Round Robin No.4 (Kenneth)

Round Robin No.3 was headed "Christmas 1974", and you may have wondered what made the series dry up. It was not because our lives suddenly became dull. Rather the preparing and sending out of a round robin in 1975 and 1976 became technically difficult. Let me bring you up to date.

We left Laos in February 1975 not quite certain of our future. I was two years past the magic age of sixty, the mandatory retirement age for most professionals in the United Nations system, and this had been achieved by taking a field post. Now with the Laos job terminated at my request (climatically two years eight months of Laos was enough), we could scarcely hope for any further extension. But luck was with us. Even while I was debriefing from Laos in New York I was unexpectedly told I might be offered the post of Resident Representative, United Nations Development Programme (UNDP) in Israel. And so it came about. There was, as always in such cases, a long delay before my candidacy was cleared within the House and by the government of Israel, but in due course we were informed that we should arrive in Jerusalem by 6thMay 1975.

Before this decision was taken we had to determine what to do if work with the UN were indeed ended. Our closest American friends, Tib and Chuck Rice, whom we knew first at Choate School, Connecticut, had retired in New Hampshire. We therefore decided to take a look at New Hampshire ourselves as a possible place for our own retirement. Chuck, after being Director of Admissions and Head of the English Department at Choate, had spent five years as President of Athens College, Greece, and then completed his career as Director of Admissions at Philip's Academy, Exeter,NH. On Chuck's suggestion we had been offered the use of a house near theirs which was owned by a lady who spent her winters in Florida. Carolyn and Phil at this time lived in West Newton, a suburb of Boston, and so would be reasonably near to us.

With Katherine Meyer's house as a base we explored the area in the short waiting period until we had definite news about the job in Israel, looking at houses in a rather half-hearted manner. After some hesitation we bought one, a small "extended ranch-type" house in woody surroundings. Phil had changed his job from teaching high-school mathematics in Massachusetts to working with a computer company in New Hampshire, so we suggested that Carolyn and he might like to keep the new house warm for us while we were in Israel. This they agreed to do.

Now Chuck is a man of many parts. After retirement he remodelled his own house and took to painting pictures with remarkable success. He offered to remodel our house before Carolyn and Phil moved in if we cared to let him have a few thousand dollars for materials. We cared, and the results are quite spectacular we think. Now we are back from Israel, and living in it, and Carolyn and Phil have their own house in Watertown, Massachusetts. They need a house with room for expansion because on 6th March 1977 Carolyn, after eight years of married life, had a daughter, Megan. We're glad they're only an hour and a half's drive away, as Megan is the apple of our eye.

Although I believe these "round robin" letters give a fairly accurate picture of the background to our life in Laos, I should also like to mention other aspects of our stay there which concerned us at the time. After our return to Vientiane from Malaysia our chief concerns apart from work were three: the extension of my contract, for I was already older than the normal retirement age of sixty; the visit to Vientiane of Carolyn and Phil; and the re-validation of Phyllis's permanent resident visa. Headquarters offered us an extension until December 1974, but for reasons of health and Phyllis's longing for a more bearable climate, we accepted an extension only until 30th June. Carolyn and Phil could obtain leave from their respective jobs about Christmas time and the New Year, so, to have something in hand, we booked rooms for all of us at the Lone Pine for 15, 16, and 17., December

The re-validation of Phyllis's permanent resident visa proved to be much more of a problem than we thought possible. We had been told to work through the US Embassy in Vientiane, and this we did. But we had nothing to prove that she had applied to the INS (Immigration and Naturalization Service) in New York to stay out of the country for more than a year, and we found later that her fingerprints sent to New York had been held up for eight months, because a pouch from the United Nations Development Programme in Vientiane had just disappeared for that length of time.

Towards the end of August we found ourselves up in Luang Prabang, again on royal invitation, to participate in the Fête des Pirogues and to watch pirogue races on the river. An average pirogue is a long canoe-like boat in which about twenty people can sit and paddle. This boat racing we found interesting, but it went on much too long. We had to be seated by noon in designated places under attap canopies – men, white-suited, ladies in semi-Ascot attire – to await the arrival of the King. The King came to the tribune by royal barge, in which he sat enthroned under a palan-quin. The boat-race crews made deep obeisances, and then the races started on the swiftly running Nam Khane river, which is a tributary of the Mekong.

All the pirogues were narrow hulls of teak, each pirogue a single tree trunk hollowed out. The paddlers were dressed in bright colours – some crews were all in blue, some in red, some in yellow, etc. They sat two abreast except fore and aft where the boat nar-rowed. In the larger boats there were as many as fifty paddlers, who, when racing, paddled like mad to the beat of a whistle or gong.

Towards the end of the afternoon a pirogue with an expatriate crew of young men from various embassies tried their hand at rac-ing. The crowds on the river were greatly amused by their efforts, especially when their boat turned turtle and they ended up in the river. But sitting watching this sort of thing from 12 noon until nearly 7pm under a boiling sun without food was really too much. It was naturally very difficult to withdraw before the King did. Nevertheless Phyllis managed it. I'm sure she did not mind missing the final races of the knock-out competition, even though these and the winners' acceptance of their prizes – large silver cups in Western traditional style – were the most impressive part of the day, for then the last rays of the setting sun made the scene magic, throwing into high relief the colourful garments of the spectators lining the steep banks of the river, and gilding the tops of the sur-rounding hills.

We were supposed to be back at the palace for the reception, dinner and dancing by 7:45pm. Poor Phyllis could not manage that but she had quite a good dinner in her room before I left. Dancing went on until after 1am, both Lao dancing, in which the man and woman slowly turn around opposite each other, moving their arms and hands in graceful undulations, and Western ballroom dancing, mostly decorous and old-fashioned. During this time, His Majesty graciously received ambassadors in protocol order – Vietnam, Thailand, USSR, France, Germany, Britain, and so on – until the dancing ended.

In Laos we found any occasion of this kind tended to be beset with a certain amount of frustration. On this particular evening the frustrations were three-fold – the air-conditioning failed, the lights went out, there was no water – all while we were trying to change for the ball. After a time the air-conditioning and the lights came on again, but there was still no water in the taps when we left for Vientiane. The Mekong had risen too high and upset the whole town system. After a time one found such frustrations seemed to erase themselves. We realized that Lao people do not understand or care much about what gives Westerners concern. These races were the great event of the year for most of the local people, and they did not mean to lose a minute of it. For us it was a good change from Vientiane anyway.

Indeed it was a remarkable change for us to be up in Luang Prabang at the end of August, because earlier in the month there had been an attempted coup in the capital. We first heard about this at 7:30 in the morning of 20th August, although it had started at 5:30am. We had our own security system to contend with such a situation. Key UN personnel had been provided with walkie-talkie sets, and I broadcast bulletins from the UNDP office for the information of our experts roughly every hour to keep them informed of what was going on. The experts and their families knew that they should remain in their houses unless explicitly ordered to do otherwise. It turned out that the insurgents were a splinter group led by a General Ma and had nothing to do with the Pathet Lao. It started with an attack on the airport, some bombing of the Army base camp, and the temporary taking over of the government radio station. But the attempt was poorly organized, and when some of the early moves faltered, those in the services who had agreed to defect to the insurgents changed their minds and pocketed the colourful scarves which were supposed to identify them. It was really all over by noon, and I joined the rest of the Diplomatic Corps at 4:30pm to congratulate Prime Minister Souvanna Phouma in his house on the suppression of the coup.

While waiting for the plane to take us back to Vientiane I wrote to Carolyn and Phil:

"You may be wondering how we feel able to take a trip up here, when the dust of an attempted coup has hardly settled in Vientiane. It is extraordinary, but the key to it all is that in theory everyone is loyal to the King. So we have up here the Prime Minister and his chief ministers and all the Diplomatic Corps behaving as though nothing at all had happened. It is noticeable, however, that most of the generals are absent."

Now we are back in Vientiane, and only just in time, because the airport is flooded. We may get some quite serious flooding in the town if the Mekong gets much higher.

In September 1973 I was smitten with a superficial phlebitis which kept my right leg elevated and tightly bandaged for some twelve days. However, with files shuttling from the office and a telephone at my elbow I felt I did not miss much. I'm sure my indisposition was much more of a nuisance to Phyllis and the office than it was to me.

On the morning of 14 September, as a member of the Diplomatic Corps, I attended the historic signing of the Peace Treaty of Laos in the home of the Prime Minister. The treaty, which ended ten years of hostility between the Royal Lao government and the Pathet

Lao, ultimately gave birth to a Provisional Government of National Unity, but for a considerable time there seemed to be an authority vacuum, and our letters to the government remained unanswered. Although the new government was understood to be a coalition government, it was apparent from the start that the Pathet Lao were going to be the dominant party in it, and as the months went by, the tone of life in Vientiane began to change. It was decided to dispense with the National Assembly and rule by "Royal Decree". The American presence diminished. The French proposed to double their aid. Many people who had been in Vientiane a long time began to leave. Signs which had until this time been written exclusively in French, as for example the "Hotel Lang Xang ", now had to be written in the Lao script also. The letterhead on government documents was now in Lao rather than in French. This was understandable, but it did not help the smooth implementation of our programme of external technical assistance.

  But all this came later. In October we moved into the dry season, and the roads turned from mud to dust. We learned that Carolyn and Phil had been able to finalize their travel arrangements. They would visit us in Laos between 22nd December and 9th January. Through Colonel Henry, a tall Texan who took a service at our little church one Sunday, we learned of the visit of some fifty wives of US servicemen believed to have been taken prisoner in Laos. However, we did not meet these ladies. Later in the month I had responsibility for back-stopping an international mission on the control of drugs. There were ten members of the mission including representatives of INTERPOL and the British Home Office. I went around with them on some of the visits, and learned something of the opium traffic in Laos and its contiguous countries. We were invited by the Chief of Police to a Chinese dinner at two round marble-topped tables, each of ten people. At my table with the Chief of Mission, an Australian, were the Chief of Police, the Chief of Customs and a general of the Royal Lao Army in charge of drug control from the military standpoint. Though the conversation centred on "an opium substitute project", they called themselves

272

jokingly "the golden triangle", A sad comment on the situation I thought.

Carolyn and Phil actually arrived in Vientiane on Christmas Eve, and were entertained by many of our friends. The social highlight for them and everyone else was the Prime Minister's Ball on New Year's Eve in his house and garden on the bank of the Mekong. Shortly afterwards all four of us left for Penang so that Carolyn could show Phil where she had been born. We had two pleasant days with them at the Lone Pine, then returned to Bangkok while they moved on to Taiping, Kuala Kangsar and Kuala Lumpur. So Carolyn made her sentimental journey back to Malaya separately from us. She had lived in Kuala Kangsar until she was seven, and then in Kuala Lumpur until she was ten, before leaving Malaya with Phyllis in 1956 for schooling in England. She and Phil returned to the United States via Hong Kong.

By the end of May 1974 our plans for the rest of our stay in Laos had firmed up a good deal. We were to leave Vientiane on 11th June and fly direct to England where we would spend three weeks with family and friends. We would then fly to the United States and visit our friends in New England. On 24th July, I would go to UNDP Headquarters in New York for consultations on the Laos Country Programme, then leave New York for Singapore where I had been asked to represent UNDP at the World Assembly of the WCOTP (World Confederation of Organizations of the Teaching Profession), which ran from 31st July to 7th August. We would then return to Vientiane to finish the work there, before leaving Laos finally in February 1975.

I had a special interest in WCOTP because at one time I had thought of joining its staff, after my retirement from UNDP. I had known its management well in Washington, DC, especially Raymond Smyke, Assistant Secretary, before the organization had moved its headquarters to Morges in Switzerland. WCOTP's Secretary General, John M. Thompson, had in fact invited me to

Morges to meet him and Raymond specifically to discuss the possibility of my joining their organization, and I went to Morges for that purpose. However, that possibility faded as I felt unable to join WCOTP immediately, and I did not intend to leave UNDP before I was obliged to do so. I felt a stint with WCOTP would have been an interesting experience, as its influence as a worldwide teachers' organization is much greater than commonly supposed. In 1974 it had five million members, and its publication, the ECHO, appeared in ten languages.

As usual our three weeks in England passed very quickly. We stayed briefly with Elsie and Ronald and my sister Barbara in the London area and visited old friends like the Tods in Cambridge, and Celia Barkway in Gloucestershire. Then in the United States we visited the children in Watertown, Gerry and Janice Dartford in Connecticut, and our Choate friends, the Rices, in North Hampton, the Atmores in Twin Lakes, and Annah Preble in Rockport, Maine.

After consultations in New York concerning the programme in Laos we were soon on our way back to Vientiane via Singapore. We did not enjoy our Quantas flight very much. The plane was full and the journey bumpy. There were tiresome stop-overs in Frankfurt and Bahrein.

But when we arrived in Singapore we were at once restored to well-being. We had forgotten the beauty of the city – its red soil, the red crinkly Chinese roofs, the dense green jungle trees, and the white stone government buildings. It had been a languid, leisurely place in our time. Now it was not. Everywhere there was air-conditioning and high-rise buildings – not close together as in New York City, but spread out among trees and lawns. The population and the speed of life had trebled. We stayed in the Phoenix Hotel on Orchard Road, which was quite new to us. From its windows we could see the contour of the Orchard Road we knew, leading down to the "Singapore Cold Storage" supermarket we remembered, but the skyline had changed completely. Our hotel was in a group of buildings which contained a branch of Robinsons department store, a modest branch of the Robinsons which had been a land-mark in Singapore until it had been gutted by fire a number of years before our coming.

The theme of the 23rd World Assembly of WCOTP was "Pressures for Educational Change". The conference was attended by four hundred teachers' delegates from forty countries and eighty organizations. The Prime Minister of Singapore, Mr Lee Kuan Yew, addressed the participants at the opening ceremony in the well-equipped Singapore Conference Hall. I read the message of the Secretary General, Dr Kurt Waldheim, in plenary session, and on 1st August presented a paper to Working Group D concerning international pressures for Educational change such as development, population, environment, women's rights, the energy crisis, and their implications for teachers and teachers' organizations. I also introduced a paper written by the Chief of Education Information Programmes, UN Office of Public Information, Mrs.Sally Swing Shelley, who was unable to attend the conference. I left the assembly on Sunday 4 August, as its latter part comprised special seminars, workshop sessions and WCOTP business of no special interest to UNDP.

While in Singapore I was able to meet with my old Oxford dig-mate, George Thompson, now a permanent Singapore resident, and follow through with our arrangements to pay a courtesy call to Tun Razak, the Prime Minister of Malaysia in Kuala Lumpur, on our way back to Vientiane.

I am not sure now whether George was still running the Singapore Civil Service Political Centre at this time, or whether he had moved on to lecture in government at the new Nanyang University, as he certainly did later. I remember we met for a curry tiffin at the Cricket Club, where he was Secretary, and watched a slow cricket match on the padang while we reminisced over the past. His rich Scots brogue and shock of black hair were the same as ever. We had both witnessed the official surrender of the Japanese to Mountbatten in 1945, in very different circumstances, a few hundred yards from where we were sitting.

Our stay in Singapore was rounded off by our attendance at the 7am Sunday morning service at St Andrew's cathedral, where the Bishop of Singapore, our old friend Chiu Ban It, preached. He spoke with us afterwards, and sent his special love to Carolyn in the United States. In the 1970s Bishop Chui had become widely known for his faith healing, and as we left, numerous cripples and sick folk were going in to take part in a faith healing service. It was like a picture from the Bible.

I had written ahead to Kuala Lumpur, asking whether Tun Razak would be kind enough to receive us. Inche Ismail Rasali, the Charge d'Affaires for Malaysia in Vientiane, and a former sixth former at MCKK, had also written to the Prime Minister separately. However, we were not sure that the visit would be approved until the PM's Office called me at the Merlin Hotel, where we were staying, inviting us to dinner at the Prime Minister's residence. Phyllis wondered whether she ought to decline the invitation, thinking it might be an all-male affair, but the secretary assured her that Tun Razak's wife would be present, and that "the Tun" would be disappointed if she did not come too. So Phyllis quickly slipped on her purple Thai silk evening dress and joined me in the waiting car. It turned out we were to have a buffet supper en famille with just two other invited guests, both old boys of the MCKK with whom I had been closely associated – Dato Hamzah, whom I remembered well as a soccer and hockey goalkeeper, but now Minister of Defence; and General Ungku Nasaruddin, whom I knew as Head Boy and captain of cricket, now Army Chief of Staff. We had a delightful, relaxed evening. Tun Razak presented Phyllis with two beautiful dress lengths in materials of local design, and me with two Malaysian batik shirts.

The next day Phyllis was successful in tracing Aw Ah Wah, the eldest of the Ah Soon children. She spent quite a time on the telephone, and tracked him down from the firm we knew he had been working for – Sime Darby. We discovered he was now the Kuala Lumpur sales representative for Carlsberg beer, and we met him in the Merlin coffee-shop. Ah Wah was a tall, slim good-looking Chinese. He had married a trained nurse, and lived in Klang. Ah Soon had died in 1972. After being our cook for eleven years, on our departure from Malaya he became cook to Malaya's first United States Ambassador. Ah Chee, now thirty-six, we were sorry to learn, appeared to be dying of cancer. Ah Fook was still the wild young man who could not stay with any job for long. Ah Lin had been knocked down and killed by a truck on Circular Road a few years earlier. It was interesting to hear Ah Wah talk about his "Granny". He seemed much more "anglicised" than we had expected. We agreed to exchange family photographs. He particularly wanted some of Carolyn. It was a great joy to us to find Ah Wah so happy and prosperous.

After returning to Vientiane from Malaya we witnessed the progressive assumption of power by the Pathet Lao, and a deterioration of conditions for the common people. The Pathet Lao chiefs moved into the more elegant houses and the price of everything soared. Repairs to the bicycles of Pha, Heung and Boune could not be effected. Only the centre pieces of their bicycle pedals remained. We raised the salaries of the servants, but we could not keep up with the rocketing inflation. Strangely to us the Lao people we met seemed to keep their unruffled outlook and inner Buddhist calm. It was little consolation to learn from experts who visited us from Bangladesh and India that conditions were often worse there.

A quote from a letter of Phyllis's to "the children" shows how Lao character can surmount the most depressing of circumstances. Heung the gardener always reminds us of the quintessential qualities of the Lao people at their best. She wrote:

Heung is just taking down the UN flag – a bit early because it is going to rain. His new pullover that I bought for him from Marks & Spencer's in London he puts on proudly after his shower. Then he cycles off on his ramshackle bicycle to his English lesson, to be followed by a meal of glutinous rice and an evening of mending radios in the Thai Dam village. If his friends can pay him a little they do. If not, he mends the radios just the same. Now he has stopped at the far end of the lounge and called out, "Goodbye Mem", and has given me a ravishing smile – gone. To look at him you might think he had inherited all God's Kingdom. Perhaps he has.

Our return to the US and what we did there do not stand out clearly in my mind now because so much happened in a very short time, and I was preoccupied with the possibility and then the actuality of my service being extended and our being posted to Israel. Again we were greatly helped by Chuck Rice who arranged for us to live in the house of a close friend of his, Katherine Meyer. She was away in Florida and generously allowed us to stay there for only the cost of utilities. Charles Rice had elected to live in North Hampton, New Hampshire, after retiring from being Director of Admissions at Philips Academy, Exeter– a post he had taken after leaving Athens College, Greece. His own house, which he had remodelled himself during the summers of his appointment in Exeter, was close to Katharine's. In this way we were able to get a feel of New Hampshire and, attracted by the thought of being near to the Rices, we even started looking for a house. In the end we bought one without much conviction. I felt we needed a pied-à-terre, something to fall back on, and Phyllis, without any great enthusiasm, went along with the idea. After all we would be with friends, and reasonably near Carolyn and Phil.

Having put down a "closing" fee we both felt qualms at what we had let ourselves in for. Phyllis was progressively less and less happy about the transaction, and I think we might have sacrificed our deposit of $1000 to be free of it but for a most generous and time-

ly intervention by Chuck. Why not, he said, leave him a few thousand dollars while we were away in Israel, and let him remodel the
house? We accepted this solution to our problem with relief and
gratitude, for we had the greatest respect for Chuck's artistic and
practical abilities. We were pleased to be rid of the responsibility,
and Chuck enjoyed having a free hand to do virtually what he
pleased with the money available. In the event he redesigned the
major rooms, turning two at the end of the house into an elegant
living room with a new fireplace, and adding a bathroom to the
large upstairs bedroom so that it constituted a self-contained apartment for guests. Later he helped us with furnishing the house, in
particular by providing some of his own paintings for the bare
walls. It was a unique act of friendship which we shall never forget.

After the main alterations were completed, Carolyn and Phil
moved in to keep the house warm. Phil was working in New
Hampshire by then, so they were able to enjoy a rent-free house
while we were away, and of course we were delighted to have them
occupy it. I should add that Phil, an excellent handyman, contributed to the remodelled with most of the electrical wiring.

We left New York for Israel on 1st May 1975, and soon were receiving from Chuck comments on the progress of his work on the
house. Here is an extract from one of his letters which clearly
reflects his enthusiasm and sensitivity:
"Jim (his helper) and I lit the first fire on 10th June, and warmed
our hands at the grill in the living room as well as the one in the
bedroom. The chimney draws eagerly and seems to admit no rain.
A painting of Jockey Hill hangs under the light above the hearth,
quite an appealing and finished sight. The decision about the fireplace facing was dictated by cost. Brick facing which I didn't favour
anyway, as too dominating, would have added $200. Simple unob-
trusiveness is my inclination with the suggestions of elegance
simplicity permits."

We had a few days in London before proceeding to Israel, and again touched base with Elsie and Ronald and my sister Barbara. On the Monday night we saw A Touch of Spring with Hayley Mills at the Richmond Theatre, a comedy which put us in a good mood for our journey. We left Heathrow on the Tuesday morning and arrived at Ben Gurion Airport by 9:30pm the next day, 6th May

Israel

It would be difficult to imagine two so-called developing countries farther apart in level of development than Laos and Israel. Laos is listed by the UN as one of the twenty–eight least developed countries of the world. Israel on the other hand has an advanced technology in many fields to such a degree that its government decided in 1973 that it would not accept UN technical assistance after the completion of the first UNDP programming cycle 1972–1976. It was my task to round out the UNDP Country Programme for Israel by the end of 1976, and to close the UNDP Office in Jerusalem on 31st December 1976. The office did in fact close on time, and thus twenty-six years of UN technical assistance to Israel came to an end.

Being a representative of the UN in Israel was a delicate business, for the UN was not popular during our stay, and became increasingly unpopular after the UN resolution on Zionism, UNESCO's resolutions on Jerusalem and the Education of Arabs in the occupied territories. Informed Israelis who knew of the non-political technical assistance being afforded to Israel by the UNDP applauded it, but our office and those associated with it were often castigated for being "the UN", and I did represent the whole UN family on special occasions such as UN Day. The UNDP Country Programme actually consisted of one hundred and eighteen projects executed by ten specialized agencies, providing technical assistance to every important sector of the economy.

Partly because of our special situation vis-a-vis the government of Israel, Phyllis and I chose to live in a very Jewish quarter of Jerusalem on the side of a hill overlooking the valley in which

Christ is believed to have taken up his Cross. Across the valley the skyline is cut by the sweeping lines of the Knesset building and the rectangular flat surfaces of the Israel Museum. These buildings are floodlit at certain times of the year and present a spectacular panorama. We lived in a block of six flats, the only non-Israelis in the block, and on Friday afternoons we watched the candles being lit in the windows around us in preparation for the Sabbath, and families trouping off to the synagogue on the morning of Shabat, which of course was our Saturday. On Shabat the end of our road was closed to motor vehicles. Their place was taken by somberly dressed men, some with velvet fur-trimmed hats and prayer shawls walking in the middle of the road.

Unlike Laos, where I had five internationally recruited colleagues, I was the only international in the Jerusalem office. It was a stimulating experience. The Lao's on the staff in Vientiane were courteous and soft-spoken with a Buddhist acceptance of fate. The Israelis were uninhibited, fiercely energetic, forthright and boisterous. At first I thought the staff were constantly quarrelling, until I discovered that most of the ruckus was reckoned normal conversation. But what a wonderful group to work with. They were intelligent, industrious, devoted and competent. However, when you know that all our mimeographing had to be done by the Prime Minister's Office you can guess why we (Phyllis and I) refrained from preparing a round-robin from Israel.

We were met at the airport by: Yaacov Saphir, Director of the National Council for Research and Development of the Planning Ministry, who was to be my Israeli counterpart; Bob Bruins, a Dutchman, chief technical advisor of a dredging project, who had been left in charge of the office by Finn Munch-Petersen, my predecessor as Resident Representative; and Leon Teboul, the driver. We did not have a smart Mercedes as in Laos, the car we drove off in was a white Volvo. We soon discovered there were no other cars attached to the office, and that Mercedes were rare indeed in Israel even at government ministries.

It takes about an hour to get to Jerusalem from the airport. The first part of the journey is through low-lying land, but for the last twenty minutes the road rises steeply some two thousand feet, and suddenly you are there. It was late and, of course, dark when we eventually checked into the King David Hotel. From our window we could see the floodlit walls of the Old City, and some of the illuminated towers and domes inside. In our room we were welcomed by a large bowl of dark red roses. At that moment we felt the magic of Jerusalem. It never left us.

On Saturday when the office was closed we went through the Jaffa Gate into the Old City, and found many streets only eight or nine feet wide, with shops on either side, all built of stone, and often with steps up or down. There were shops selling vegetables, meat or bread, together with others where people worked at weaving, making clay pots or metal objects, and a plethora of souvenir shops. Occasionally a light-coloured donkey with his double pack would push his way through the pedestrians.

We quickly became aware of the Shabbat – the Jewish sabbath. From sundown on Friday to sundown on Saturday, except in the Arab quarter, all is quiet in Jerusalem. No shops are open and little work is done. We stayed only two nights in the King David, it was so expensive, and then moved to the Moriah, which was nearer to the UNDP office – only seven minutes walk away. There we were introduced to the normal Israeli hotel buffet breakfast, which features stewed fruits – prunes, figs, apricots, fresh grapefruit and fruit juices; uncooked vegetables – grated carrots, sliced cucumber, quartered tomatoes and whole spring onions, yellow and white sliced cheese, herrings, gefilte fish and yoghurt. Rolls, jam, butter, eggs and coffee seemed to be offered rather as a concession to international guests.

Though we wanted to get out of our hotel as quickly as possible, we soon began to enjoy Jerusalem. Phyllis and I met most of the experts and their wives at a cocktail party given in the UNDP office at 39 Jabotinsky Street, which had formerly been the residence of a prime minister of Israel, Eshkol. My own office was a fine long room which lent itself admirably to meetings and interviews and, from time to time, receptions and cocktail parties.

We spent a good deal of time looking for accommodation, and while doing so savoured the beauties of the golden city. One free day Leon took us to visit the Holy Sepulchre, and then out to Bethlehem to see the Manger. On the holiday for Pentecost we called on the Munch-Petersens' best friends, the Gelobters. Shimshon Gelobter is a lawyer, while his wife Sara collects works of art and organizes exhibitions of paintings around the world. And then, from the outside of the house of one of our experts, set out on a sort of artists' colony built in light honey-coloured stone, we looked out across the valley to the Mount of Zion. While we were there a rabbi called me over to him, put a yarmulke on my head, and urged me to enter a nearby synagogue. I gently explained that I was not Jewish, and after some quick explanations from one of the bystanders in Hebrew, I withdrew with what grace I could muster.

The problem with our housing was that there was very little unfurnished accommodation in Jerusalem, and we had a fair amount of furniture on its way – some from Bangkok and some from New York. The unfurnished house which attracted us most was that of a Professor Friedlander, who was on sabbatical to the University of Geneva. However, we tended to favour the furnished apartment of an Israeli diplomat, Pinhas Eliav, who was about to leave for New York to become Deputy Permanent Representative of Israel to the United Nations. It was this apartment in Ibn Shaprut 15, that we finally decided upon. We would manage to accommo-date the bits and pieces we would receive from Bangkok via Eliat, and cable New York not to send us the furniture we had in store with the Neptune company.

To our surprise and pleasure walking in Jerusalem is quite a usual way of getting around. The sidewalks are of stone, meant for pedestrians, and the streets are tree-lined and often flower-bordered. The trees are mainly dark green cypresses, and the empty spaces rocky, sandy and stoney. Those in charge of the city, led by Teddy Kollek, Jerusalem's ebullient mayor, have done much to beautify it. Tucked away in small places are charming little playgrounds for children, and connecting lanes between streets display over garden walls fine bursts of bougainvillea and plumbago. Often, because Jerusalem is hilly, the views are striking. There are places where one can look down on the city. As for the climate, we arrived in May and were told that we could expect no rain until November. Until then the temperature would be agreeable, the weather dry and sunny with never a cloud in the blue, blue sky. At dusk the city is briefly transformed by a halo of rose pearl light. At the summit of the Mount of Olives, just below the formal gardens of the International Hotel, is a place from which we learned to watch the sun go down. The city is touched by a pearly pink light as by a benison, with the golden dome of the Dome of the Rock glinting in the last rays of the sunset.

An unforgettable panorama.

My official working day at the office was from 7:30am to 3:00pm, unbroken by a meal. I wondered how the staff made out with such a regimen, and soon discovered that they ate snacks while they worked. I had in fact asked Finn Munch-Petersen when the staff ate. He had replied laconically: "All the time!" Phyllis and I found this timetable difficult to live with while we were in hotels, but life became easier when we finally moved into our own accommodation. But that did not come quickly. After a couple of weeks at the Moriah, we moved to the President, because Leon, the driver, got us a 30per cent reduction there. The President's manager was from Morocco too. Leon, I must admit, had quickly assumed a position of something more than a driver. He became a sort of Jeeves – Moroccan style. He had a strange history. When Hitler came to power, anti-Semitism was widespread in Morocco, and one day all Jewish men in his small Moroccan village near Fez were massacred.

At the age of seventeen, although he was left for dead with his throat slashed and his head bashed in, he alone out of thirty-eight survived. As he spoke French as well as Hebrew and Arabic, we always spoke French together. He had a sense of service which was quite foreign to most Israelis.

Finally, to get away from hotels, we moved into a small apartment on Berlin street until our own in Ibn Shaprut could be vacated. Phyllis wrote to "the children" about it as follows:

"I think I told you we had rented a small apartment for the month of June. It is really a humble little place and quite dirty. Nevertheless we are enjoying it better than the hotels. It is in a very orthodox section of town (but perhaps they all are), and on the Shabbat we live under the influence of the Jewish religion. As the sun goes down on Friday a calm falls over the city. The cars all park along the roadside, and many people go to the synagogue. Dooze and I usually take a walk at this hour, and Dooze wears his hat. I think some people are a little surprised at the kind of hat. There are a few trilbies about, but they are mainly black ones small and high on the head. It seems always to be accompanied by a flourishing black beard. Apparently not many blond Israelis grow beards, or if they do they do not wear hats. Boys and girls go to the synagogue – at least I suppose that is where they are going. They are neatly dressed – all the boys wearing kipas, mainly white embroidered ones, and the girls carry their holy books. There are also many young men, usually together, wearing long black coats and broad flat black felt hats, and each of them has a couple of long curls hanging down on each side of his face just in front of the ears. When you visit us in Ibn Shaprut on Friday evenings you will see every kind of orthodox attire, and interesting faces from many parts of the world. The children here interest me very much. Some of the little ones come and talk to me and cannot accept the fact that I do not understand them. One little girl (perhaps four years old) from the opposite apartment takes my hand and tries to shake me into comprehension. Hebrew is a living language again, and it is binding the people together. Moreover, the little children here are still full of curiosity and the joy of learning. The blasé, cocky spoiled child of Europe and the US seems not to have arrived."

The staff-member who had been with the UNDP longest was Hilda Ben-Nun, once Miss Weller from Manchester, now married with three children. At first she looked and sounded to me like a busy housewife from a Manchester suburb. But there the likeness ended, for her work was first-class in content, speed and presentation. She had originally been engaged as a secretary, but after a number of years had become an excellent programme officer. Isabel Mazliach was my secretary. She had also lived in Manchester, but was born in Cork. She was younger than Hilda, married with two children, also excellent in her work. Both answered many routine letters off their own bat, just presenting fair copies for my signature. But when I needed to draft myself, each was a near perfect stenographer.

My administrative assistant was Willie Weintraub from Baltimore, a highly competent accountant of impeccable integrity. Dina Toledano was an Egyptian who had lived in Cairo until she was eighteen. She did not stay long with us. My special assistant, Ephraim Halaban, had many close contacts with the Israeli government, and was to prove extremely useful in this respect. But he had had a heart attack, and was not back in the office when we arrived. So to my astonishment I found I was the only internationally recruited staff-member surrounded by first-class local staff. As I wrote to Carolyn and Phil: "These six plus me are the Office – very sleek. Laos by contrast was labour intensive."

Because we had to move out of the apartment on Berlin Street by 1st July, and the Eliavs had not quite moved out of the Ibn Shaprut apartment by then – indeed Mrs Eliav had fallen ill with the strain of packing and had to take to her bed – we decided to have a spell in the non-profit-making St George's hostel attached to St George's cathedral, where we had been regular worshippers since our arrival in Jerusalem. We felt very much at home in this Anglican/Episcopalian setting with its gracious solid stone buildings and cloisters, its beautiful garden, and refectory-type meals around long tables. The people we sat next to at table or chatted with in the garden were priests from around the world, experienced archeologists, or young people on digs. I remember speaking to one woman from Canada who was studying archeology. She had graduated from Oberlin, so when I told her Carolyn had been at Earlham (also a Quaker college) we became friends at once.

In the large compound which comprises the cathedral, cloisters, theological college and hostel, we occupied a room in the college, which was on vacation. It was entirely peaceful there, and the walled garden at the height of its beauty. Trained over a wide-topped wall was an old vine with twenty or thirty bunches of grapes hanging down from a wooden framework. Along a low stone wall beside the well was a lavender hedge – scented and very blue with flowers. There were pomegranate trees with the fruit swelling and colouring up to a russety red, and crowded close to them fig trees with small green unripened fruit. Old olive trees were dotted around, with olives as yet the size of a little fingernail. Hollyhocks grew in the nooks and crannies of the stone walls and buildings. In the flower beds clusters of flowers of almost every kind and colour thrived, except, we were told, lupins and delphiniums. Lemon, orange and grapefruit trees had been planted for decorative purposes, and picking out the pale golden buildings against a blue cloudless sky were tall slim pointed cypress trees and broad grey-green olives. It was a garden which would live in the mind's eye for a lifetime. However, although we enjoyed the peace of St George's, we felt we could not stay in its hostel long, because it was in the Arab area, and our work was in the Israel of Hebrew speakers.

Our 4th July was a rather unusual one. I was on the X-ray table of Jerusalem Hospital for a routine check-up to see whether or not I was growing any more kidney stones, and chatting pleasantly with a pretty Canadian technician from Toronto, when there was a flurry in the corridors. I was whisked off the table and hustled away, because casualties from a bombing in Jaffa Street were being brought in – ten dead and thirty wounded. It was a devilishly ingenious bomb-plant. A refrigerator packed with explosives had been left on a small cart in the city's main business thoroughfare. Because all Israelis are extremely aware of explosive devices – even shopping bags are inspected at the doors of supermarkets – the refrigerator door had been opened many times by passersby. The refrigerator was empty. But the explosives had been packed in the insulation part of it where the electric motor is normally housed. Jaffa Street is the busiest street in Jerusalem, and 4th July 1975 being a Friday, the day before Shabbat, the street was crowded with shoppers. A shock wave ran through the city, but there was never the remotest sign of panic. The scene at the hospital was one of swift, purposeful activity.

The same day we paid our respects to the US Consul in Jerusalem, where 4th July was being celebrated, and early that evening we attended another celebration of 4th July in the American Embassy in Tel Aviv, which was very exciting because news was being passed round quietly that a commando raid had been made on the airport in Kampala, Uganda, to rescue a number of Israeli civilians who had been captured and held there by Idi Amin. Except for one casualty, the shooting dead of the commando leader, and the refusal of one old lady to join her would-be rescuers, the raid had been 'a complete success. Amin's prisoners were flown back to Israel in triumph. It transpired afterwards that an Israeli undercover man had been in telephonic conversation with Idi Amin during the whole rescue operation.

While at that exhilarating cocktail party I had the opportunity to speak with Aba Eban who had become world famous for his speeches as Israel's Ambassador to the UN. We had been together in the same matriculation class at St Olave's School in London, and I had called on him in New York when he was head of the Israeli

Consulate there. At that time we had had a very cordial exchange of reminiscences, but in Tel Aviv I discovered he held a very poor opinion of the UN, so our meeting was much cooler.

Shortly after the 4th July cocktail party Phyllis and I attended a dinner party in honour of a Foreign Service official going to New York. Phyllis and I were the only non-Jews among four couples. There were readings from the Torah, for which I wore a kipa, before we started, and we were served by the young son of our hosts. We made some new friends, including a lady who was a seventh–generation Israeli, and Professor Kamon, Professor of Geography at Hebrew University, and his wife. The incident of the morning was barely mentioned, and taken in stride. That evening I felt a great admiration for the courage and resolution of our hosts and fellow guests, and for the unshakable faith Israelis in general felt in their cause. Later I drove down to Ben Gurion Airport to meet a high official from UNESCO, whose mission I surmised was, if possible, to heal the wounds the government felt the agency had inflicted on the Israeli people. However, he was not on the flight, and I returned to Jerusalem at 1:30am, disappointed and somewhat frustrated.

Our apartment on Ibn Shaprut was really quite a modest affair – a third-floor walk-up with spacious balconies overlooking flowering trees. But it was coolish in the hot weather and near the office, and these advantages offset our lack of enthusiasm for its furnishings and furniture. Towards the end of July we were beginning to feel much more at home.

Among our extra-office activities at this time was a visit we paid to the abode of an interesting and unusual priest named Murray Rogers. He wore a beige-coloured monk's habit complete with a rope-like girdle and sandals, and lived with the two elderly English ladies who wore Indian dress constantly. These three had been for twenty-six years in India together, but had left their work there because they thought the Indians to whom they had been ministering should now be on their own. They lived high up on the wall of the Old City near the Damascus Gate, and called themselves the Jyotiniketan Community. Jyotiniketan, is seems, is Sanskrit for Place of Uncreated Light. The Community was interested in spiritual and human interaction between Hindus, Muslims and Christians. From the windows of their dwelling one could see the holy places within the city on one side of the wall, and on the other a view of the Garden Tomb in a place reputed to be Golgotha. Surprisingly, the man in charge of the Garden Tomb grounds was a Colonel Dobbie, who we learned after conversing with him was the son of General Dobbie, the GOC Malayan Forces before the war. It seemed an extraordinary job for him, but he was enthusiastically devoted to it.

About this time we had an office picnic. We went, twelve adults and twelve children, to a place called Aqua Bella, about half an hour's drive out of Jerusalem. Willie Weintraub and his wife Ruthie were great hikers, and it was they who planned the outing. Phyllis and I provided the meat for the party, and the other families brought drinks, vegetables and fruit salad. I joined in games of soccer and frisbee-throwing in the sun, and the young children fished for tadpoles in the nearby stream. The restrooms were in the ruins of a twelfth–century crusaders' abbey. Phyllis greatly enjoyed this outing because there was adeqaute shade and everyone seemed happy.

In mid-August, I wrote to "the children":

Our social life has been rather lively recently, partly on account of two semi-political invitations to the Jerusalem Hilton. When we first arrived we took note of the Hilton as being the highest building in Jerusalem, and having learned its prices, made mental reservations that we would refrain from going there. Now we've visited the place twice in one week. The first visit was in response to an invitation from the Japanese Ambassador to meet a group of Japanese representatives from the Japanese Diet. There were seven hundred guests sitting down to a splendid dinner. While the

Ambassador spoke the lights were suddenly dimmed and in came a line of waiters with dishes of bombe Alaska crowned by lit sparklers. A pretty idea, but the timing was unfortunate. The main Japanese speaker then went on to say he "was not for Israel" – all this in Japanese which did not translate very well no matter what the interpreter did with it. Afterwards a little white-haired American stood up and said that Israel and Japan were "very close to his heart", and we learned that he had paid for the dinner. His name was Armstrong and he obviously had pots of money.

Our other Jerusalem Hilton visit was as guests of President Echeverria of Mexico. We had all been summoned to a garden party at the president of Israel's residence to meet him, and so Mr Echeverria was reciprocating. He declared, among other things, that Israel should give up its occupied territory, but the party was so jolly and so lavish (there must have been about one thousand, two hundred people there), that nobody seemed to mind very much what anyone said in Spanish. Echeverria is certainly trying to make an impression, and he had a good try to get Sadat and Rabin together. The open secret, however, was that he hoped to succeed Waldheim in 1976.

We have also been able to return hospitality in the last few days by taking some people out to dinner, as we cannot invite anyone to the house yet. We took the Bar Yaacovs and Jan Schumacher to Chez Simon and it seemed a great success. Bar Yaacov is a special adviser to Teddy Kollek, Mayor of Jerusalem, and was once Israel's ambassador to Nigeria. What made the party especially successful was that Jan, a Dutchman, Chief Administrative Officer for UNTSO (United Nations Truce Supervisor Organization), had found that Mrs Bar Yaacov, a Polish refugee, had been to the same school as he had been to in Montreux.

Tomorrow evening I shall go down to Ben Gurion Airport to meet Kouros Satrap, Director of the European and Middle East Division of UNDP, which deals with Israel. He is coming to take part in our Country Programme Review. I shall take "the workers" Yaacov Saphir, Nizhia (his girl Friday), Hilda and Kouros to the Jerusalem Theatre restaurant for lunch after Monday morning's session, and then in the evening there will be a cocktail party in the office for Kouros to meet all the staff, the experts and their wives. We hope to map out what will happen to the Country Programme to the end of 1976, and just possibly beyond. Israel has decided to become "a net contributor" to the UNDP overall programme by that time, that is to say, after 1976 the country will pay for itself for any UN technical assistance it receives, so we expect to close this office by 31st December 1976.

Did Mummy tell you about our trip to Beersheva? It was to participate in a little get-together of first-year students starting off on a new kind of medical doctor training, which combines medical Education with medical care. The student studies physics, chemistry and biology alongside medicine proper and clinical practice, i.e., he or she is in contact with patients and hospitals from the word go. Our invitation to Beersheva University came from Dr Asher Segall, who has come as a short-term (nine months) WHO consultant from Harvard to help prepare and oversee the curriculum and the project. The authorities probably chose Beersheva because the university is new (right next to the desert), and they believe a course with new approaches to medicine will suffer less in Beersheva than elsewhere from the attacks and forecasts of doom expected from conservative medical practitioners. We met quite a number of the students. They were young, brown as berries, casually clad and enthusiastic.

While in Beersheva we visited the retirement home of Ben Gurion himself. It is a tiny modest bungalow on the very edge of the desert, but it is clear from the memorabilia preserved there that a steady stream of distinguished people in many walks of life had made tracks to his door. We also visited some remarkable experiments in arid zone irrigation.

On our return to Jerusalem we met some Israelis who had been travelling in Europe. They seemed to be unanimous in their poor opinion of the Jerusalem winter. We were told that it rains and occasionally snows during the period November to February in an amount equal to the average precipitation in Britain for a whole year.

And so indeed we found it. The cold was never really severe, but the heating arrangements in our apartment were inadequate. The stone walls seemed to hold the cold, and the central heating for the whole apartment block was only turned on from six to eight each evening for reasons of economy. After a while we bought a little dish-type electric radiator, which threw out some heat but focused it on a very small area.

Part of our reading with regard to the history of Israel had been Herbert Samuel's "Memoirs". Carolyn, in a footnote to one of her letters, had mentioned that their landlord had brought her a gift of three golden peppers attached to one stem. It reminded me of a comment Viscount Samuel had made on a photograph of Palestine dignitaries which appeared in his book. Samuel wrote: "I noted that there was an olive tree at one side of the picture, and hoped that this was a good omen for the future." But Storrs (afterwards General Storrs), who also figured in the photograph, chimed in: "But may I draw your attention, Sir, to the pepper tree at the other side of the photograph!" This was not a green pepper plant, of course – the pepper tree in Israel looks rather like a weeping willow.

We had been interested in Herbert Samuel partly because he had been the first High Commissioner in Palestine after serving as a Cabinet Minister in various governments in England, and also because we had met his son Edwin several times. Edwin, a viscount like his father, had written a number of books, including a collection of short stories which we found rather attractive. He returned to England for several months of the year to take his place in the

House of Lords, but the rest of the year he lived in Jerusalem in an apartment near ours. Sometimes on my morning walk to work, I would meet him taking home the groceries from one of the typical tiny grocery stores which were tucked away in the suburbs. At seventy-seven he wore his years well. He was meticulously punctual in his attendance at functions, and once, being the first arrival at a cocktail party in our office, remarked to me: "As far as I am concerned, there is only one eight o'clock!"

During his tour of duty it is customary for the Resident Representative of a developing country to make visits to the various headquarters of the specialized agencies which are executing the projects of his country's Country Programme, and on 19th September I received approval to make these agency briefing visits from 1st to 18th November in respect to Israel. I would visit Athens, Rome, Vienna, Geneva, Paris and London, and Phyllis would accompany me. As I explained to Carolyn and Phil in a letter:

You ask how the agencies are involved. Well the system is that UNDP provides the funds for a Country Programme, and then in consultation with the government (with which the Resident Representative. has collaborated in working out the programme) invites (again through the Resident. Representative.) the specialized agencies (UNESCO, FAO, etc.) to execute the individual projects which are within their field of competence. The agencies for which we have projects in Israel are – in Athens UNIC (United Nations Information Centre); in Rome FAO (Food and Agricultural Organization); in Vienna UNIDO (United Nations Industrial Development Organization) and IEAE (International Atomic Energy Agency); in Geneva the UN Technical Assistance Office, ILO (International Labour Organization), ITU (International Telecommunications Union), WHO (World Health Organization); in Paris UNESCO (United Nations Educational, Scientific and Cultural Organization); and in London IMO (International Maritime Organization).

Towards the end of September Phyllis and I were invited to Isabel's house to see their "succa". At this time of year, "succas" are put up by devout Jews for a week during the Festival of the Tabernacles to remind them of the journey of their forebears in the wilderness, and so less work than usual seems to get done. A succa is a kind of outdoor shack open to the stars and decorated by the family with branches of trees and gay objects, in which the whole family take their meals during the week, and sometimes sleep as well. In practice everyone goes around to the succas of friends and takes pot-luck meals. In the case of Isabel all the neighbours' children piled in and had a wonderful time. As Isabel explained: "We have only two children and the neighbours feel sorry for us, so they send us theirs!" No family planning in Israel!

Back in the office I found myself interviewing candidates for the post Dinah was vacating for family reasons. We had advertised in the papers, and immediately received about forty applications. Ephraim Halaban did the preliminary screening and passed on to me some remarkable people. I liked especially a sixty–two–year–old lady with a Glasgow MA and fluent English, French, German and Hebrew. She was feeling bereft after losing a son in the Yom Kippur War. Another candidate had a degree from Queen's College, New York, and was a regular contributor to Good Housekeeping. She needed a little money to keep her writing going in the evenings. A third, a mother of three, brown as a berry, and wearing a broad-brimmed summer hat, wanted to escape from an empty house. She had a typing speed of one hundred and twenty and had quit her degree course in Madison, Wisconsin, to marry her husband – an international bridge player. Most seemed over-qualified. In the end I chose Ilana Baram, the lady with the hat, as we thought she would mesh in best with the rest of the staff. It proved a good choice, as apart from being a good office worker Ilana was an invaluable help in organizing receptions and the final arrangements for closing the office.

She came from a wealthy Chicago family, and, we heard later, returned there with her husband shortly after the office closed.

Before she joined our staff we found she had won considerable publicity in Israel because when her husband had been held in a highjacked plane, she agreed publicly with the government that it should not yield to threats even if it meant the death of the hostages, including her husband.

And so almost before we knew it we were in the throes of closing the UNDP office in Jabotinsky Street. We gave a party in the long room of our office for all those Israelis in government and outside it who were associated with the work of the UNDP in Israel. Many high–ranking officers of the Israeli government attended as well as Teddy Kollek, the Mayor of Jerusalem, President Harman of the University of Jerusalem, and his wife Zita Harman, who had accepted the Nobel Peace Prize on behalf of UNICEF when she was its president. Parties in honour of our office were also given by Zita Harman and Yaacov Saphir.

On 29th December 1976, in an editorial, The Jerusalem Post had this to say:

END OF AN EPOCH

It is a cause of sentimental regret that the small but always busy office of the UN representative will be finally closed this week, after a quarter of a century of devoted service to Israel's development.

Israel had outgrown the need for aid in basic skills and knowledge, thanks not a little to the work of the UN and also in its time, to the American Four Point programme.

The impact of UN assistance has always been bigger than it seemed in money terms because its purpose was to teach the teachers. Every expert had an Israeli counterpart who was supposed to pick his brains.

Training centres were established–among them one for Technicians and Foremen, one for Industrial Research, one for Science Teaching, one called the Small Industries Advisory Service. The organizers and lecturers were originally UN men, handpicked from the industrialized countries. Today they are Israelis.

In contrast with the political aims of the United Nations the technical assistance administration has always shown impartiality. It is distinguished from the various programmes by its exclusive devotion to the interests of the recipient country.

Disappointment is all the keener that the number of fellowship-holders coming to learn in Israel under the UN programme has dropped – for political reasons. The responsibility lies not with the UN Development Programme, but with African countries that want to avoid ruffling Arab feathers.

They should take inspiration from the UN offices that continue operating in their various territories, and whose success derives from a scrupulous determination to keep business and politics apart. Israelis can happily say thank you to the United Nations in this area, with a clear conscience.

Reprise

When I left Israel in 1976 I was sixty-four. Now I am eighty-seven, and would like to mention some of the events which have taken place and some of the experiences I have had in the interim. Since retirement I have been on a number of missions for the UN family, most of them for UNDP. I list them here, with a few comments on two of them.

Consultant Missions since retirement in December 1976

For UNDP	Geneva (WHO) – to participate in Ad Hoc Committee For Global Project in Rural Water Supply	1978 (3wks)
UNDP with UNESCO	Indonesia Preparatory Assistance Mission Development of General Secondary Teacher Education in Five Fields of Study	1979 (6wks)
ADB with UNESCO	Indonesia Upgrading of the Technical Faculties and Development of the University of North Sumatra at Medan (Team Leader)	1979 (14wks)
UNDP with UNESCO	Sri Langka, India and Thailand – Review Regional Education projects in the Regional Education Programme of the Bureau for Asia and the Pacific	1980 (5wks)
UNDP with UNESCO	Afghanistan – Review of Country Progamme Projects in the Education Sector	1980 (2wks)

UNDP with UNESCO	Malawi – Evaluation of Primary Teacher Education and Curriculum Development Project	1983 (3wks)
UNDP with UNESCO	Zambia – United Nations Institute for Namibia Evaluation Mission	1984 (3wks)
UNDP with UNESCO	Thailand – Strengthening of Educational Radio	1985 (2wks)
UNDP with UNESCO	Laos – Improvement of Science Teaching and Secondary Teacher Education	1986 (2wks)
UNESCO	Establishment of a National Polytechnic	
UNFPA	Evaluation of UNFPA supported FAO Inter-country Programme Manila, Bangkok, Nairobi, Comoros Islands, Rome	1988 (7wks)

As indicated above I spent five months of 1979 on two missions in Indonesia. The first, a preparatory assistance mission of six weeks for the Development of Secondary Teacher Education in Five Fields of Study, I remember especially for the delicate political atmosphere that surrounded it. In particular we became aware of the interesting over–riding consideration of the Indonesian government for consensus among the various national departments and agencies concerned with the project. This was the Indonesian philosophy of "pancha sila", or consensus in operation. All participants in the project had to agree in general on what action was to be taken. "Consensus", as far as we were concerned, meant a considerable wait before a final decision could be made as to the size and shape of the project.

The second mission to Indonesia in 1979 was different from the others that I had undertaken in that it was funded by the Asian Development Bank, and was by far the largest in scope and funding that I had ever been closely associated with. Its title, the Upgrading of the Technical Faculties and Development of the University of North Sumatra at Medan, called for recommendations in the content of courses and for buildings in which they could be conducted. We were a nine–person mission, and I had been chosen as team leader partly because I had a knowledge of the Malay language, which in many ways is similar to Indonesian.

Although most of our time was naturally spent in Medan I was obliged to visit the UNESCO offices in Jakarta and Bangkok, and it was in Bangkok that the mission was completed and its report written. Because this was such a long mission, and missions had been separating me from Phyllis for long periods, we had decided that she should accompany me on this one. Unfortunately she fell sick with pneumonia in Bangkok and was confined to hospital there. She recovered slowly under the wonderful care of a Dutch woman doctor.

In Medan we moved about in four cars which were seemingly commandeered from the university staff for our use. The hotel in which we stayed was not very reassuring. The manager looked after our valuables personally, as the security boxes in the hotel vestibule were not secure, and had from time to time been rifled, it was presumed by members of the hotel staff. On our first day in Medan, as three of us were walking on the sidewalk just outside the hotel, a young man jumped off the pillion seat of his accomplice's motor cycle, snatched the brief case of our expert for architecture, an Indian national from Brisbane, and then jumped back onto the pillion seat and made his get-away. The briefcase had all the expert's money and papers in it. In due course the money which had been stolen from him was reimbursed by UNESCO after I reported the heist to UNESCO Headquarters, but this beginning was a clear indication of the conditions we would be working under in Medan.

Having made a number of recommendations with regard to programmes and buildings I thought our mission might be able to help with teaching personnel. As the local language in Medan, Sumatra, apparently was not excessively different from the Malay spoken in Penang, I thought I would see if my old friend Hamdan Tahir, who had been a member of staff of Clifford School, Kuala Kangsar, when I was Headmaster there, might be able to help us, as I knew Hamdan had become Head of the College of Science in Penang. Trying to telephone across the Malacca Straits at that time, however, turned out to be extremely difficult, as the reception was very bad. I nevertheless did manage to speak with Hamdan, who later was to become Governor of Penang, his full title Tun Dato' Seri Haji Hamdan bin Sheikh Tahir. Hamdan promised to help us in any way he could.

The mission to Sri Langka, India and Thailand – Review of Regional Education projects in the Regional Education Programme of the Bureau for Asia and the Pacific, which took place in 1980, I remember now chiefly for the vast Educational resources of the area. India had a tremendous supply of PHDs for example which it seemed most willing to share. I noticed in meetings with the Government Education officials that my colleagues in the mission team not infrequently and half in jest raised the question of how difficult life must have been for them under the British Raj. However, I was interested to note that these Indian officials never felt the need to lambast or even criticize the British. The reputation of the Indian Civil Service was still very much in place.

In Afghanistan, which I also visited in 1980, our mission comprised of two UNESCO officials, Burmese and Iranian, and myself. Our business was to evaluate a secondary teacher training institution project supported by UNESCO and funded by UNDP. Our visit was a strange validation of the independence of the UN family from politics, for Kabul, the capital, had at that time been over–run by USSR troops. The international experts whom we met recalled the invasion of the Russians, bombing and fighting in the streets, and the evacuation of all international personnel from the various embassies located in the capital.

I remember this mission vividly because I fell sick and had to be visited by an Afghan doctor in our hotel. It had been decided from the start that I would be entrusted with the writing of the report, so my speedy recovery was vital to the mission. In the end the report was completed within the time we had available, with the usual burning of midnight oil and the help of the Bulgarian Resident Representative's wonderful English secretary. At a farewell reception, at which we met with some twenty or thirty Afghan and Russian officials, I found I could communicate with the Russians in German. I remember our recommendations were conditioned on the expectation that the political situation was likely to change.

Early in such free time as we had in Kabul we were escorted around the town by our Iranian Deputy Resident Representative. I remember sitting back deep in the car we were using as I did not wish my white skin to be taken for a Russian official's. The Russians were not popular and moved around the town unescorted at their peril. We went with him to a bank to get some money. However, the bank seemed unable to give us service, so the Deputy Resident Representative said he would take us elsewhere. Accordingly he took us to what he called the "souk", a sort of huddled marketplace with all kinds of stalls squashed in together. We were taken into a small tent-like office and seated before a tiny desk, behind which sat a huge turbaned Afghan. We were told he would exchange our money for us. Traveler's cheques? No, we understood, our own bank cheques! And so to our amazement I made out a cheque on my local New Hampshire Bank in the United States for a number of dollars, and in exchange received Afghan money. "Suppose", I said to my Iranian friend afterwards, "my cheque bounced?" He replied "He would find you wherever you were, and kill you!" We also visited a tailor in Kabul, and I ordered a suit because the materials on display were excellent, and the work could be done very quickly and cheaply. It was an interesting experiment. But I never wore the suit.

Before our departure we were each given an Afghan carpet by our hosts. Since we, as international civil servants, were not allowed to accept gifts from Governments I left mine with the Resident Representative in Kabul. My one regret on leaving Kabul was that I did not buy one of those wonderful fur hats.

After settling down in the house we had bought in New Hampshire, Phyllis and I led quite a quiet life. Unfortunately the lack of energy which she had suffered from after her return from those years alone in Africa seemed to intensify. At first she seemed to enjoy a daily meeting with Tib Rice who would ride round from her house on her bicycle, but her lassitude increased, and after trying daily help in the house for some weeks I at last found it necessary to resort to a nursing home. I tried Goodwin's of Exeter, New Hampshire, first and then another nursing home in Exeter. There followed a long spell in the Brattleboro Retreat in Vermont, to which I would pay a visit every week end. But in the end Phyllis returned to Goodwin's.

During the time Phyllis was at Goodwin's our lives were made less burdensome, and from time to time were uplifted, by a visiting therapist named Sheilah Rose, who was very highly qualified and most agreeable. She would breeze into the nursing home like a breath of fresh air. Several times Sheilah took special care of Phyllis while I went on mission. One day it was suggested by a member of a support group of care-givers to which I belonged, which met regularly at Goodwin's, that I should take Phyllis to the Mayo Clinic in Massachusetts for a thorough examination to see if anything could be done to alleviate her condition. When I mentioned this suggestion to Sheilah she immediately offered to come with us. I was touched and delighted, and accepted her offer immediately, as by this time Phyllis needed a wheelchair to move around in whenever she was not in bed. The report of the clinic was inconclusive. Phyllis was suffering from acute headaches from unknown causes, which made her severely depressed.

Unhappily from this time on there seemed to be nothing we could do to improve Phyllis's health. Her condition steadily deteriorated until she died in her sleep on 1st September 1987. We held a service for her at St Andrew's -by-the-Sea in North Hampton, New Hampshire. The Rev. Warren Deane took the service, and Carolyn and I shared in the eulogy. I found it strange and touching to be able to tell the story of our long separation, and of Phyllis's extraordinary war-time years alone as a headmistress almost in the centre of war-time Africa, while I was prisoner of war of the Japanese in Malaya and Thailand. Carolyn told the story of her own childhood in Malaya, her time as a student in the Froebel School in Roehampton, England, to which she commuted across the Atlantic, until it was time for her to go to a secondary school in the United States – always under the watchful and supportive eye of her mother. It was a lovely service. Phyllis was cremated. I spread her ashes over the little North Hampton garden overlooking the ocean, a garden maintained by the Gardening Club of Little Boar's Head.

Alone in North Hampton I felt in limbo for some time. I had taken comfort in the friendship of Sheilah, but after a while in the fall of 1987 she moved to Arizona because New Hampshire was not a State which paid personnel in the medical field well, and pay opportunities were much better there. I had been pleased to receive a letter from Marjorie, the girl friend I had left behind when I went to Malaya, whose name when she was single had been Bliss. I had lost touch with her because I did not know her married name or her address. She had read Phyllis's obituary in the "Times" and, concluding that there was only one Kenneth Dudley Luke, wrote to me from Hampshire, England. I picked up the telephone, and we had a good talk. Marjorie had been married twice since we last met. She had two fine sons, and was now alone. I was not uninterested. But when I received an invitation to visit Sheilah in Arizona and talked with her on the telephone I decided not to pursue the friendship I had had with Marjorie.

Sheilah had become Social Co-ordinator at Sun Grove Resort Village in Sun City when she invited me to visit her in Phoenix. I flew down. She met me in her Nissan van, and we found out more about each other. I discovered that besides being a therapist and having excellent qualifications in that field, her main interest was in painting and that she hoped to spend as much time as possible doing just that. She had impressive qualifications in fine art from McGill University in Canada, the National Academy of Design in New York City, and in Art Therapy from the University of New Hampshire. I found I enjoyed her company immensely. On my return to North Hampton I realized I was in love. So one evening while lying in bed in North Hampton, New Hampshire, I tele-phoned Sheilah in Phoenix, Arizona, and asked her to marry me. To my delight she agreed.

Sheilah had no special church associations, but I had been Senior Warden at St Andrews-by-the-Sea, Little Boar's Head, and was anx-ious to have a church wedding. So I requested a letter of introduction from Bishop Douglas Theuner, Bishop of New Hampshire, to the Rev. Carl Carlouzzi, Vicar of All Saints church, Phoenix, Arizona so that our wedding could be celebrated in All Saints Church. Bishop Theuner kindly wrote a letter, and our wed-ding accordingly took place in All Saints church on Saturday, 18th June 1988 at 1pm. Afterwards there was a reception at the home of Dr and Mrs Gerald Rosenblum (Sheilah's cousin). As I write now Sheilah and I have been happily married for more than ten years.

Return to Malaysia

The second chapter of my story is entitled "Departure for Malaya", and the reader may well wonder why the change in the name from Malaya to Malaysia in the heading of this chapter. The reason lies in the history of the development of the region. In 1936, when I first went out there, Malaya comprised the mainland part of the peninsula to the border with Thailand and included the island of Singapore. However, Singapore broke away from Malaya in 1948 under Lee Kuan Yu and became a separate State. Today Malaysia comprises two noncontiguous regions: Peninsular, or West, Malaysia on the Malay Peninsula and East Malaysia on the island of Borneo. West Malaysia contains the bulk of Malaysia's population and has the capital city of Kuala Lumpur. The country's estimated population in 1988 was 14,005,000. East Malaysia consists of the states of Sabah and Sarawak on the northern part of the island of Borneo and is separated from mainland Peninsular, or West Malaysia by some four hundred miles of the South China Sea. East Malaysia's estimated population in 1991 (prelim.) was 3,385,119.

In May 1993 I received a letter from Azlina Ariffin, the daughter of Datok Ariffin bin Nam, who with Che Salleh bin Datok Hussein, seemed to be the only two surviving Malay members of staff of the Malay College of my time. I had written hoping that Datok Ariffin and Azlina might be able to visit us in our home, particularly as Azlina had trained as an architect in the USA. Azlina in her reply regretted that she felt unable to accept our invitation because her father was old and infirm. However, she made what turned out to be a most fruitful suggestion. Her uncle, Tuan Haji Azmil Daud, was the Secretary of the Malay College Old Boys Association, and she felt sure that if I wrote to him the Old Boys would be very inter-

ested in inviting Sheilah and me to the MCOBA dinner on 23rd
October 1993

And so it turned out to be. Haji Azmil, in reply to my letter wrote:
"You may like to know that most of the older members of MCOBA
still remember you and are anxiously looking forward to meeting
you again. On behalf of the MCOBA Management Committee I am
happy to convey to you our invitation for you and your wife to
attend this year's MCOBA Annual Dinner to be held on 23rd
October 1993 at the Istana Hotel, Kuala Lumpur. Please let us
know your itinerary while you are here so that we may make
arrangements for you to meet some of the old boys."

Accordingly Sheilah and I set out for Malaysia. We chose
Singapore Airlines for our trip, perhaps because we wanted to see
if we could meet Dr Chuah Chong Yong and his wife Kim Kee in
Singapore. I had always wanted to see these two again ever since
they left Clifford School, Kuala Kangsar. (As I write I have "The
Cliffordian", dated January 1948, before me with Chong Yong's
striking design on its cover.) We were later to regret having done
this because Tunku Adnan, the organizer of our travel inside
Malaysia, hinted that MCOBA would probably have upgraded our
tickets to first class had we been travelling with Malaysian Airlines.

Upon our arrival by taxi at our hotel in Singapore we were dis-
mayed to find that Sheilah's handbag was nowhere to be found, but
even while we were trying to assess the seriousness of our situation
we found to our delight our taxi driver appearing at the hotel
counter with the missing bag. Honesty in the controlled Singapore
certainly paid off for us. The driver would not accept a reward.

As soon as we had recovered our composure I searched through
the telephone directory among the many Chong Yongs and found
one which looked promising, and sure enough it turned out to be
Kim Kee who answered the phone. Unhappily Cheong Yong had
died some years before our coming, but Kim Kee met us at our

308

hotel with her son, who had also become a dermatologist, and we had a happy time time talking of early days in Kuala Kangsar. I had last met Cheong Yong and Kim Kee when they were attending a dermatological conference in Washington, DC. Through Kim Kee we also met Teoh Teik Lee who was working for the Duke of Edinburgh's International Schools Programme.

We spent three days in Singapore during which time I had a quick look at Changi Gaol again. We could not go inside because apparently it is still in use as a gaol. I would also have liked to have seen Belakang Mati again, especially as we understood it has been turned into a vast amusement park connected to the mainland by an overhead railway. Our time, however, was short, and our arrival on time in Kuala Lumpur important. Accordingly we duly caught our scheduled flight, and on arrival were immediately escorted to the VIP lounge where we were greeted by a delegation of Old Boys of MCOBA, chief among whom was Tunku Dato Seri Adnan bin Tunku Besar Burhanuddin, who was to be our mentor, guide and friend throughout our whole stay in Malaysia.

Sheilah and I soon realized that our visit to Malaysia was to be completely taken over by the Old Boys. We were to be their guests for the whole time we stayed in the country. We were taken without delay to the Istana Hotel, a five–star establishment far more luxurious than any I had stayed in during my twenty-one years in the old Malaya, and after some time a programme was worked out which was thought to combine our wishes for nostalgic visits with the Old Boys' desire to show us some of the highlights of modern Malaysia. I append a copy of the programme here. We felt almost overwhelmed by the Old Boys' generosity.

Programme of Mr & Mrs K.D. Luke

Wed. 20/10/93	ETA 1320 hrs	Subang by SQ 112 Check in at Hotel Istana KL (Guests of MCOBA)
	ETA 2000 hrs	Dinner at No. 1 Lorong Duta 1 Persiaran Duta, KL (Guests of YA Tan Seri Mohamed Azmi)
Thur. 21/10/93	ETA 1000 hrs	Tour of Kuala Lumpur Lunch at Lake Club (Guests of YM Tunku Adnan)
	ETA 1550 hrs	Tea at Istana Negara (Guests of DYMM SPB Yang Di Pertuan Agong) Accompanied by Y. A. Tan Seri Mohamed Azmi)
Fri. 22/10/93	ETA 1000 hrs	Tour of Shah Alam Lunch at Royal Selangor Golf Club (Guests of Mr Kassim Aris)
	ETA 2000 hrs	Dinner with Senior Old Boys at Royal Selangor Golf Club Green Room (Guests of MCOBA)
Sat. 23/10/93	AM ETA 2000 hrs	FREE Istana Hotel – MCOBA ANNUAL DINNER (Guests of MCOBA)
Sun. 24/10/93	ETA 123 hrs	Lunch at Carcosa (Guests of YBhg Dato Hamidi Osman)
	ETA 200 hrs	Dinner: Shangrila Hotel (Guests of Y. Bhg Dato Malek Merican)
Mon. 25/10/93	ETA 1100 hrs	Leave for Penang by MH 1140 Check in at E&O Hotel, Pulau Pinang

		(Guests of Tuan Hj. Sidek Lassim)
	ETA 1940 hrs	Leave for Sri Mutiara Penang
		(Guests of HE Tun Dato'Seri Hamdan Governor of Penang)
Tue. 26/10/93	ETD 0930 hrs	Leave for Penang Hill & Temple Tours
		(Guests of Tuan Haji Sidek)
	PM Free	
	ETA 2000 hrs	Dinner at Penang Club
		(Guests of Tuan Hj. Sidek)
Wed. 27/10/93	ETD 0700 hrs	Leave Butterworth for Ipoh (train)
	ETA 1100 hrs	Ipoh
		Lunch in Ipoh
		Short tour of Ipoh
	ETA 1400 hrs	Leave Ipoh for Lumut (Car AAY 1)
	ETA 1500 hrs	Leave Lumut for Pangkor
		(By Pan Pacific Boat)
	ETD 1530 hrs	Check in at Pan Pacific Hotel
		(Guests of DYMM SPB Yang Di Pertuan Agong)
Thur. 28/10/93	AM – PM	In Pangkor
Fri. 29/10/93	ETD 0930 hrs	Leave Pangkor for Lumut
	ETA 0945 hrs	Lumut
	ETD 0945 hrs	Leave Lumut for Ipoh (Car AAY 1)
	ETA 1045 hrs	Ipoh
	ETD 1100 hrs	Leave for Kuala Kangsar (Car AAY 1)
	ETA 1145 hrs	Kuala Kangsar – stay at Rumah Tetamu
		(Arranged by Istana Iskandariah)
	ETD 1145 hrs	Leave for Malay College, KK
	ETA 1200 hrs	Lunch at Malay College, KK
	1630 -1800 hrs	Tea at Istana Iskandariah 2000 hrs
		Dinner at MCKK
Sat. 30/10/93	AM – 13.20 hrs	Guests of Clifford School
	ETD 13.30 hrs	Leave for Ipoh
	ETA 14.00 hrs	Ipoh Airport

311

	ETD 14.00 hrs	Leave for Kuala Lumpur (MH 1615)
	ETA-14.30 hrs	Kuala Lumpur
	ETD-14.30 hrs	Leave for Genting Highlands
		(Guests of Y Bhg Tan Seri Alwi Jantan)
Sat. 30/10/93	PM	Dinner with DYMM Sultan Selangor
		(Guests of Y Bhg Tan Seri Alwi Jantan)
Sun. 31/10/93	AM-PM	In Genting Highlands
		(Guests of Y Bhg Tan Seri Alwi Jantan)
Mon. 1/11/93	ETD 1100 hrs	Leave for K. – Istana Hotel
	ETD 1400 hrs	Leave for Tuanku Jaafar College
		(Guests of YM Tunku Adnan)
	ETD 2000 hrs	Dinner
		(Guests of DYMM Yang Di Pertuan Besar)
	PM	Leave for Kuala Lumpur, Istana Hotel
Tues. 2/11/93	AM	FREE
	ETA 2000 hrs	Dinner at Bankers Club, Kuala Lumpur
		(Guests of Y. Bhg Tan Seri Abu Zarim)
Wed. 3/11/93	AM	FREE
	ETA 1600 hrs	Tea
		(Guests of Y Bhg Dato'Ariffin)
	PM	FREE
ThUr 4/11/93	ETD 0600 hrs	Leave for Singapore – SQ
	ETD 0900 hrs	Leave for Los Angeles – SQ

Prepared by Hj Azmil bin Hj. Mohamed Daud

Honorary Secretary, MCOBA

This remarkable programme of our stay in Malaysia needs some interpretation, partly because the hospitality of the Old Boys was almost overwhelming in its generosity. I was delighted for us to have dinner with Azmi and his wife at the beginning of our visit, because Azmi had been Head Boy in my final year as Headmaster of the Malay College, and we had a solid respect for each other. Azmi is a High Court judge in Kuala Lumpur, but as a Government servant he lived more modestly than many of the Old Boys who had done well in business. Sheilah and I enjoyed the informality of being his house guests and meeting his charming wife and family. Azmi was President of MCOBA at the time of our visit, and was therefore anxious to oversee the programme that had been prepared for us.

The whole programme was, I believe, largely prepared by Tunku Adnan, who was at the time Vice-President of the MCOBA. We could not have had a more efficient adviser, trouble-shooter and friend. It was he who also worked out the details of our programme, and arranged for our transportation from place to place, if not in his own car, a Jaguar, then in a Mercedes supplied from some other source. Every car we were driven in was chauffeured by a uniformed Malay chauffeur.

In the time which we had together Tunku Adnan explained that he, unlike Azmi, had been very young when I was Headmaster. He recounted several episodes of his school days which I found very amusing. He remembered particularly an occasion early one Sunday morning when the tiny swimming pool outside my bedroom window was reserved for Malay College staff. I had stepped out onto my verandah to breathe the morning air. Little Tunku Adnan's head emerged from the water at the edge of the pool. Our eyes met; but we "agreed" not to see each other. When we visited the College in 1997, Sheilah and I were conducted round the grounds and particularly admired a full-sized swimming pool which had been built since my time. However, we were later shown my old wooden bungalow, empty but still standing, and alongside it the old tiny swimming pool with its sloping sides. For some reason, I do not know, my name was printed alongside it.

Our visit to the College itself was particularly rewarding. The college had created a special garden named after me, complete with a commemoration plaque which I was asked to unveil, and the trophies room had a number of photographs recording incidents which had taken place during my headmastership. Sheilah and I dined with our hosts at a dinner served alongside the new swimming pool.

The Malay College Old Boys had also graciously set aside a day for us to be the guests of Clifford School, which we also greatly enjoyed. Clifford School put on a show of "bersilat", the ancient Malay/Indonesian art of self-defence, demonstrated without actual combat. I was particularly pleased to see that the headmaster of the Malay College had also been invited to participate in this reunion. His presence signified a happy cooperation between the two schools rather than the troublesome rivalry which had existed in the past.

This closing P.S. to "Luke's Log" dated February 28th 2004, gives me much satisfaction.

Eric and Elizabeth have visited us in Escondido, California, where Sheliah and I now live. We have had a wonderful time together, Eric is a fine young man, as tall as I am (over 6 feet), with an interesting job in New York City. His special interest, however, is flying, for he intends to become an airline pilot, and is already flying solo!

Elizabeth also has had a good job in New York City, but has given it up for now as she has had a baby boy Alexander on 15th January 2003.